My Soul To Keep

My Soul To Keep

THE WAR HAS BEGUN...

Kayli Coffman

This is not an official publication of The Church of Jesus Christ of Latter Day Saints. The opinions and views expressed herein belong solely to the author. Permission for use of sources, graphics, and photos is solely the responsibility of the author.

ISBN: 0996806229
ISBN 13: 9780996806220

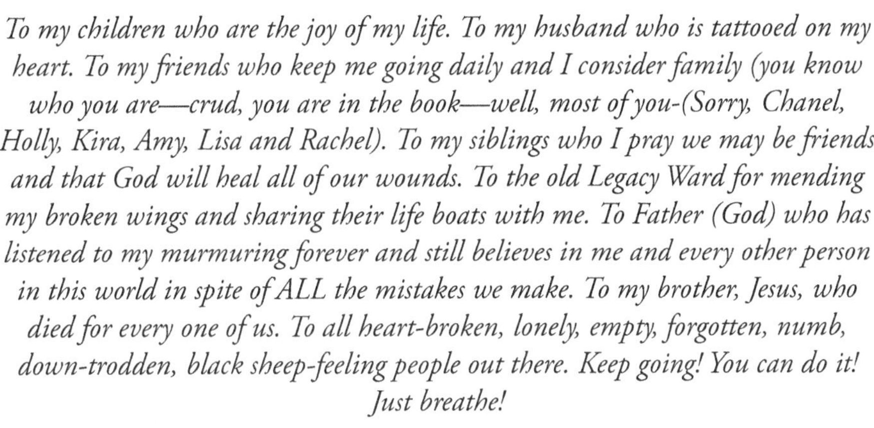

To my children who are the joy of my life. To my husband who is tattooed on my heart. To my friends who keep me going daily and I consider family (you know who you are—crud, you are in the book—well, most of you-(Sorry, Chanel, Holly, Kira, Amy, Lisa and Rachel). To my siblings who I pray we may be friends and that God will heal all of our wounds. To the old Legacy Ward for mending my broken wings and sharing their life boats with me. To Father (God) who has listened to my murmuring forever and still believes in me and every other person in this world in spite of ALL the mistakes we make. To my brother, Jesus, who died for every one of us. To all heart-broken, lonely, empty, forgotten, numb, down-trodden, black sheep-feeling people out there. Keep going! You can do it! Just breathe!

Contents

Preface

I never planned on writing a book. I have never even read a whole one, except children's stories, and perhaps that qualifies me as illiterate on some level, but I feel pushed and driven—or, as some may say, "inspired"— to write one now. Please bear with the first bit of my life story so you can get an idea of what I experienced, how I dealt with it, the way it shaped who I am, and why Heavenly Father personally intervened in my life.

This book is about physical, emotional and spiritual survival, hope, love, freedom, and most importantly who we are in our relationship with Father, our REAL father, God, who loves us all so much! I want my friends and family who have heard these stories or have been part of them to understand, truly understand, our purpose on this earth and our relationship as brothers and sisters.

We are not sent to the earth to just endure the experience; we are here to have joy, truly. As every day is considered a gift, my experiences are a gift from God, whether I wanted them or not. Most of all, with God (and many spirits and angels) as my witness, they are all true! As shocking, frightening, terrible, inspirational, wonderful, unbelievable, and unimaginable they may seem, I promise you they are true.

I believe my experiences will answer questions for many about why we are here, where we are going and who we are. My family and close friends always ask, "Why you?" I ask myself that same question all of the time. I don't know. I do know that Father uses the weak things of the world sometimes to accomplish his work, and that is definitely me! I hope this book helps those seeking answers to some of the mysteries of the other side.

Not all of my experiences are written here. Several are random and it would take too long to explain the people or events surrounding them, but the more phenomenal ones are written.

CHAPTER 1
In The Beginning

We are all spiritual beings having a human experience
—Pierre Teilhard de Chardin

Father in Heaven

One day recently, I found myself sitting with God in his office in Heaven. I wasn't asleep, in fact I was very much awake, trying to figure out how I could have possibly gotten there. Was I dead? No! All of my senses were very much alive, and some I didn't recognize. My mind seemed to open up in a way I didn't know it could. The longer I sat there, the more I remembered things, remembered my Father and this place. Why was I so comfortable here? As I looked around I thought, "I have been here before, many times. I am home." Then, Father began to speak.

Whoa, back-up. Before I can explain this experience, I need to catch you up on who I am and where I came from. This life is all a big personal puzzle that we find and decide what pieces we want to use to complete it. It is all about our agency, our choices. We can make a beautiful masterpiece if we desire, or leave everything to chance. The point is, we are all very important people with incredible talents, some we know about and many we have to discover. We are each the "Columbus'" of our own life. Where we go, what we do, and what kind of impact we want to leave behind on the earth is purely up to us.

We all came from, and will return to, that same place in Heaven. If we behave ourselves, we will be lucky enough to return right there in that familiar office with the big man in the sky, affectionately known as "Father."

Home Sweet Home

D&C 58:2-4

If God gives trials to those he loves, than I am his favorite!

I was born in what I call, a "house of horrors." Every kind of abuse you can think of was in that house. Fortunately it was semi-short-lived. Unfortunately, it was so horrible and vile it has stuck with many of my siblings and me all of our lives.

It wasn't all bad, thank goodness. I had a wonderful mother who I knew loved me, no matter what my biological father felt or said about me. She was sweet and tender, with kind words always. She was never angry—well, almost never.

If she was unhappy, I only knew because she would sit down at the piano and start playing a song that belonged in Dracula's castle, loud and eerie as she pounded those keys. The louder and longer the song, the more anger she had.

Mom sang or hummed all of the time. I was awakened every morning, as she opened my curtains, with a song that went like, "Good morning, good morning, a happy good morning, happy good morning to you. Fathers, Mothers Sisters and brothers, grandmothers, grandfathers too." Because my middle name is Sue, I sometimes would get the 50's song, "Wake up little Susie, Wake up" or "Susie, Que-sie, I love you-sie, just the same." I don't know if some of the songs were made up or where they came from, but she was always singing a happy song like a darling princess in a Disney movie. On our birthdays, very early in the morning, we would awaken to mother singing in a quiet, not-to-startle-you whisper, "Happy Birthday to You." It was a tradition, even if we were away, it didn't matter, she would call and sing.

Somehow, despite Mom's own rough childhood and her heavy and sorrowful adulthood, she was always positive and saw the good in all mankind. Her glass was always at least half full. I think sometimes that was the contributing factor to her many trials. People seemed to prey on her goodness and willingness to trust. I believe that is the trait my father took advantage of when he pursued my mother. To make sense of my own experiences, I have to give a briefing on my mother's background.

My mother had a very hard childhood. When she was seven, her own precious and loving mother became very ill with tuberculosis. There was no one she loved more than her mom, whom she was kept from and never allowed to touch again after the diagnosis. Crying and pleading, she would only be allowed to stand at the door of the sanitarium room and wave at her mother—when what she really wanted was to run to her and hug her tight. If she could just be in her mother's arms again, she knew she would be safe and happy. She didn't care if she got that terrible disease. She wanted her mom.

When she was nine years old, her mother, age twenty-eight, died, leaving her and her seven year old sister Glenda motherless. Their father, caught up in his own grief and despair from losing the love of his life, couldn't deal with those little girls mourning the loss of their beloved mother. Through the worst part of the illness and after the death, they were placed in foster care, leaving my mother to take charge of her younger sister.

Eventually, Grandfather came back. In order to give his girls a place to sleep, he ran a motel. Soon after, however, he left town again, this time to find work, leaving mother for weeks, sometimes months, to care for her sister and run the motel alone. At the young age of ten, she would be checking weary travelers in and out at all hours of the day and night. Grown men would ask her, "Aren't you a little young to be working this place?" My mother said that, as scared as she was inside, she would put on a brave face and tell them that her father was in the other room and that she was "very capable of handling the motel patrons, thank you."

The Wicked Step-Mother

Things became a lot worse. Grandfather brought a woman home to be the new mom of the house. She brought with her two children of her own who were definitely given priority over these two little girls. It was like a scene out of Cinderella, but worse. To say her step-mother was abusive would be an incredible understatement.

My grandfather adored his daughters from his one true love, especially my mother who looked just like her own mom. His new wife was very jealous of

Mother. Unfortunately, Grandfather was still traveling to find work, leaving his little daughters to be tortured and tormented until his return.

My step-grandmother's threats would keep my mom and her sister awake at night. They were truly terrified of this woman and were convinced if they told their father of the abuse, there was a possibility of death coming their way. This woman used any and every excuse to pull out belts, wooden spoons, anything she could think of to pound on those little girls. She was in every way a wicked and evil stepmother.

Their new "mother" was quick to fill Grandfather with stories of how terrible his girls were while he was away and how lucky he was that she was there to keep them in line. She wouldn't leave their side for fear of them tattling and the truth coming out, but they were too afraid for that.

The fabricated tales of their misdeeds didn't seem to matter to Grandfather; he loved his girls. They could do no wrong in his eyes. This made the jealousy and rage skyrocket and the beatings much more severe in his absence. As her father readied to leave, Grandmother would whisper in her ear that she was "going to get" her as soon as he was gone.

Eventually, Mother got old enough and started to fight back. She would joke to make her sister laugh when the threats were silently whispered. When Grandmother said, "In 2 days, I am going to get you!", my mother would lean over to her little sister and say, "Not if I get you first" or "In that case, until then, you better sleep with one eye open!" They would both burst out in giggles, which made Grandmother irate.

Grandmother went from initially abusing Mother, to turning on the younger, easier victim, her little sister, Glenda. My mother, who was very protective of Glenda, would tell me stories of her and Grandmother toppling over furniture in horrible fist fights, scratching, and hair pulling. The whole house would be in ruins as they threw each other into walls and over tables. She said they would tumble over the couch clenched together. If Grandmother was throwing her over, she was taking Grandma, too!

She never knew when Grandmother was apt to throw dishes, vases and other items at her. Once at the dinner table, she threw a fork, striking my mother perfectly between her eyes. The fork stuck there for a few seconds before dropping on her plate below. Mother said she sat there glaring at Grandmother, not giving her the satisfaction of crying as blood came down her face and onto her plate.

When Grandfather returned, Grandmother hovered close to my mother, trying to make sure nothing was told. She, of course, had threatened the girls beforehand and concocted a story of the clumsiness of Mother "to get such an injury on her face." Needless to say, Mom wanted to get out of that house as soon as she could.

Cowboys and Cops

Grandfather, I've always said, was "the last real American cowboy." He was a large man, around six and a half feet tall, with tons of muscle. A cowboy hat always dressed his head, making him look even taller. I never saw him without cowboy boots on his feet.

Grandpa swore all the time and Mother would tell us to cover our ears and not repeat any words he said. You knew he liked you if he called you a no-good varmint or a good-for-nothing-blankety-blank. If he didn't like you, he wouldn't say anything at all.

He believed in the old ways, everything settled with a handshake. If you wouldn't honor your handshake, he would shoot you. We always made jokes about how many people grandpa probably killed or shot and nobody ever corrected us that it wasn't so. Grandpa was a very old-fashioned and honest man, so if he really did shoot someone, we were sure they probably deserved it.

He believed in the old-school, take-care-of-business way towards animals. If a creature is hurt and suffering, shoot it in the head. When his dog Shep chased and killed the chickens, he shot him in the head. I never saw the same dog twice while visiting grandpa, but he always had a dog named Shep.

The rules and laws of the town he lived in didn't apply to him. They truly didn't. I heard the story of a salesman driving past his "private property" signs and onto Grandpa's mountain. Grandfather went out with his shotgun and started firing. The man tore down and off that mountain to the police station. When he finished his tale of terror, he asked the police to arrest my grandfather. They laughed and said, "Our advice is, don't bother old Bill and stay off his mountain!" The man argued that my grandfather was a lunatic and his actions were attempted murder. The police said, "He was nice to you. If he meant to hurt you, you would already be dead on that mountain." Old justice, that's my grandpa.

At 16, Mother was a high school cheerleader and started beauty school to be a hairdresser, or beautician, as they used to call them. It was during this time that she met her future true love, Carl. He was two years older and had graduated already. He was smitten with Mom and although she played a little hard to get, he pursued and won her heart. They were married in a Catholic ceremony when Mother was twenty and he was twenty-two.

Carl was deeply loved by Grandfather. He was the son that Grandpa never had. As rough and tough as Grandfather was, he had only three real soft spots, Carl and his girls.

One time Carl was helping out on the farm when Grandfather's horse purposely attacked him. It turned around, backed up, and kicked him squarely in the chest, throwing him backwards, knocking the wind out of him, and breaking some of his ribs. Grandfather was so angry he took his huge fist and punched that horse squarely between the eyes, hard. The horse dropped to his front knees, then fell over. Grandpa had knocked it out cold. He then began to yell at Mother to go inside and get his gun. Mother pled with him not to shoot the horse, but he forcefully insisted she get his gun. Mother never disobeyed her father but cried and begged him again not to shoot the horse, as she walked toward the house to retrieve his gun. Only when Carl caught his breath and pleaded with him for mercy for that horse, did Grandfather listen and spare the horse's life. He truly loved Carl.

Carl joined the army and was sent to Germany with Mom and that is where their first two sons were born. The Latter-day Saint missionaries had knocked on their door, and there in Germany they were taught the gospel of Jesus Christ and baptized. They later went to the Switzerland Temple and were sealed together for eternity.

An interesting thing about Carl is that he began to tell my mother that he would be leaving the earth by the age of thirty. My Mother did not want to hear that kind of "rubbish" and refused to listen. Carl continued to prepare for that event by working hard to pay off things, setting up savings accounts, getting a life insurance policy, and reminding Mother every once in a while.

They finished with the Army in Germany and settled in Oregon where two daughters were added to the family. Carl had taken work as a logger, or lumberjack, because of the growing industry there. Mother said it was very good money because it was very dangerous.

Carl had come home once with a gift of a beautiful, full-length mink coat. When Mother told him that they couldn't afford it and she didn't need it, he insisted that she have something special from him so that she knew how priceless she was.

I remember that coat from when I was young. Sometimes I would sneak into her closet and try it on with some of her very fancy hats, put on a pair of her heels, and look in the mirror at how beautiful I was. She never got angry when she caught me. She would just kind of sit for a minute and look at me, probably reminiscing of when Carl gave it to her, then smile and tell me to be careful with it and to gently hang it back up when I was finished.

Mother told me an experience that she repeated many times in her life to many people. She said that she and Carl had gone on a walk around a large block of homes on one side and businesses on the other. They were holding hands as they walked, quietly enjoying the peace and beauty around them. When they turned the corner to a street that began businesses and shops everything changed. They were in the afterlife, the spirit world. It was the same street but a different sphere. There were all of these people walking quickly and busily in and out of shops, filling the streets, doing their daily business. No cars were there, just many people. She recognized individuals that had passed on, looking at them as they walked along. Mother said that the people were wide-eyed and just as surprised to see mother and Carl as they were to see them. Even those that mother didn't know stopped and stared at them out of curiosity as to why this couple who were still alive, were in their environment. As they reached the end of the street and turned the corner, they were back in the regular world. Mother and Carl hadn't said a word to each other as they had walked that stretch until then. Carl said, "Did you see that?"

Mother said, "Yes!"

As I learned later in religious study that mother was right, the afterlife is all around us. Those that die only leave this sphere but not the earth. They are all around us and understand the difference of where they are and where the living happen to be. They can see us much clearer and with a better knowledge and understanding of what we are experiencing. It is we that cannot see them.

Mother had told me about what an amazing and handsome man Carl was. He was an excellent father who adored his children like no other. He put the kids to bed at night, every night, with a horsey ride on his back to their bedroom, the kids laughing and squealing with delight. It was a ritual for the three eldest children, something that the boys have always remembered. Every day when Carl came home from work, the boys would be waiting on the porch.

When they heard his blue VW Bug that Mom loved so much coming down the long gravel driveway, they would run to greet him before he could even open the door.

That horrible, fateful day came when Carl didn't return. He was killed by what was properly known as "the widow maker." That is when one tree is cut, falls against another tree, then while cutting the second tree to get them both down, the first falls one way and the second another. Carl's logging partner said that a strange wind came up right before the tree fell. He ran to check on Carl and found him alive but unconscious under the huge tree. Carl lived about an hour while his partner was trying to get help, then he died.

My mother was informed of the news and quickly called Grandfather. When he got on the phone and heard the alarm in her voice he asked "Is it Carl?"

"Yes, Dad."

"Is he hurt?"

"No, Dad, he's dead!"

She said she had only heard Grandfather cry two times in her whole life and this was the second. He got in his car and drove the two hour drive to get to Mom in less than an hour.

Mom said that she didn't want to break the news to Willy, age 5, and Dougy, age 4, but they were waiting on the porch for their daddy to get home and he was late. She went outside and told them that he wasn't coming home and that he had died. Willy began to cry and ran off. Dougy just stood up, stiff and firm, as if it were unacceptable. Putting his head up into the wind and looking off in the direction Carl would come from, he locked that pain inside, as if he had swallowed it. After that, he became a serious, quiet child, no longer the laughing free-spirited boy he once was. He did not speak for two years and never talked about his father's death.

Carl was thirty when he died, just as he had always said he would be. He was buried on a beautiful grassy hill between two of the biggest and most beautiful pine trees I have ever seen. At twenty-eight, Mother was left alone with four children, ages three months to five years.

Grandfather, worried about Mother, built her a house. She acquired the loan to pay for the supplies, but Grandfather put his hard work and love into building a three bedroom, two car garage home with an office. It was small like most homes in 1968, but he put it in a cul-de-sac for child safety reasons.

He also tried to spend more time with Mom to be a father-figure for Willy, Dougy and the girls.

It wasn't long before my father came into the picture. Frank was a science major and had gone back to school for his teaching degree. He knew my mother previously, as she and Carl had gone out on a double date with Frank and his wife. Now divorced, he had two children, ages two and three. Frank pursued Mother. He knew what he wanted and was not going to stop. He went so far as to join Mother's church, trying to get more of an opportunity to date and possibly marry her. Mother felt a lot of pressure from women in the Church to give her four very young children a father by marrying the new single convert pursuing her.

The House of Horrors Begins

Three days after my mother wed my father his ex-wife called and told Mother the real reason behind their divorce. She said that Frank had been sexually abusing his own son, just three years old.

My mother's first reaction, of course, was to confront him about the allegation. Frank went nuts, yelling and screaming about how absurd that was, that this was his ex-wife, and how dare Mother ask him about that! He told her how she was in the wrong to believe something from an ex-spouse. Mother, always seeing the good in others and giving everyone the benefit of the doubt, apologized, and everything went back to "normal".

Frank joined the family with a vengeance. Once he got comfortable, the abuse began. He was extremely jealous of anything having to do with Carl and decided to begin his takeover with having that cute little blue VW hauled away, bringing Mother to tears.

He constantly criticized mom, telling her she was fat, stupid, ugly, anything to bring her down. He also used the funds Carl had left for mother and the kids to finish his education. The money went fast and the family was broke. This stressed out Frank and made him more violent then he already was. My mother didn't have much of a say and was afraid of Frank and his takeover and control of the family.

Carl's youngest, who was only a few months old when her father died, once told me that she had to have been about three when she couldn't get her tricycle to work properly. She walked up to Frank and said, "Dad, can you fix my bike?" He turned around and yelled, "I am NOT your father! Don't you ever call me that again!" She said she remembers the pain of that moment and turned her heart forever away from him and said, "I am on my own." She hardly spoke to him again after that.

Carl's eldest daughter was sick all of the time. She was allergic to everything. She needed to be kept in a plastic bubble but since that wasn't possible, she just stayed sick. She was the only one of Carl's kids Frank had a soft spot for. I believe that was taken from his own childhood in which he had only one sibling, a sister who was gravely ill her whole childhood. Frank told me how he was always so concerned for his sister. She was in and out of the hospital for years. In those days, they didn't have technology on their side so never discovered what was making her so ill. He said his parents were always at the hospital with her. Ironically, she out-lived everyone.

Frank became very involved in the Boy Scout program. He was a scoutmaster for many years. I heard he was pretty good as that was right up his alley with science experiments and camping expeditions. The fact he was amongst many young boys may have also been a motive for him.

The Model

Frank had an interesting childhood in the 1940's, as his mother was kind of a big deal. She was one of the original, what we would call in this day and age, supermodels. She was said to be in magazines and her beauty was unsurpassed.

My mother told me that my grandmother, Frank's mother, was probably the most beautiful woman she had ever seen in her life. She said she was breath-taking and if they walked into a restaurant that you could hear a pin drop as every table would stop and look at her. Men pursued her and women wanted to be her. Frank did tell me stories toward the end of his life about how proud he was in his youth, especially high school, to walk next to his mother. All of this classmates would "ooh" and "ahh" over her beauty. He said everyone was in love with his mother.

On the other hand, Mother said that she was a very mean and cold woman and I can only guess that is where my father got his anger. I had never heard my mom say an unkind word about anyone, including my father, so I knew this grandmother most likely was pretty unkind. My paternal grandfather was said to be a really kind guy but became an alcoholic for reasons I don't know, drinking himself to death by the time my father was 18. He died of liver disease.

Grandmother married again to what I believe was a self-made millionaire, although I don't know how much money he really had. I did see his estate when I was ten and it was breathtaking, something I imagined that a movie star would own or that would probably be on a television show.

My grandmother was diagnosed with bone cancer in her leg and was told it would have to be amputated to save her life. Her response was, according to mother, "I would rather die!" So, she did. She died a month before I was born.

I have had many people say I share physical traits of hers, a great compliment to me, such as long legs and "piano playing" bony, extra- long fingers. I have never had weight problems, even after five children. It takes some serious work for me to gain. All I can say is, "Thanks, Grandma!" My face has mostly my mother's features such as the big brown eyes and small nose, even her smile, so I've heard.

Shortly after marrying Mother, Frank left the Mormon religion. He did not encourage us to go or have Mother take us. I don't know why she didn't. Did she feel threatened? Was it too much work? We did go a few times over the years, as I was even baptized at age eight, but I didn't understand the baptism, or why I was there. The fact that we were going to Farrell's Ice Cream Parlor after was all of the push I needed to do just about anything. I loved Farrell's so much I would have let kids throw mud pies in my face if it meant going there.

There were probably six kids getting baptized and a huge room full of onlookers. My brother baptized me. I was embarrassed as I heard kids saying they saw my underwear "and it had holes in it" when I came up. With all of these people looking at me, it was scarring more than some kind of spiritual experience.

Mother took Carl's children to church weekly who all graduated from seminary. Both of the boys served missions and all four of his children were married in the temple.

Mother had four children with Frank—well, more like three, since my youngest sister was conceived ten years after I was born and after Mom and Frank hadn't been together in five years. Frank must have been feeling kind of frisky so invited Mother on a date to a ball game. Mom must have been frisky too because that was the first time ever she didn't come home. Nine months later, my sister was born, just in time for the divorce to finalize.

Middle Child Syndrome…You Think?

Frank never knew his youngest. When I refer to the kids in the house, I refer usually to the seven of us older kids and not to my youngest sister. Not for a second does she not count, she just wasn't there. I was Frank's second child in this marriage with a sister one year older and a brother two years younger. My brother was the favorite or maybe the most un-disliked (a word I think I just made up) and I was loathed. I tried really hard to figure it out, but Frank did not like me at all!

One day Frank came home with a surprise in his truck. As we ran out to see what he had, he pulled a mini dirt bike from the back of his truck and gave it to my younger brother, telling him it was his. He then pulled out a second one and gave it to my sister. I sat there waiting for mine and he closed up his truck and said, "That's it." My sister and brother were happily checking out their new motorcycles when I said, "Dad, where's mine?" He looked around and said, "Uh, share with your sister." My heart sank. Of course he hadn't purchased one for me. I was purely an afterthought. My kind sister said, "It's okay Kayli, you can share this one with me." I was so used to getting the scraps Frank dropped on the ground. We got so little anyway and I didn't mean to complain and seem ungrateful, it just hurt a bit. I wanted to feel special.

When Frank would return from work or school, as he came in the front door, you would see four to six children scattering like cockroaches out the back door. My half-sister told me how if she saw Frank's truck in the cul-de-sac when coming home from school or a friends, she would turn right around and go to another home. Nobody was glad when Daddy came home!

We bonded together as siblings even though four were Carl's and three were Frank's because he didn't particularly like any of us—he hated us equally (well, maybe me a bit more). He brought abuse of every kind into our home. There was emotional, verbal, psychological, physical, and sexual abuse represented here. Did I miss any? If so, it was probably there too. He was pretty thorough and didn't miss much. Different kinds of abuse were given to different kids, but physical, verbal, and emotional for everyone (lucky us).

Physically, aside from the countless spankings, I was neglected medically for treatment that was needed. Kidney issues have been a constant trial in my life and it was discovered I have only one oddly shaped working kidney that is supposed to have already failed me. I also possess a second one that quit growing around four or five years old, completely full of scar tissue that doesn't work at all. The doctors said it was due to untreated urinary, bladder, and/or kidney infections as a child.

Emotionally, Frank would completely humiliate me by tearing me up one side and down the other about how I wouldn't become anything, had no talent, was a "runt" and, worst of all, punish me by pulling down my pants (what I believe is one of the worst forms of abuse) and exposing my privates prior to spanking the tar out of me.

Although the physical pain was great, due to no clothes to protect the skin, I have emotional scars that have never healed from that traumatizing practice. I have taught my children that "your privates are yours and nobody has a right to see or touch them." I have never allowed that terrible, awful form of abuse to be practiced in my home. I would rather have been put in stocks in the town square.

Rescue of the Bumblebees

When Frank became angry, which was anytime around us kids but seemed like every minute of the day, his ears became very red which we decided was due to his Scottish blood and us kids knew to start running or hiding. If he caught you, you would be very, very sorry.

I never really thought about it before but maybe that is why I was an amazing track star in school and a great basketball player who could run that court like nothing. I should have given Dad credit for my amazing speed and capability to get out of any situation by scaring the life out of me daily. Thanks, Dad!

I spent a lot of time hiding from my dad in closets or under beds. I would watch through the metal vents of the closet, holding my breath, and wait for him to pass by and enter into his office. If I was under my bed, I would put clothes or other items in front of me so a quick glance wouldn't expose me. The fear I had seeing his long bony feet still gives me heart palpitations. I was sure he could hear my heart pounding and would hold my breath until he left. If he was looking for me, I would hide behind the coats in the coat closet up against the wall and put everything in front of me, just listening for him to leave the area so I could sneak outside and ride my bike away.

When Frank would finally go into his office—to drink, as I came to understand—he would close the door and put on very, very loud music. He usually played classical, which I didn't mind. My favorite thing he played was "Flight of the Bumble Bees." When the music was on, he rarely came out and everyone knew then it was safe to come out of hiding because he would be in there for a long time. That music was pure joy to my ears!

Nobody was allowed to ever interrupt Frank or you would suffer the consequences, and nobody did. If you wanted or needed anything, you always spoke to sweet Mother. In fact, I don't even know what he was good for. He didn't help with anything. He certainly didn't fix anything. You couldn't even speak to him. If you got too close, spilled your milk, dropped a plate, made any kind of childhood mistake, his wrath was unleashed and you were terrified for your life or for the life of whichever sibling was at the end of that anger.

I truly understand why children don't say anything or request help at school or from police when they have a sibling that has been singled out, beaten, locked in a closet and starved at home. It is out of sheer terror, the kind that keeps you up peering out of your covers at night, hoping that monster doesn't come looking for you.

That monster wasn't under my bed, he consumed the whole house. We were the ones hiding under the bed. Frank would grab a child and take them to another room, closing the door and your heart would sink as you tried not to cry knowing what hell they were going through. I remember hearing the hitting and the screams of others. You knew that you would be in trouble when Frank returned if he saw you looking at him or the victim. To survive you would just pretend nothing was going on, pretend they deserved it and keep doing what you were doing. Don't wince, don't flinch, don't look up and especially don't look him in the eyes.

I remember Frank spanking me at age five until his hand was bleeding from the crown of his watch digging in. As soon as he finished his punishment and saw the blood he began yelling, "See, look at what you made me do!" as he threw me over his knees and began to spank me again but this time, much harder.

I don't know how my mom could emotionally handle the screaming from our spankings or beatings. I remember putting books in my pants a couple of times, hoping he wouldn't notice so I could handle the spanking. My square bottom gave me away. Thinking back, that was pretty creative. When he said he was going to spank you until you couldn't sit down, he meant it! What possibly could a small, half-starved, undersized little girl have done to deserve that rage? Needless to say, Children's Services visited our house a few times.

My mother never told Grandpa about the abuse by Frank. She knew Grandpa would shoot him. She did not want him to go to jail. He could have cared less! Grandpa never liked Frank and would have gladly put that rabid dog down. She didn't want us to mention it either. It was a pretty big secret.

My Comforter, My Angel

I will not leave you comfortless; I will come to you
John 14:18

When I was about four or five, I had been sent to my room after being spanked and humiliated by my father, again, for being the "horrible" and "bad girl" he thought I was. I remember wiping my eyes and thinking about how I was going to be in that room for a long time. I was murmuring to myself at how much I hated that mean man in our house and referred to him with whatever cuss words I could come up with like "poopoo-head" and "dummy" and said that I would never be married to someone like him. I remember wishing I could call him those bad words to his face, but my bottom couldn't take any more.

All that I wanted was someone to be nice to me. I just remember repeating the word "nice." "Why can't he just be nice? Why is he so mean? I want a dad that is happy and kind. I want to grow up and get married and my kids will like their dad because he will be nice." I was very concerned as to how I would find this "nice" person in my future.

I don't remember who or what, but I began talking to what I remember to be was an angel of some kind standing in my closet. Although I don't believe as an adult that angels have wings, this one I think did—maybe for the purpose of me knowing who or what he was. I don't remember exactly what he looked like but can only suppose it was a guardian angel there to comfort me after a lot of abuse. I was not afraid! In fact I enjoyed his peaceful company. He was gentle, non-threatening, and felt like an old friend. I opened up my heart about my concerns for the future. I remember telling him about my mean father and a desire to have a boy when I grew up "be nice to me and my kids."

Although I cannot recall what was said to me, I do remember asking, "How will I know it's him?" Whatever he said wasn't good enough for me because again I pressed, "But how will I know?" He then told me that our "names would match." I only knew that either our first names would be something like Kayli and Cameron or the last name would match my first, like Kayli Christensen.

It is funny how much time in my dating years went into pondering that experience and the names of my dates until I began to discount it and started to think of it as a silly childhood fantasy, yet something about the truth stuck with me. Maybe the fact that this was my first "spiritual" experience and that deep down I knew the experience and that angel was for real. I had no idea that there would be many, many other experiences to come.

As an adult and relaying this experience about the angel to my older sister, she replied, "Oh, he was in the closet the bubbles would go into."

"What are you talking about?"

"Don't you remember at night, so many times we would be frightened to go to sleep and then we would see all of those bubbles—at least that is what we called them—coming down the hall and into our room. They were so peaceful and would go into our closet. It meant we would be safe that night. They were there to protect us."

I vaguely remember, but we were very young.

The Devil Has Left the Building

I am not here to write a book about my siblings. In fact, I will try to keep them out of this book as much as possible. I am not here to share their experiences, although I know some horribly vile and disgusting things that happened to a few of them at the hands of my father that didn't happen to me. Yet, I experienced things that didn't happen to them. That is their story and they may want to keep it hidden forever and I don't blame them. This is my story.

I will also spare details of experiences that happened to me that belong in child abuse, psychology or psychiatry books. What I will say is that most of my vile abuse happened at night, making it very hard for me to go to sleep. Sometimes I would just pretend I was asleep, hoping things would be over soon. There was something wrong with me and I always felt dirty, like I had done something bad. I just wanted to take a bath and wash the filth off, but I was polluted on the inside and that horrible feeling that I had felt as long as I could remember wouldn't wash away.

I couldn't wait to get married to have a protector next to me, finally to be able to sleep in peace, snuggled against someone who loved me so much and would never let anything happen to me. To this day I have problems sleeping alone when my husband is out of town. No matter how much therapy I have received, and I have had a lot, it is the same. I am up and down all night and have to sleep with a light or music on. When my husband does come back into town, even just being in the house, I sleep like a baby.

The hell continued in our home and my father started moving in and out during a period of a lot of fighting. I was five when he left the first time after I told my mother some disgusting and vile things he was doing that I didn't understand. It was enough for her to first, in shock, spank me and put me in timeout.

As I was sitting there crying, she came back to me and got down on her knees, eye to eye with me. I guess she had thought about it for a few minutes and realized I shouldn't know things like that and why did I? She asked me a bit more about it. I told her what I knew, had seen, heard, etc. She forgot to let me be finished with my time-out as I watched her marching away from me at a brisk pace. Then, a war ensued. As I remember, it lasted all day until dark and my father packed some things and left.

Running to the window with my sister, I remember watching him and his old truck drive away. I was afraid of how this was going to change things but said to myself, "GOOD!" Just then my sister started crying which made me cry. Mom was trying to comfort both of us, mainly my sister and was saying kind words, but I couldn't tell her what I was really thinking. I knew it seemed bad for thinking of how happy I was that my father was gone. Mom actually thought I was crying because he was gone? I was rejoicing, tears of joy. It was true what I had told her. I don't lie, never have.

Do I feel guilty for being the catalyst for breaking up my family? That was the question a therapist asked me once. I said that I never thought of it like that. I guess I may have subconsciously had a little guilt as a child due to the poverty we all had to be subjected to, but mostly not. As an adult I can see that our family was already broken. I think I started the mending process. My therapist told me, that was a lot on my tiny shoulders. Somehow, my old soul knew he had to be gone, that it was better for our family. I wasn't sad about it. The thing I was sad about was that since Frank had the job, there was no money coming into our house after that, which meant no food. I hated being hungry. We went hungry a lot.

My Best (Pet) Friend Beau

One positive thing Frank had brought into our home was a darling cocker spaniel named Beau. When Frank moved to an apartment, Beau stayed with us. There was no money for human food let alone dog food and before long, he was skin and bones. We had no business owning a dog. Someone should have called animal control to have that poor thing picked up. I was glad no one did because it would have been devastating to me, but it would have been the humane thing to do. Beau was almost dead when I asked my mom if I could make him my dog and I would care for him. She said that I could try but thought it was too late for him. It wasn't.

Beau was a lot like me, a survivor and a vacuum cleaner. He would eat anything edible and some things not. Everything I could find such as bread crusts, fruit off the trees out back, anything went to Beau and before long he put some weight back on. Sometimes Frank would buy some cans of food and drop them off. We would both be hungry so I would open the can and take a bite, then give the rest to him. He ate the majority of the can because I wanted him to live, but I would take a bite or two. Later my sister told me she would do the same thing out of hunger.

For exercise I took Beau on regular walks or runs with me. I wanted so much for him to be happy. I had never had anything special belong to just me so Beau was my prized possession. He could do all sorts of tricks. I taught him that when he was hungry to bring his food bowl, an old plastic cool-whip container to the back glass door. Beau was also the star of the "circus" that the neighborhood kids would put on. We would then charge our families to watch. Beau would jump through a hula-hoop (that we would explain was "on fire") from one chair to another.

Beau was a great friend and I sure loved him. One day I took him out for a run. Thinking he had become a bit fat, the run was a little longer than normal but not unusual. When I arrived back at the house he went through the side gate to the back yard as usual as I would run through the house to get his food. When I opened the back curtains to the glass door, he was dead. I panicked as

I saw him lying there and started calling his name over and over but he didn't move. Hyperventilating, I ran to my mother and told her he was dead. She jumped up and ran to the back door and kept repeating, "Oh no, Oh no!"

My beautiful Beau was gone. This was the first time I felt true loss. My heart was broken as we put him in a black garbage bag and in the trunk of our car. I wasn't ready to say goodbye. We drove his body out in the country to the property of mother's friend. After digging a hole for my dog and helping mom place his body in it, I couldn't take any more. There was no way I could watch her cover him with dirt so I ran back to the car and laid my head down. I never looked back out that window until we got back into town. The pain was too much.

Mom kept talking about where he had gone and about God and Heaven between her tears. Numbness was the only thing I felt, mixed with anger at this man in the sky that would take him from me. Part of me hoped there was a real place called Heaven for my sweet boy. He had been through a lot in his short life and deserved the best.

Stinky Shoes

There were so many kids in our family that there wasn't money for clothes. Everything was handed down. By the time it got to me, it was completely trashed, usually with patches sewn to cover holes. I was constantly teased at school about my clothing, especially my shoes. Mom could only afford cheap shoes to begin with and, again, they were handed down. With all of the playing and sports, it wasn't long until holes appeared. Being the youngest girl, I was the last in line for anything.

The most embarrassing thing to me was when my toes would show through the top of my sneakers and kids would say, "Nice shoes!" It was worse when they would notice beyond that and say, "Wait a minute, you have socks on too and we can still see your toes. Those have holes, too?" Then they would begin to laugh and tease me, pointing it out for everyone else. It was difficult, but I knew this was the way it was and not much I could do about it.

The best thing happened one day when my mom came home with my first pair of new shoes I can remember. I was probably seven years old. There was a warehouse that contained shoes that had a fire. All of the smoke damaged shoes were $5. That was a lot of money for us at the time, but Mom got shoes for all of us. To say I was thrilled was an understatement! Finally, I had a pair to be proud of with no holes. I wore those stinky new shoes proudly to school until those toes came back through.

All I Want For Christmas

My father came back a few months after he had left and moved back in for a couple of months. He, for once, was actually nice to me, playing with me in our sunken front living room one evening.

Our living room had two wooden steps down into it and a big comfy couch on one side with two matching chairs on the other. There was a round cherry-wood coffee table right in the center of the room and two matching end tables with lamps on either side of the couch. At the end of the living room was a big stone fireplace with large grey rocks ascending to the ceiling and covering the entire wall. My grandfather had set each of those huge, heavy stones himself and I had spent much of my short life in that room, lying on the carpet or pulling a chair near the fireplace, admiring them.

My father actually wanted to play with me? Was this a new beginning for him? Was he trying to reconcile with Mother by becoming a better father to us children? He began swinging me around by one arm and pulling me as to run in a circle around him, faster and faster. I was laughing and enjoying having a dad for just a minute but then…then he let go, right toward the stairs. I flew uncontrollably, face first into the wooden steps, knocking out my non-loose front teeth. I was screaming, blood was everywhere, and mother came running. I couldn't hear their exchange of angry words over my own screams, but my father stormed off into his office and the loud music went on.

One of my siblings found my teeth and brought them to me in the bathroom where mother had rushed me to the sink. She stayed with me rinsing my mouth and fat lips over and over, telling me that it was an accident and that Frank really was sorry. Frank never came and told me that. He actually avoided me for weeks while my mouth and lips healed. Even later he never spoke about that incident to me. I've always wondered if that was punishment for me telling on him. I never played with or trusted him again after that.

I grieved over the father I had. My heart ached to be loved, held, kissed, and played with like the fathers I saw on television (when we could pay the bill). What was wrong with me? Why was I so un-loveable? What could I do better so that he would love me? I ached for approval from him. Deep down at a very young age, I knew it would never come. He was so incredibly mean and angry all of the time. I have only one memory of him showing any affection to me. It must have been my birthday or something. I had to learn to let go of the many insults and negativity thrown my direction. The pile alone would crush my tiny frame. If you asked Frank, I was never going to amount to anything in this life. I was dumber than a doornail, a loser in his book. There wasn't anything I could do that was good or correct. There wasn't much of my self-worth growing when he was around.

Sweet Dreams

Frank must be the reason I have obsessive compulsive behavior traits. My room became immaculate. I cleaned the bathrooms to a perfect shine every Saturday for my chores. In sports I had to be the best basketball player on the team or I was a loser. I broke school records in track. Still, it wasn't good enough to receive a simple, "Good job." Approval is all I longed for. I just pleaded on the inside for something to say that I was normal, or even just alright. It never came.

Years later I would have a very detailed dream: I call it a memory because the details checked out. I must have been around six months old. There I saw myself in our sunken living room. I was alone in a cheap, plastic baby carrier on top of our round cherry-wood coffee table. The room was dark and I must have just woken up. It looks like the family came in from somewhere and I was asleep so was just put into the dark, quiet front room. I could see my arms flailing around like I was screaming. All of the sudden, I was inside that baby, right then, myself. I felt everything from the one-piece, zip up pajamas on my skin to the hard plastic against my back and the curve of the seat I was sitting on. There was no control of my body or its movements. My hands and feet just seemed to do their own thing, thrashing around as I cried. I did not feel a safety belt holding me in like the seats these days. Looking out toward the hallway there was a light shining across the wall from what I know now was my parent's bedroom. I saw a shadow crossing the wall coming to get me. I was so excited because I wanted my mommy. I remember that feeling of, "Oh, she's coming. The excitement! Everything is going to be fine now." Around the corner and into the room was my worst nightmare, Father. I gasped and screamed, as if the devil himself was coming to get me.

Right then I sat straight up in bed. I was sweating, with my heart pounding and lungs breathing hard. There I was, terrified of my father as an infant. This truly was a memory and his mean and evil spirit was easily recognized by me, even then.

Good Riddance

Father moved in and out several times. During that time my eldest brother had the opportunity to go to Japan as an exchange student with another high school in Japan. He went for a year and upon returning was a black belt in judo, along with the talent of speaking fluent Japanese. I don't believe Frank was living back in the house. This time with my brother, things were going to be different.

One day I heard Mother yelling and screaming for help in a very frightened voice. All of us kids ran to the hallway leading to the bedrooms to find mother on the ground, on her rear-end, holding her head as she was being dragged by her hair by my father. She was crying in pain and fear, trying to get to her feet but she was backwards so didn't have her knees to help get up. We were all terrified and frozen. I wanted to get to her to help even though I was the second smallest in the house. I wanted to run to Frank and punch and kick him so he would let go of my mother. As I made my move to help, my eldest sister grabbed me tight and held me from behind in a bear hug so I couldn't intervene and possibly get hurt. I felt so helpless and insignificant knowing there was truly nothing I could do. We were all just lined up, helplessly watching this abuse to our beloved mother unfold. My other half-sister ran to the back of the house and yelled to our eldest brother that Frank was hurting Mom.

Right then my eldest brother appeared. He came down the hall in two leaps, almost like magic, and I don't think my father knew he was home. Frank looked a bit surprised and she cried, "Will, help me!" Will, in more of a manly deep voice than I remembered him having stepped up and said, "Let go of my mother!"

Frank said, "I just want to talk to her."

My mother cried, "Don't let him take me into the bedroom."

Will stepped over my mother who was still on the ground holding her head, and in that thin hallway got eye to eye with Frank. He still had a tight grip on Mom and a handful of her hair when Will repeated, "I said, let go of my mother!" It was silent, a stand-off. All of us kids were scared for what can and may happen next. Nobody stands up to Frank and gets away with it. They stood there looking at each other for another minute and I think that Frank for the first time realized he wouldn't win this battle. He let go of Mom and just stood there looking in Will's eyes as if to say, "Okay, I let go."

Will then said, "Get out of our house."

We were all already surprised that Will had intervened like a superhero but then, Frank just walked off, right then, out the front door. We didn't see him much after that.

That experience changed my brother forever. He once told me that was the day he became a man.

Little Bums

When Frank left, he took his money again. We knew what this meant, a repeat of no food, raggedy clothes and toeless shoes. We definitely would have no telephone. Television had access to 3 local channels. The power and gas company shut us off on a regular basis—oh, those cold showers!—for nonpayment until mom got enough money to turn it back on. Even our water at times was turned off. We were broke.

Sometimes at night when Mom thought we were all asleep—remember, I didn't sleep—I would hear her crying in her room, real heartbroken sobs into her hands or pillow. I knew she didn't want us to hear her so I never told her. One night I quietly slipped out of bed and peeked in her room. I saw her on her knees, pouring her heart out to God. For some reason that seemed useless to me and I felt sorry for her. This made me angry and sad to see her in so much anguish as I tip-toed back to bed. Maybe I was mad at God then. Maybe I had been through so much I didn't believe in God and for sure didn't know Him. He seemingly didn't know or like me either so I didn't care much for Him.

As just a little girl, my heart ached for Mom. I felt so helpless and hurt I couldn't ease her pain. I couldn't wait to grow up one day so I could work hard and help Mom. She had done so much for us, sacrificed so much, that I wanted to ease her burdens and take care of her. Much of my time was spent trying to be the best little girl I could, the best helper. That is all I could do.

With the concern of how to feed her children with no money and no real job, I cannot imagine the sleepless nights she bore. I believe that she stayed with Frank as long as she did to keep food on the table. It must have been a terrible double-edged sword to walk in her shoes. My mother, without an education and on her own, couldn't afford to feed and care for seven hungry little mouths.

My sister and I were always scrambling to make a few dollars in the neighborhood to help buy food. We would weed flower beds, rake leaves, and sweep porches, anything to get a few bucks for food. You have never seen younger paper girls than us. We must have been seven and eight years old taking over our elder sisters' route every day. That big paper carrier vest practically went to our toes, but we had no problem working hard. Mom had purchased what was called a "bugger." It pulled two small kids on the back of a bike. My sister and I would attach that to one of our small bikes and fill it with papers. We would take turns pedaling the bike or riding in the back throwing papers. It was much better than those heavy vests. We had that job for years, along with the daily terror of a little dog named Pudd.

Do You Want Fries With That?

All through elementary school and starting junior high, my sister and I had to work in the lunch room every day, if we wanted to eat. I think nowadays that is called slave labor or violates child labor laws, but in the 70's if we wanted to eat lunch, we had to work. The funny thing is that it was called "free lunch" but we actually worked for it. I don't believe it was a bad concept at all. It taught me not only how to work, but that if you want something in life, even lunch, you need to get up and get it. No spoon-feeding. These days they do give out free lunch to almost anyone.

My sister and I weren't the only ones working in the kitchen for our lunch. There were a few others. The advantage was that we got out of class about ten minutes early to get to the cafeteria for set up. The lunch ladies had the food prepared and we would get in line to start dishing it out buffet style to our peers when the bell rang. It may have been a little embarrassing but my friends were used to seeing me all through elementary school and the first year of junior high. It was no secret we didn't have money for lunch. Sometimes other kids would make unkind comments such as, "You have to do that because your family is broke." I couldn't help myself but make a comment similar to, "Actually I do it so I can spit in your food" as I dropped a big spoonful of mashed potatoes on their plate." We missed the lunch recess in elementary school to wash dishes after everyone ate, but I was happy that I could get extra helpings of food that were left over. Every job has its perks. I also learned to work hard for everything I have.

Mom also had side jobs to get a little bit of food. She could earn a few bucks cutting hair. She cut anyone's hair at our house for $3-5, except the Mormon missionaries who would stop by. Theirs were free. Anyone who didn't have money like us also got free cuts. There was only one other family in town that I knew for sure was as poor and destitute as us. As one of my best friends told me, we were so beyond poor we "made poor look like a step up."

Mom was very giving and loving. Manners were a priority to her. We may have looked like orphans but we were extremely polite and grateful. Mom was the greatest example of Christ's love that I ever knew. She didn't have enough food for us but tried so hard. Sometimes random money would show up (I guess from Grandpa) and we would have a few weeks of food.

Mom was a great cook. When we did have groceries, Mom would make roasts on Sundays and cookies after school. During those times of plenty it seemed she always would bring someone home for dinner. She found people on the streets. Once, I remember a homeless lady with a couple of small kids, an old man, a dirty bum, and a prostitute she met on her late night job another time. They never left without her giving them a coat or gloves, something useful. The money and the food always came and then, unfortunately, would always run out.

Beans, Beans the Magical Fruit

For far too many dinners, Mom would fill a big pot with water and soak pinto beans overnight, then cook them the next day for what seemed like the whole day. My brother would sing that horrible little poem about beans, while making obnoxious noises by blowing on his arm. If you don't know it from the title, it's a good thing. The beans were horrible but cheap, a good source of protein, and something to fill our bellies. If we were lucky, she would get a few pieces of bacon to throw in too. We had beans a lot! Many times I would go to bed hungry because I couldn't stomach any more beans. I have never made them for my own children, although I have threatened.

Another of Mom's favorites during famine was liver and onions. When that smell came into the air my heart would sink as I knew I was going to bed hungry. Don't think I didn't try to eat them to rid my hunger pangs, but it made me want to hurl. I would watch out the window, hoping my friend Kim's family, who lived next door, would come home so I could escape there for dinner.

I think the liver came from Grandfather, along with roasts and money for food. He butchered his pigs, chickens and cows yearly on his farm. Even though mother never told us he had given her anything, I would see him stuff what looked like a bill in her pocket when he would visit and thought no one was looking. I am sure we certainly couldn't afford those roasts mother made without Grandpa's assistance.

Bills, Bars, and Steaks

Character is what you do when no one is watching
—J C Wells

Let me start this chapter off with reminding the world about the Ten Commandments which, if obeyed, would bring about peace, comfort, respect, love, safety, and security. Adherence to these ten simple concepts could change the world. This chapter is about one of them.

The best example of honesty in my life was Mother. She was 100% perfectly honest, no matter how much it hurt. Once in our cul-de-sac, my sister found a $100 bill and went to show Mom. I don't know if Mom had ever seen one; we certainly hadn't. We all sat there staring at its beauty for a minute. Mom was trying to figure out if it was real. As much as we could have used that money for food, Mom quickly said, "Let's find the owner of that. I am sure they are distraught and looking for it." She went with my sister to a few doors and quickly found the owner who was outside looking on the ground and had just cashed their check from work when the wind swept up their money. They were extremely relieved to have it back.

Another time, I rode my bike to the grocery store, using my paper route money to buy maple bars for the family. The cost for twelve bars was $1.99. Checking out, there was a man in front of me, obviously wealthy and in an extreme hurry. As he exchanged words with the clerk, it sounded like he would be attending a barbecue. The clerk bagged his groceries and quickly rung up mine, finishing with me in no time. The man was putting the cash back in his wallet, slowing me down from leaving. He then grabbed his bags and rushed out in a hurry. I picked up mine, followed him out and started home on my bike.

The bag seemed awfully heavy as I rode, and by the time I got home my wrist was hurting from holding it. Walking into the kitchen, I pulled out my maple bars only to see meat, great big cuts of red beef. I had never seen meat like that in my life, just hamburger and some roasts. These slices had to be something special. They looked very expensive. My mother said they were called steaks.

"Well, I guess we get to eat these instead of doughnuts," I said.

Mother quickly wrapped them back in the grocery bag and said, "Those aren't ours. You take them quickly back to the store."

"Mom," I protested, "I saw the man leave in a very nice car. It's his fault because he took my maple bars and left me this bag. He traded with me. That means we can have these, plus, I don't want to go back. My arm hurts."

Mom again repeated, "Get on your bike and take those immediately back to the store. We do not take things that aren't ours, even by accident!"

I rode back to the store unhappily and gave the cashier the package of meat. The manager and cashier said the man had not come back for the meat, but gave me a new set of maple bars and thanked me for bringing it back. Riding again home I was relieved the bars weighed almost nothing. It seemed like such a waste of my time, then, but this has been the one lesson that has stuck with me more than any other my entire life.

My children know the story about the steaks and maple bars. They are also expected to be exact and honest in all of their dealings as well. I hope I have done the same kind of job instilling that in them as my mother did for me. As Sheldon F. Child taught, "Honesty is the ONLY policy."

The Night Job

Mom's greatest attribute was her positive spirit. She whistled and sang all of the time. You would have thought her life was perfect. She seriously was that happy. She may have cried at night, but she gave every new day her all, hoping or having faith for it to be better than the last. Some of my best memories are of her playing old vinyl records from the 50's and 60's on the huge antique stereo in our front door entryway at the top of the stairs by our sunken living room. On Saturday mornings the whole house would wake up to the stereo blaring "Yellow Polka Dot Bikini" and many others. To this day I can sing the words to every song off most of those albums. All of the songs were super old and I must have heard them 1000 times. Totally loved it!

Mom began to work at night for the local paper, delivering bundles to stores and filling the newsstand boxes that used to be in store fronts. She had to be at work at about midnight to get the bundles. She usually finished deliveries around 4-5:00am. She was thirty-eight years old, widowed and divorced with seven hungry mouths to feed. She didn't believe in welfare but hard work. Surely she only made minimum wage and it was part time work, but every dollar meant a loaf of bread or gallon of milk. Mother was grateful for the work.

I enjoyed going with her to work on the weekends. She appreciated my company and it went much faster. We owned a big, red VW hippy bus with the sliding side door and a luggage rack on top. It was totally ugly. I would open the bundles and count the papers, having them prepared before we drove to the next stop. That way Mom could hurry around the car, slide open the door and put the readied and counted papers right into the news stand. It was much faster. She would reward me for going with her by looking at the bottom of her purse for change and stopping by the 24-hour donut shop on the way home. There were many times I didn't want to go that Mom woke me and pleaded for help. I may have murmured a bit but would go because I loved her.

The sound of the car engine humming as I lay on top of those nice warm newspapers hot off the press would put me to sleep. Back then cars only optionally had seat belts so I would use bundles of papers to make a little "crib" as to not roll when she went around corners. When I think back, I bet Mother was a bit afraid of many of those dark stores and truck stops in the middle of nowhere at night. I was afraid, too. At a couple of them, Mom would say, "Lock the door as soon as I get out." So inside the bus I would lock her door, unlock and open the sliding door, hand her the papers, close and lock the sliding and wait for her to run toward her door which I would unlock again. It's not like someone couldn't still get to me if someone grabbed her out there. I may be locked in, but there were no cars, phones, people, any sign of life at several stops. Whoever she feared would have been able to get me as well.

Those are still good memories I have of time spent with just me and Mom, in spite of the dangers that could have been lurking there. Carl was probably watching out for his sweetheart anyway.

Carl's Ghost

I know my mom missed Carl immensely. Sometimes I would watch her doing dishes at the kitchen sink and as she did, she would stare out into the backyard and just drift off for a moment. For a brief second I could see her pain and longing for Carl. She didn't have to tell me what she was thinking about, I knew. I wished so much that he was here to love and protect her but most of all to make her happy.

I wished that Carl was my father. Sometimes, when I was fighting with one of my half-siblings, they would try to be hurtful and say, "Well, you have the crappy dad." What could I say to that? I would be like, "Yeah, I know." They would win the fight EVERY TIME by saying that. There wasn't anything I could say to trump it, except when I got smarter and started saying, "Well, your dad is dead." Not very nice, I know, but they kept winning the fights. I had to be creative. At least it stopped them from bringing up my dad. Either way, we all were dad-less. (Did I make up another word?) When I would cry to my mom about the "crappy dad" comment, Mom always said, "Carl is your father, too." I am sealed to him in the temple and you come through me. I never understood how that worked or what in the world it meant, but it was good enough that my mom sounded like she knew what she was talking about. I trusted her as the only person that was a sure thing. As long as I was with her, everything was going to be alright.

One of my half-siblings had a spiritual experience in which Carl appeared to them during some rough teenage years when they really needed a dad. Mom talked to us all about it and no matter what she said to comfort us—how he watches over our family, etc. It was a horror movie to me. I had never thought of that possibility that a ghost could appear to people I know in my house. Mom tried to explain that it was Carl's spirit, not a ghost, to comfort, not to scare us. That was not good enough. I decided quickly I would start to pray. I would say, "Please, God, whoever you are, don't let any ghosts come to comfort me." I never thought about the one in my room as a tiny girl being a ghost; it was a friend and definitely a comforter, but not a scary ghost.

The interesting thing about Carl is that he visited three of his four children at different times in their youth. My two older brothers both had a visit from him on their missions in foreign lands. I remember thinking, "Wow, he must be really up there in rank to have privileges like that."

What my mom had said about us, Frank's kids, being equally important didn't then make sense. Obviously my older siblings were more loved because he appeared to them. He clearly was their dad, not mine. He visited them, not me. I had to remind myself that I really didn't want to see him. I even prayed to not see him but was envious that he cared enough to send his very best, himself. I couldn't even get a birthday card from my dad, if I sent my dad the card stamped and asked him to send it to me. I think he would have sent it to someone else's kid. The interesting thing here is that Carl appeared to all of his own but one. Why not my other half sibling?

When the idea of ghosts freaked me out one time, Mom told me a story about a friend of hers. She said that as a couple they wanted a child badly. One day, her friend's husband was in the bathroom, looking in the mirror shaving with the door open. A small red-headed boy came in and started to watch him. The husband, thinking it was a neighbor kid his wife let in, didn't pay a lot of attention until the boy said, "Hi, my name is Randy and I am your son."

The husband in shock spun around and the boy disappeared. Sure enough they had a son with red hair about eight months later and named him Randy. Mom wanted me to understand that I didn't need to be afraid of spirits. They were people like us without their bodies but regular people.

Sunshine and Roses Next Door

Back to my half-siblings, even if Carl was their dad, good for them, they got the good dad. My feelings were that God didn't love me anyway to put me in this crappy life with an even crappier dad. I didn't understand dads much anyway. Mine only brought me fears, tears, and pain. What was a dad good for?

Other people seemed to like them. The only other one I knew was the super, duper, nice one that lived right next door, Donald. I really believed he was supernatural, abnormal. He was like the ones I saw on television, except they were phony actors and he wasn't. From my experience, normal was my crappy dad. Donald was my best friend Kim's dad, lucky girl. Kim had moved next door when I was two years old. She was adopted and when she was, she won the mega lottery! I wanted to be adopted to get a dad like Donald. I loved my mom, but I loved her mom, too. Donald and his wife lost their two only daughters to a tragic car accident that killed four of the five occupants when the girls were returning from a high school game as teenagers. I can't imagine their pain losing both of their only children at the same time and going from teens in the house with friends to just silence. It must have been excruciating! Kim's mom sat a lot at their kitchen table, looking out the window like my mom. I bet I know what she was thinking about. She had that look of deep thought which was probably longing or pain, same as my mother but would quickly put her smile on if she saw you enter the room.

I still remember the last high school pictures of Kim's sisters always sitting, perfectly dusted, in their living room. It was the room we almost never played in.

Kim's house was my only escape when my father was around. I would see him come home, and would sneak quickly out of the sliding back door or run through his office and go out the side door, through our back gate to the front and sneak through the bushes between our houses to freedom. There were no fighting or harsh words at Kim's, only laughter and love.

Kim was extremely protected and very spoiled. She had every toy on TV. If she wanted it, she got it. It made it fun to be her friend because I got to play with all of her toys. Most of my happy childhood memories and thoughts come from Kim's house.

Donald was such a great father figure. He would play basketball with us, especially during basketball season since Kim and I always played on the same team. Summer nights we had endless games of horse or pig. He also taught me to bowl and would take us bowling on Saturdays. The best memories (if there is a best because there are so many) were in the summertime when he would take us to the county fair. He didn't particularly care for the rides but would go if I wasn't there. That was the only time I was able to experience fair food like cotton candy and corndogs. There was no way I would have been able to pay for those luxuries and definitely was not going to miss a chance to go with Kim.

Donald bought and set up things for Kim and I to play with like tetherball in her driveway and a teeter-totter and swing set in her backyard. She had all of the new board games that would come out before I finished watching the commercial. Her world was an amusement park to me.

My sister and I would only get one toy a year which was usually on Christmas. One year my sister had received a Little People house and I, the treehouse. Kim had an awesome castle, cars, the barn, house, you name it. We would spread all of it across Kim's garage since Donald would back up the cars so we could play. One summer day, Kim's ping pong table fell over and crushed my sisters' wooden house. My sister and I knew what that would mean. We would have to share my toy until Christmas. We sat there with horror on our faces for about five seconds before Donald told Kim to give us her house as replacement. When she fussed, he said, "Kim, give it." He knew there was no way we were ever going to get another one. It wasn't even their fault about the ping pong table. My sister leaned against it. Donald knew that. He didn't have to do what he did but didn't think twice about it. Kindness consumed him. He was exactly as God would want a man to care for his family, a perfect example.

The only thing missing in that perfect world of Kim's was religion. They didn't practice a religion. However, Kim did have a terrifying and unexplainable spiritual experience that she shared with me when we were around eight years old. It isn't my experience so I won't share it but it was the first time I thought about the possibility of evil existing on the other side that we couldn't see.

I knew evil existed on this side in the form of my father. Even recently when questioning Kim about her experience and asking if it was possible for it to have been a dream, she firmly stands with "NO!" With that experience, it may have scared her away from religion, one of Satan's works. It is like the "see no evil, speak no evil, hear no evil" monkeys. In a way, if I pretend it's not there, it's not there. He keeps people from receiving blessings on earth and eternally in Heaven by keeping them away from prayer and religion. Remember the whole "ask and ye shall receive" scripture? In fact that scripture repeats like 100 times in the Bible. The "asking" is usually going on during a prayer.

Even without religion in their life, I believe Father above is very happy with that family. Her parents were so wonderful they were given Kim as a gift and put right next door as a gift for me. That family rescued me. I was such an abused, lonely little girl who wouldn't be who I am today without them.

Oh, and the food. There was never food at my house. They had everything at theirs. Even Kim knew the drill when playing at my house. We would start to get hungry and Kim would say, "Let's go to my house to eat." Kim's mom made us grilled cheese or fresh tomato sandwiches and tomato soup every day in the summer time as we played Barbies from sunrise to sunset. There was Chocolate pie and double-chocolate cookies, butter horns, and chili with cheese. It was heavenly! I was so skinny and scrawny, and always hungry. I know they kept me alive.

Her family went out to eat a lot. I tried my first Chinese food, pizza, everything with Kim and her parents. Her mom was a great cook, but always in the house, so they would go out for dinner regularly and to entertain Kim, I was invited along. Kim would request that we sit at our own table sometimes and, funny enough, the restaurants and her parents would oblige. It was so much fun.

Laughter wasn't common at my house, but I laughed a ton any time with Kim. She is hilarious, to this day. At dinner I wouldn't know what to order, but Kim took care of that, too. She walked in with confidence, like she owned every restaurant.

On weekends Donald cooked and I would stay the night. He would make us whatever we wanted. Kim and I would giggle late into the night and sometimes he would open the door fast with a "Boo!" We would scream and laugh, diving under the covers. It was great to feel safe and to be a kid.

Years later when coming back to Oregon with my husband, we met up with Donald at a restaurant for dinner. When the bill came, we wanted to and had planned to pay but Donald flatly refused. I argued that it was my turn to do something for him. This was definitely the one time we can and had planned to do this. I said, "Donald, you have bought me a thousand dinners at least." He answered back with, "Then what's one more!" He's just so amazing. Thank you, God, for that family!

Special Memories from the County Fair

My older sister and I would go to the county fair every year by ourselves. Sometimes mom would drop us off, but at nine or ten years old we were pretty comfortable taking the city bus alone. We enjoyed getting there right when it opened early as people brought in their horses and livestock or set up for the bake-offs. The rides were totally open to walk right on so we would go on our favorites over and over.

My favorite thing to do, even more than the rides, was to walk around and especially go look at the horses and other animals in the barns. I could fantasize about what it would be like to raise and train a horse—I had already named it Wildfire—and then enter it into the fair.

In the barns by each stall there were ribbons of what place the horse had come in during some sort of judging I couldn't understand. They were all beautiful and winners to me. The horses would put their heads over the stalls so I could pet them. It was a dream come true and I would spend hours just in those barns talking to and petting the horses.

Having all access to the rides was never a possibility for us. Only when I came to the fair with my neighbor, Kim and her dad was that dream a reality. One particular year we brought used soda cans with us for the "kids get in free" promotion. We had saved paper route money for a few rides that had mostly been depleted by 3:00pm that afternoon. Now we were hungry. We needed to save 60 cents each to get home on the bus so eating anything there was out of the question. The smell of food at the fair was unbelievable. The smell of corn dogs and cotton candy mixed with barbecued chicken, ribs and buttered popcorn filled the air. My sister and I were so hungry but that was not an unusual feeling. Walking past the barbecue area, we spotted our father who we hadn't seen in several months or even a year or longer with his future 3rd wife and her 2 boys. They were sprawled out on a blanket having a picnic near the barbecue vendors. They all had big plates of a barbecued chicken with baked beans and corn on the cob. It looked heavenly and our stomachs were growling.

We had just planned on walking past the food area to get some good smells in when Frank was spotted. My sister said, "Let's go over there, maybe he will give us some food."

"No," I said. "Let's pretend we didn't see him. I really don't want to go over there."

Driven by her stomach, she said, "I am so hungry, aren't you?"

"Yes," I said "but let's just keep walking."

"Let's just try. They look like they have a lot of food. You don't have to say anything, I'll ask."

How I dreaded going anywhere near him but I hesitantly followed behind my older sister. She said, "Hi dad."

"Well, hello" he said, surprised to see us.

I was standing back away from him, behind my sister and not in arms reach where I felt safer. He surprised me by first acknowledging us, then introducing us to his date and her boys as his "daughters." I never said a word, just nodded politely. Sister then said, "Dad, is it possible that you can buy us some lunch or give us a couple of dollars so we can get something to share? We don't have any money for food."

Frank, not surprising me at all, said, "No, sorry dear. You need to plan that out when you come to the fair to bring enough money for food. Well, have a nice day." He then excused us to leave.

I was eyeing the large plate of food one of the small boys only had half eaten and threw down on the blanket for the garbage. Certainly I would have finished that but wasn't going to give Frank the satisfaction that I would request anything at all from him or that he was needed. I refused to be a beggar to him of all people and would rather starve! So I did.

As we walked away, my sister teared up and began to cry. This made me steam inside. Why did she let him do that to her? I said, "See, I knew that answer was coming. He's not worth crying about. He sucks!"

She said, "That's our dad, not those boys'. Why couldn't he invite us to the fair and buy us food?"

"Don't expect anything from him and you won't get your feelings hurt," I piped in. "When are you going to figure out that he doesn't love us and doesn't care?"

This was a pretty mature and grown-up conversation coming from two little girls.

Through the Looking Glass

When you reach the end of your rope, tie a knot in it and hang on

As I grew to the ripe age of ten, depression moved into my soul. Not understanding why I had to experience severe poverty, extreme abuse, humiliation, often times hunger, in addition to a father that despised me for no reason was more than my brain could process. My father would occasionally come by the house and take my younger brother motorcycling, then out to dinner.

Sometimes my brother would come home with new clothes or shoes while we were in rags. He had never asked to take me anywhere and when I would ask for a day of motorcycling, I would sit on the porch waiting for hours, only to have my mom tell me he wasn't coming. I began to believe that my father was right; I was unlovable.

Believing there was something wrong with me, I decided to start seeing a counselor. My mom had told me about therapy and went with me to my first session. Why did she take just me? Was there nothing wrong with anyone else, just me?

In my parents' divorce the prior year, my father had to provide insurance for all of his kids, making these sessions possible. It felt so good to talk to someone about my feelings. Her name was Ginny. She was young and starting out in her profession. The first time talking was a bit weird, but it was nice to have someone who cared about how I felt, even if they were paid. Every time after that first session, I had to go by myself. Not wanting to miss these and looking forward to them, I would take the city bus from a stop on the big street near my house to the bus station downtown. From there I would walk to the counseling center. After my hour-long session, I would go sit at the bus stop downtown and wait for up to 30 minutes for a bus to come along and take me back home. The whole process took me a good 2-3 hours. Looking back, that commute terrifies me. I cannot imagine my children doing that at such a young age.

Severely depressed at one session and talking about suicide, Ginny told me that anytime I thought or felt like that, she wanted me to take a breath and think for a second. She said I had to wait one year from that day to kill myself; I could even mark it on the calendar. When the year was up, if I could remember what made me so depressed that I wanted to die, then I could do it. She promised me that I would never, ever remember, so it wasn't worth doing. "If you can't remember in only one year, then why die and lose the fifty years after that?" she asked. "Obviously, it wasn't THAT bad!" She made me promise to at least think of that when I was down which I always have.

CHAPTER 2

Change Begins

The Moves

I'm not quite sure what happened and why, but one day when I was eleven my mother told us to pack up, that we were moving to Utah. It came out of the blue. All I have been able to figure in my adult years is that my absentee father had decided he wanted custody of my brother and she panicked. He did have another son and daughter that he left from his first marriage. Why did he want this one? I'm not sure if that is what happened. I am just trying to piece together small bits of conversations I overheard through the years. Whatever the reason, we put our house up for rent and within three days packed my life into a moving van and were heading out. My mom thought Utah would be a good place to raise kids, ha! I laugh about that now.

At this point in life, my three older half-siblings were gone from the house, the youngest of Carl's kids had moved in with another family, and my sister had begun to run away and refused to go with us. We were leaving the only stability I had which was my home and friends.

Even with all of the abuse I had to endure, that moment seemed to be the worst experience I had yet. I had to say goodbye to Kim. If my mom had just shot me, I think I would have preferred that to leaving my other family with whom I felt so safe and loved. As our moving van was preparing to leave, Kim's family came out onto their driveway to watch. Kim was crying and so was I. I couldn't take it. I leapt out of the van and ran to her, hugging her with everything in me. It was if one of us was dying and would never see the other again. The pain was terrible and I cried for days.

Now that I think about it, Mom probably could have left me there with Kim. They were used to two daughters. They probably would have gladly taken me in.

Happy Valley

The first place we moved to was Provo, Utah. We moved to a rental home directly behind the Missionary Training Center into a neighborhood my mom couldn't believe. All of these "famous" Mormon people lived there. I wasn't really a Mormon—just baptized—so I didn't care but heard names that were supposed to mean something like Nibley, Madsen, Easton and Skousen. I can't remember them all, but Richard Anderson, a long time religion professor at Brigham Young University and writer of Church books and other articles, lived directly across the street from my new house. As I had finished unpacking our moving van, some neighborhood boys came by to say hello. All of the sudden, a girl came out of our bushes and said to them, "If my dad comes by, tell him you didn't see me." She then went back into the bushes. Her dad a moment later came by on his bike and asked if anyone had seen his daughter. Good thing I didn't know her because even though I'm amazing at keeping secrets, I don't know how to lie. That was okay since the boys answered, "Nope." He rode off down the road and she came out and introduced herself. This was my next best friend, Chaney.

Chaney was a great distraction to heal me from my loss of Kim. She was also adopted and the baby of her family. She was the apple of her father's eye, too, which I envied a little. Chaney had been through some early trauma in her life that was on a smaller scale than mine but still difficult for her. We had each other to talk to about how we felt and that bonded us. She had a sweet but rebellious spirit about her. I had never had a friend that did things they weren't supposed to, but it was fun. We would sneak out at night and meet up with the other kids in the neighborhood. It felt good to rebel, if all we did was walk around in the dark and hide in bushes when cars came by. That was a great adventure for me. I had always been such a good girl and this little bit of release let some pressure off.

I am not going to go into all of the experiences of that wild and crazy year across the street from her and those years following but to say that she was instrumental in helping me grow up. There was no way I could talk to my mom about anything. I am pretty sure she never wanted to know what I had experienced with abuse and I didn't particularly feel comfortable talking to her about it. Chaney is who I went to for everything. When puberty changes started happening in my body, Chaney had all of the answers. She was, however, three years older than me. She had two awesome friends her age as well who would do things with us. Sometimes they were like a panel. All three would sit together on their trampoline as I drilled them with hundreds of questions about any teenage thing I could think of. I learned things definitely beyond my years. At least one of them always had an answer. It may not have been the textbook answer, or what our parents would have said, but it was a real life answer. I could write books similar to Judy Blume with my many experiences of becoming a teenager and a young woman.

As I was pretty naïve, Chaney and friends taught me everything to know about boys and what to watch out for. They also taught me to drive and by the age of thirteen I was driving full-time, easily passing my driver's test later in life.

Therapy Please!

During that same year living across from Chaney, I was attacked by a man who moved into the neighborhood to rent a home. He had a daughter my age who invited me to her aunt's house. I never met her aunt, even though we were there for a few days, but her father attacked me in the pool. I thought he was going to drown me, but my friend came to the rescue, jumping on her father's back, screaming and hitting him until he let go. I think it's safe to say that some not good things were going on in that house. When I got home, I was ashamed, just as I had been as a kid with things that had happened to me, and certainly didn't want to talk about it. I was used to keeping secrets so I didn't tell. One day, my sister asked Mom if she could go to this same girl's aunt's house. I told her not to, and when pushed I finally told my mom what had happened. She called her bishop who called the police and that family disappeared in the night.

Had I seen a family therapist or someone at that point, it would have really helped me unleash what was building up inside me. Mother's generation kept everything hush-hush, leaving time to somehow heal the wounds. It didn't. I was a very innocent little girl inside. Even though I had seen and been through much, I didn't understand what men wanted and why these different men kept trying to hurt me. I have always thought about those poor girls in that home, wondering what happened to them, especially my friend.

A year quickly passed and we moved again. In fact, we moved frequently, as often as every three months. It wasn't worth it for me to make friends anymore so I just stayed in my room, waiting for the next move. I was used to my bedroom from my childhood and Father always putting me there. Wherever we moved in Utah, Chaney and I would have to be together every minute and all of the time. Unfortunately we would move away to California, back to Utah, out to California again, back to Utah. Finally, at fifteen, my sophomore year of high school we moved back to Oregon to our home.

My mother said we were only moving back to Oregon to clean the house and prepare to sell it. Years had passed and things changed. Kim had new friends. I was happy for her and, of course, understood. She tried to include me as much as possible but it wasn't the same. I just didn't fit in anymore, anywhere. With all of the moving and time spent alone, I felt weird inside, like a black sheep or the ugly duckling. The high school I attended had mean girls that bullied me regularly. At lunch I would go into the library of our high school, grab a cubicle, and do my homework from morning classes. There was nothing else for me to do and I couldn't take the nasty comments. They were wearing me out. The cafeteria would be suicide for me. I don't believe I ever saw that room. There was no way I was going to work for my lunch in high school. I was fine with going hungry. There wasn't a time I remembered being so alone, such a loser. I cried all of the time. The depression was getting to me. I felt like I didn't belong anywhere, that I was unloved and forgotten. It was a dark time and I wanted to die.

My father lived across town, but I never saw or spoke to him. He made no effort to see us. I didn't understand what was wrong with me, why I was so unlovable. During this period of depression, suicidal thoughts began to get the best of me. Honestly, I didn't want to be dead, really; I just didn't want to be anywhere. If there was a way to be non-existent, that is the place I wanted to go.

Changing Things Up

While in Oregon, I met a new friend, a true life-saver, Georgene. She became my third best friend. She was a few years older, like Chaney, and a lot wiser than me. We met at a teenage dance club when, after trying to find some kind of relief or escape to no avail, I walked outside behind the club, grabbed a broken bottle, and slashed my wrists. I wanted to die! A bouncer had walked out back to have a cigarette and saw me bleeding, while trying to dig deeper still. He ran over, picked me up, and, as I kicked and screamed, ran with me to the girl's bathroom inside. Georgene was there and saw several bouncers run to my aid. They cleaned my wounds out, covered them with pressure bandages, and wrapped both wrists like a mummy. Georgene began asking me questions as to why I would do this and why on earth had I wanted to die? She surprised me that she would care so much about a complete stranger. Georgene had white hair, not blond but white like snow. She had long nails and cat eye glasses. She looked like someone from an antique magazine. I had never met anyone as intriguing as she. She was such an amazing and positive person, enjoying life completely, looking at every day as a new adventure. She was so motherly and friendly and decided to take this poor stray and injured girl to her home. I stayed the night, and then stayed again and again. Her mother, Grace, was very concerned about what I had done.

Grace also had white hair, just a bit blonder than Georgene's but still white. She spent a lot of time just listening, then talking about life and surviving hard things. She quickly became another mom to me. Grace was fun and unusual, different from any mom I had ever met. She would read my tarot cards and look at the placement of the sun, moon and stars and how they aligned when I was born. It was a different kind of religion to me, magical and interesting. The constellations I don't completely understand but believe there is definitely something to them. Grace lost a baby the same year I was born so felt a closeness towards me. I just enjoyed having a cool new surrogate mom. Grace was always right about what was going on with me. She could read my feelings quite well. I don't remember all of the hippy-type things that she could do, but she was brilliant. Georgene was a hippy child, born right in the middle of the 60's, which explains a lot about Grace, too. She was a younger clone of her mother which was great. Grace was so real and understanding. She understood the struggles of teenagers like nobody I have ever met. I asked her many questions and could talk to her about everything.

I cannot forget about Georgene's step-dad, James. The first time I stayed the night, he walked out of the bedroom and across the living room in front of us to the kitchen and I said, "Wow, is that your dad?"

Georgene said, “Yeah, my step-dad. All of my friends are in love with him.”

I said, “Yep, I understand why!”

James was one of those quiet, strong dads. I gave him the nickname of Grizzly Adams. He wouldn’t say much and let Grace handle everything, but was solid as he stood behind her. He was kind and strong, rugged and very attractive. He was always fixing something and, while he worked, he would listen to us girls talking about the universe and our place in it. Once in a while he would say something. When he did, it was very meaningful, helpful, and profound. It was great to have another father figure as an example in my life. We are still close to this day. I love James, Grace and Georgene.

Moving Out

Mom was moving again, away from my new family and I was angry. She moved to California this time for another six month lease. This was the last straw! I couldn’t do it any longer. I was breaking. I’m a homebody by nature and need a stable environment. Nothing I needed for my sanity was getting fulfilled. That was it for me. I was moving alright, but this time not with Mom. I helped her with driving the moving truck and her car to California, but that was all I would do. It was time for me to take a break. My little piece of junk $400 car I had saved for had plenty of room for the minimal personal items I proudly called my life. A phone call to Chaney found that she and Becky, another friend of ours, were moving in together. They invited me to join them for the summer, so I did. I drove several hundred miles across a couple of states toward Utah where the three of us would be renting a three bedroom house.

I was sixteen years old.

The Murderer

It is given to us to be aware of evil. We can sense evil thought or evil intention in those around us

—Richard G. Ellsworth

A very strange thing happened at a gas station on the border of California and Nevada. As I was pumping gas into my car and looking around, a white van pulled in, you know them, the kidnapper vans. This very dirty, scroungy (yes, I know he's a child of God too-but not a nice one) man with filth, almost dreadlocked blond hair got out and started pumping gas, too. He wasn't even that close to me, but our eyes met and locked. He was angry and filled with hate. Instantly I could read his mind. I didn't know or understand why, but he was clear to me. My mind seemed almost to talk to him saying, "You are evil and a murderer." I just knew that was true, but how? A bit startled and unable to look away from his glare, I could hear his thoughts as clearly as if he had spoken: *I would kill you if I could, but I can't.* Surprising myself more, because of my lack of fear, my soul said, "I am so much stronger than you will ever be. You can't touch me and you know it!" Just then, I forced my eyes to pull away and got in my car, and headed toward Utah again. I saw him watching me as I drove off.

Could he read my mind, too? It was actually a terrifying thought. I didn't even know that was possible. This was a first for me. More than anything, I was surprised at my lack of fear and the fact I felt so powerful in the presence of evil. It felt as if a supernatural power came over me and him for a minute and we were communicating mentally in some way, or possibly it was just one-sided. Later in life I would understand this better.

Summer Much Needed Break

After getting to Utah, Becky's very kind, faithful, priesthood-holding, God-loving Latter-day Saint father was gracious enough to give me a part-time job selling candy at his store in the mall. Not a lot was going on during the day as the three of us worked that summer. We would get together in the evenings, crank up the music in the living room, and dance our hearts out. We were all going through different personal, difficult trials at that time but bonded as sisters and friends forever. Becky would tell me how beautiful I was, something that I wasn't used to or comfortable hearing. I had always thought she was so beautiful with her Swedish-looking face, flawless skin and very blond hair. Her confidence came from growing up with a father that she knew loved and adored her. He would give and do anything for his precious daughter. That was a testament to me again that there were indeed wonderful men still on this earth. Becky told me that her father adored and believed in me, in all of us. He told her that we could all conquer anything. I had never been told that before. Someone believed in me (and adored) that wasn't my mother. I didn't even know how much I needed to hear that I had value until she told me.

Sometimes we would go to the movies. Many times I would have to sneak in due to my age, which was always a team effort. We would meet up with old friends as well or have parties and movie nights at our house. It was a good experience for me to be on my own and understand the responsibilities that came with that.

One evening Chaney and I were in deep conversation about life. I was complaining about how much I hated my life. Chaney saw things differently. She said, "Kayli, you are SO STRONG! You amaze me and always have. I have had such an easy life and have sat back and watched the rug get pulled out from under you again and again for years. You keep getting back up, dust yourself off and go again. It's incredible!"

I said, "What choice do I have Chaney?"

She said, "You can choose NOT to get back up! I couldn't do it. I couldn't go through what you have gone through and get back on my feet. I would just lay there on the ground crying."

Nowadays, I have decided when people tell me how "strong" I am, it really means "unfortunate."

The summer went fast and we had fun, but I was only a junior in high school and knew I was in need of an education if I wanted to have more in the future than my past. Finishing high school was a must for me. No one had ever talked to me about college. That was a fairy tale in my world. I never mentioned it either. Somehow there had to be a way for me to make something of myself, but at this time I wasn't sure how. The worst fear I could think of in life was to end up like Mother without a way to provide for my family and to watch my kids go without. In my heart I knew I would never let my kids experience any of the pain I did. It was important that they know about the trauma and how I lived through it, but they didn't need to feel weird inside and go through it themselves. I would be there to protect them.

The end of summer came all too quickly, plus we ran out of money to live so everyone decided to head back home to the safety and stability of parents and free room and board. At least that's what it was for them. For me it meant another school.

California Dreaming

My mother was up in the air about where she was going to be for the next year. Currently she was in east San Jose, California. Since Mom was only there a short time before proclaiming that she was moving again, I started to rethink school. My eldest brother had married a very nice girl who invited me to live with them instead of moving again. She said California had a program to keep kids from dropping out that she would help me get into. I would have to do summer school and night school for the whole next year to get my credits but could then test out of senior year. She said it was not a GED program but that I would actually graduate. This sounded like a good plan so I stayed with them and Mother moved away for the school year.

Their neighborhood would be frightening to most, but after living through my dad's horror in our house, nothing scared me. The high school I would be going to was a very rough one, but that was the area where they could afford to live as newlyweds. It wasn't a big deal, nor did I care, since we had always been poor. I would actually be around people more equal to the situation I was used to. My brother was a Japanese black belt, too, so I wasn't worried at all about break-ins or thefts.

The high school was a bit intimidating, considering that in the mid-1980's it had a chain link fence and guards to keep the peace. Violence was a common occurrence and there were very few "whites" in the school. I was definitely in the minority and knew I would be picked on or taunted quite a bit. Again, nothing was unusual there. Fortunately, in my morning class on the first day of school, a Hispanic girl, Georgena, sat right next to me and said with a Spanish accent, "You are new here, huh?"

"Yes," I said.

"Oh, do you want to eat lunch with me and my friends?"

"Sure," I said.

I didn't know she was saving my life, but I think she did. We met up with her gang—and it *was* a gang! She introduced me and they were all super nice. One of the girls was a sophomore and five months pregnant with her third child. The others were just tough. We headed for the courtyard to get lunch. Right after stepping into it, the attacks on me began. It was like I was the newbie in prison. My group went from smiling and shooting the breeze with me to screaming obscenities and threats in English and Spanish, letting others know they better not get anywhere near me "or else." The group then went right on back to joking around with me like nothing. I was like, "What in the world just happened?" The girls gave me a good talking to and stressed about never letting people disrespect me. They said, "Once you allow yourself to be disrespected, nobody will respect you. It doesn't matter how big or small you are, attitude and confidence are what is important to respecting and protecting yourself." It was a good lesson, one I have always carried with me.

A particular bully in school had her eyes stuck on me. She started her badgering from the first day and every day after. If "butch" is a descriptive noun, than that is what I would use to describe her. With a stockier frame, military shaved head and 5'9 height, she was pretty intimidating. She wore thick black liquid eye liner with black eye shadow. She had her gang, too, which consisted of a girl on each side of her. Georgena and friends kept telling me, "We aren't always going to be there, but if she picks a fight, never show you're afraid. You know you will have to fight her or things will get much worse." I had been in many fights over the years and had been suspended once, but there was always a very good reason behind it and my mother would tell me she was proud of me for sticking up for myself. She even took me to lunch once. I just wasn't used to fighting people for no reason. Just because a person is breathing or a different race is not a good reason to me; I have to be justifiably angry. Even so, apparently I would have to fight a girl I had no problem with.

That day came after months of Butch swearing at me in the courtyard and my friends yelling and threatening back. It was after school one day when I had to stay and talk to a teacher. There was nobody left on the grounds, at least visibly. Teachers were cleaning up their rooms, correcting papers and preparing to go home. There were no security officers that normally roamed the halls. Heading toward my locker, who do I see coming around the corner? It was the three musketeers, as I nicknamed them. Just my luck! I had never yelled or fought back and had no idea what her problem was with me. That makes it difficult for me to fight someone when I'm not mad at them for really anything. They were just being stupid. I certainly couldn't turn around so kept walking straight towards them. "Butch" started talking about me, loud. I won't repeat the vile things she said. The words didn't bother me anyway since I was too busy strategizing how I would take on all three at once. It certainly wouldn't be the first time I had to fight three people at once and wouldn't be my last, so that didn't stress me out either.

As the space between us closed and her terrible words got louder and louder, I just became angry. It was an anger I had never felt before, a rage! The memories of my father spanking me for no reason, the insults, how he pulled my sweet mother by the hair in that hallway, the thoughts of myself hiding in dark closets because of the biggest bully I knew all came flooding back. No more was I going to be helpless! No more was I going to be an innocent victim because someone just didn't like me. She didn't even know me! These girls certainly weren't going to hit me just because I was alive and breathing. I had been quiet and ignored them the entire year, never fighting back with ugly words, but now I was ready to make a stand.

As they walked right past me, two on my left and one on my right, Butch yelled the ugliest word ever, right into my ear where I could feel her breath in my hair. My inner rage turned outward and I snapped! Fire must have been coming out of my eyes. Throwing my books down, literally slamming them on the ground, I started yelling, "Come on! Come on! You want to fight? I am going to tear you to pieces! Let's go! You and me, right now! Once and for all, let's go! I don't even have my gang here and you do, let's go! I'll take all three of you! You said you want a piece? Come and get it!" Of course there were a few obscenities in there, but that was life at that time for me. The three of them turned around, just shocked. They didn't know what to do. They had never even heard my voice before. The two followers looked at their leader for direction, but she was bewildered. She looked at each of them, then back at me. She paused in shock, gave an uncomfortable little giggle, and said, "Huh, let's go; she's not worth it." They walked away. My heart was racing, fists were clenched, fire was in my soul, I was practically hyperventilating and they walked away? Unbelievable! That moment gave me power. I was no longer a victim at that school.

Word got around quickly because my gang knew about the "almost-fight" before I got to lunch the next day. They were patting me on the back, telling me "Good job, "Blanca" and "You crazy gringa". Nobody could believe this "white girl" would challenge those three, all alone, after school with no back-up. You just didn't do that at this school. You could get stabbed. It made me look incredibly brave, crazy, or amazingly stupid. Either way, I came out the winner. The three musketeers never bothered me after that. In fact, I hardly ever saw them. I believe Heavenly Father, again, was watching out for me and sent Georgena and her gang to teach me the ropes and, again, how to survive.

Georgena had a soft spot for me and didn't live but a few blocks from my home. I became really close to her and her family that year. Her parents called me their "white daughter." Sadly, I lost touch with them after I graduated at the end of the year.

The Nanny

Right after high school I became a nanny at seventeen. A little spoiled girl chose me when I was dancing to music blaring from my car at an ATM bank machine. Whatever she wanted, she got. She already had a nanny, but they fired her to have me. I hadn't even thought about being one but had done a lot of babysitting all through growing up for some spending cash. I liked kids.

Regie's father offered me a job with lots of money and a car to use, all of which I needed. During that year, something interesting happened. The LDS missionaries came to the house in Los Gatos, California, tracting. I answered the door and cringed a little, but they were cute and kind, plus I knew they wouldn't hurt me. Wanting to be polite, I invited them in. I told them technically I was a Mormon. They started talking to me about God. It was my first contact with religion in I don't know how many years. I could feel the goodness in them. They had a spiritual strength about them and what they taught I knew they believed it to be true. They weren't there for long because I was on my way out, but just that contact watered a seed that had been planted when I was very young.

It wasn't too many weeks after that the doorbell rang again and a different religious group of missionaries told me I needed to be baptized. It was supposed to make me feel clean which I wanted most, so I let them inside. Since I had been thinking about religion, I wanted to hear about theirs but didn't feel the same truth radiating from them.

Like the Mormons, I believe they believed what they were saying was true, but the spirit to back it up wasn't there like it had been with the LDS missionaries. Even so, they told me I needed to be baptized to be free of sin so I thought, "Sure." If they can clean me up for a bit, why not? They called some of their friends which seemed weird because all of these people showed up in five minutes and came in to baptize me in the bathtub. When I was eight years old, I had been baptized in a font with the understanding I needed to be completely immersed. This group just did my top half first, then my bottom half. It didn't feel right. I thought back at that embarrassing baptism day when I was a child and thought that it didn't seem so weird anymore. This was much stranger and more uncomfortable as I climbed out of my bathtub with soaked clothing into a bathroom full of complete strangers.

CHAPTER 3

Old "Friends" and New Friends

The Voice

Mother had moved about an hour and a half away from the area I worked as a nanny. She was now in Manteca, California. I had just ended an emotionally abusive relationship with my boyfriend from San Jose. Actually this was not without help. After months of tolerating the love mixed with nasty comments, it was beginning to wear on me. I loved my boyfriend, my first real love. He was a twin I had met at a dance club Regie's family owned. It was a mixed club with an underage section on one side. There was a small opening lined with bouncers that led to the 21 and over side. I went with the family for several concerts of my favorite groups. Regie and I were allowed to sit on the stage as the band played popular 80's hits. The bouncers, security, and regulars at the club all thought I was the owner's eldest daughter and I realized I could do whatever I wanted.

Once I snuck over into the 21 club and the security pretended they didn't see me. It was there I met my soon-to-be boyfriend. Donnie and his twin brother, Derick, were the best dancers in the club and girls lined up trying to get their attention. He spotted me watching them and quickly invited me to dance. It could have been his brother that asked, I don't know, but after that they had an argument about who would go out with me. Donnie was actually the lesser evil twin and thank goodness he was the one that won the argument.

Things started out great, but then the comments would start to come out, usually from his brother Derick first. "Do you think your girlfriend is fat? I think she is." I was 5'6, 110 pounds, hardly fat. Even so, being a teenager it was still hard for me to hear. Donnie would continue Derick's bullying with, "Yes, I agree with you, she is fat." Then a mean session of verbal and emotional abuse would ensue. I was so used to my father's abuse as a child that I kind of fell right back into that trap, as if it was acceptable behavior. I would try to ignore it and not let it get to me and sit there holding in what I could for as long as I could until tears started to run down my face. They had their satisfaction so Donnie would say, "Stop crying and let's go do something."

The abuse sessions became more frequent until one day I was sitting on the stairs of the porch. Several of their family members were sitting out there and the nasty abuse began, first directed at a sibling's little four year old daughter. Everyone just sat there and watched. Nobody said anything to defend her as they began to call her "ugly" and "weird." She was crying and went onto her mother's lap who—I was shocked—also said nothing. As soon as I came to her defense, yelling at them to leave that "beautiful little girl alone," they started on me. It was worse than ever. How dare I interrupt them! Like my father, they tore me up one side and down the other when all of the sudden, I couldn't hear them anymore. They were muffled as if someone put plugs in my ears. I then heard a very distinctive male voice that I recognized but couldn't place, at least in this life. It was stern and clear, as it said, "What are you doing here? You don't deserve this. It is time for you to leave." I could see the twins' mouths moving but heard nothing. I looked around at everyone there. The women, Donnie's mom and sisters and Derick's girlfriend and "baby momma" and, most importantly, Donnie's precious nieces all looked like I felt. They had been emotionally beaten down over time. The twins must have realized I wasn't listening to them, even though they were both walking around me in a circle like lions ready to pounce. The "ear plugs" slowly came out and their voices got louder. "Did you hear me?" Derick bellowed. Something came over me right then. *I need to leave. I can see my future, sitting on those steps, beaten down too. I am not going to marry my father! This is everything I worked to get out of. I was that little girl.*"

I didn't say a word, turned my back to them all, and walked directly to my car. I heard Donnie's voice with a bit of surprise and concern in it. He said, "Kayli, where are you going?" I felt a sense of peace in my soul for the first time. Without looking at them, I opened my car door and yelled loud enough so they could hear me, "Away!" I drove off without ever looking back. Somehow, God gave me just enough strength to leave and I did.

There were no cell phones in those days available to regular people, just the rich and famous. I knew there was no way I could see Donnie again so I quit my nanny job and moved an hour and a half away to where my mother now was. He would never find me there, and he never did. I did run into his sister once who told me I should go back to Donnie and that he was really, truly sorry. Like I would later say to Lucifer, "I can't! Wait, no, I *won't*!" I had to rephrase that to "I won't" because I really could go back but for my mental strength I needed to not be a victim, but a victor. It certainly wasn't easy to leave someone I truly loved. Finally I had love that I had wanted so badly but it came at an expensive price to my soul. Caught up in the love part of it, I had failed to recognize the abuse that crept in and grew. I cried in my room for probably two weeks and was sad and depressed for several months.

That was a defining moment. In that second I made a deal with myself to never tolerate abuse again. It was in my blood to stand up for myself. I would never, ever again tolerate anyone to treat me that way!

Manteca was a much more positive place. There was a kind LDS family directly across the street from my house we rented for half of that year who had a daughter my age named Laurel. She was always happy and came from a wonderful family who were kind and helpful to my mother. She had an inner light I envied and didn't understand at the time. Finally, I had a friend that didn't talk about boys and parties. She was about good, clean fun. With my work schedule I was busy so didn't spend as much time as I wanted to with her, but she left an impression on me. Still to this day if I think about her, I think of the light that shone around her that I desired to have for myself—the light that comes from within.

Those Beloved Pets

Beasts have spirits and shall dwell in eternal felicity on an immortal earth
Doctrine and Covenants 77:1-4

Eventually, Mother decided to move to Utah, again. The company she worked for was expanding to Utah and wanted her to go with it. I was eighteen and decided I should go, too. It was a good time in my life for a fresh start. Of course I had to bring my cat, Kitty Idol. He was my best friend at that time, especially because I felt alone so often. We moved into a small house my mother rented in a very Mormon neighborhood. The house had a split entry hall. My bedroom and another were downstairs in a basement type of setup and the kitchen and master were upstairs. There was a half window in my room almost eye level with the sidewalk. It was perfect to open and close for Kitty Idol. He roamed freely during the day and scratched on my window when he was ready to come in at night. He always slept at the foot of my bed and kept my feet warm. We had been at that house for just a few weeks when my mother came running and crying inside with my brother following right behind yelling, "Do not go out there!"

"What? What happened?"

"You don't want to go outside! Don't go out there!" my brother yelled again, grabbing me tight.

My mother was hysterical. I wrestled away from my brother and ran out to find Kitty Idol in the driveway with just his head run over behind Mother's tire. He was suffering. He was flopping around on the ground with blood all over. I felt my knees buckle and I dropped to the ground next to my sweet baby. Immediately I heard high-pitched screaming, the kind you hear in a horror movie and realized it was coming from me. I cannot imagine what the neighbors were thinking of this new California family, but I am sure people were looking out their windows. I didn't care, I couldn't stop screaming.

He finally quit moving and I wouldn't leave his side. I sat there crying for about 15 minutes or so when Kitty Idol did one last complete body spasm. I know he wanted to live. He loved me. That body spasm was all it took and my horror screams began again. I must have sobbed for over an hour, rocking back and forth, while sitting Indian-style on the concrete. Dusk came. I then got up and walked inside. A very sweet, little old LDS man from across and down the street came over and spoke to my mother. I saw him earlier come out when I was crying. He walked very slowly so I knew he was pretty ancient. He asked Mother if he could "take care of the kitty" for us. My mother told him yes. He was so Christ-like and caring and loving. He told my mother that it was obviously a beloved kitty and promised he would not throw him in the trash. I agreed to that. He took Kitty Idol away on his shovel. Just like with Beau, I couldn't watch so went inside. The man was gone for a while then came back with a hose and sprayed and scrubbed the blood off of our driveway. Someday I will see him again in Heaven and want to thank him for his true and caring heart. I never saw him again. I believe he was another gift from God to take care of the widow and her grieving children.

With Kitty Idol gone, I couldn't sleep. Visions of him flopping about and suffering kept appearing in my mind and I was completely helpless to take away his pain. It was a horrible nightmare, again and again. Sometimes, I would start to fall asleep and hear the scratching on the window. I would jump up to let him in but he wasn't there. Night after night I cried myself to sleep with the same result, jumping up to open the window and no Kitty. This went on for about a month.

One beautiful, sunny morning I woke up with sunshine peering through my blinds and across my bed. I felt well rested for a change and as I opened my eyes and looked around, at the end of my bed where my feet were was Kitty Idol. I was not asleep. I had just woken up. He was laying there where he always was before, curled in a ball looking very comfortable and content. He was looking right at me as if to say, "Hey, I'm okay." If cats could smile, he was definitely smiling. I looked at him with wide-eyes for maybe 15 seconds. I was studying his little black and white face and what seemed like emotions telling me not to cry anymore. Then, he slowly faded away and was gone. Something about that experience changed me. I slept every night just fine after that. I never heard his scratching again.

I know animals not only go to Heaven, but they are there waiting for our return. Many remain around us throughout our lives in their spirit form that we cannot see. God is so good and so understanding. The Master Creator would not give us these sweet creatures to nurture, love, and take care of only to have them nonexistent after this life. What kind of Heaven would that be with a hole in our hearts for our beloved pets? I promise you, they will be ours again.

Gerald E Jones, director, Institute of Religion, Berkeley, CA asked and then answered his own question, "Do animals have spirits and are they resurrected? Yes."

A Little Visit from Our Brother Lucifer

The only power the adversary has is the power we give him when we sin or break our covenants —Sherry Dew

My eldest half-sister married a nice Kansas guy who was called into the bishopric of a young singles ward while they were completing their degrees at

Brigham Young University in Provo, Utah. My sister lived about 15 minutes from me and had just given birth to her first daughter. Knowing that I had been looking into various religions, she called and asked if I would like to attend church with her. When I refused, she pleaded that it was absolutely necessary for me to come help her with my new niece, as her husband would be sitting on the stand with the bishop during the meeting and unable to help. When she put it that way I agreed to go, but only to help her.

My first Sunday meeting was great. I sat with my sister and looked around the room that was full of young men and women, averaging probably twenty-one years old. I don't remember much about the talks because I was trying to determine who the best looking guy in the room was, as I played with my niece. At the end of the meeting my sister introduced me to a duo of really cool California girls who invited me to come to their apartment and hang out. I did, but didn't attend church for a couple of months after that.

Over the course of about a year, I randomly attended that ward. I was asked on a date by a devilishly handsome guy on one of those occurrences. Now this made things interesting. The California duo called me, probably under a request from my sister, and pleaded for me to attend one Sunday with them. I went again but this time I paid attention. For the first time, I felt a real warmth come through my body and realized that there was something more to this church besides cute boys and cool girls. I needed to find out what it was. The sudden true interest in the Mormons changed my life forever, but not in the way you may be thinking.

It was a normal night like any other, nothing special at all. I went to bed about 10:00pm. Exactly at midnight I was awakened by a slight shake to my shoulder, similar to what a mother would do. It was not my mother. Standing next to my bed was our brother, Lucifer. Now, this wasn't the scary devil that everyone thinks of when they hear his name. This was the brother that we all knew and loved in the pre-existence in his God-made, beautiful form. He was right up there with Jesus in rank and was called, "Son of the morning." In fact, the dictionary of the King James version of the Bible describes Lucifer as "literally a spirit son of God, he was at one time 'an angel' in authority in the presence of God; however, he rebelled in the premortal life, at which time he persuaded a third of the spirit children of Father to rebel with him." The scriptures say "the heavens wept over him." I completely understand that now.

Lucifer stood next to the bed as I opened my eyes and looked at him. I knew him instantly and said, "Hello, old friend!"

Okay, first of all, who talks like that? I wake up with a man standing over me and haven't had a man in the house (except my new brother-in-law) in ten years and I don't scream, I say, "Hello, old friend?"

Lucifer then spoke to me, "Get up, I want to talk to you." He motioned towards the end of my bed so I scooted down and threw my legs over the end until my feet touched the floor.

My room was everything to me. At eighteen, I worked a job in an office, and spent all of my money on myself like any normal teenager. There was a twin bed right in the middle of the room with just the headboard touching the wall. I had a window on the left wall, the same one Kitty Idol used to come in and out of. There was also an aquarium with my specialty goldfish and black moor. I had a black and white hounds-tooth loveseat right at the end of my black and white checkered bed. The loveseat was facing my feet, almost touching, making it very difficult in my small room to get over to the window. The right wall had a TV stand that held my prized stereo and all of my music perfectly set in alphabetical order. I am a bit of a clean freak.

Lucifer sat down on the loveseat facing me and I should have felt our knees touching but didn't. He was beautiful! Let me repeat that. Lucifer was absolutely, insanely gorgeous! Any favorite movie star in his prime is a bum living under a bridge next to Lucifer. I have never on this earth seen someone even closely resembling that kind of perfection. He was tan with dark brown hair. His eyes were the bluest blue I have ever seen. He was stunning! I thought to myself, "No wonder a third of the host of heaven followed him!"

He started to talk to me and I began to remember things from the pre-mortal life we shared with God our Father, Jesus our brother, and Lucifer, our dysfunctional brother (prior to the dysfunction). I remembered that he and I were close—it figures I picked the wrong friend! He started to tell me that he missed me, missed "us." He brought up memories, things I could remember at the time he was with me. He would say, "Remember when we used to…" "Remember how we…" I would find myself daydreaming off into this hazy "yeahhh." Then he would go on to say, "I want you back with me, it will be like old times."

Considering I did not think of myself at all as religious, I was shocked at the things that came out of my mouth. My soul remembered, even if my brain did not. I would stare into his beautiful eyes and would begin to feel like Mowgli on the Jungle Book with the snake, Kaa, (the irony) singing, "Trust in me." I could feel myself leaning towards him almost like going in for a kiss, but that wasn't my plan. I was falling under his spell. I would shake myself out of the hazy trance and pull away from his gaze and say, "No, I can't…I won't follow you, I want to follow Jesus." I kind of sounded like one of those Jesus freaks and it was a little strange to hear myself. I had never talked like that on this earth. He then would start new stories and other memories of how we used to be, how we could be, if only I would be with him again, follow him. He was so smooth, so charming. As I looked at him I knew I had loved him immensely. We all did. He was a beloved brother and leader before his fall. My heart ached for him like it would for a good friend who had turned to drug or alcohol abuse and you could no longer be around him. He ruined himself, what he could have been! My heart hurt for him. In my head I kept asking, *why? Why did you do that?* He wasn't sorry, I could tell, just bitter. I knew why he came. He wanted me to rebel against Father, too. With the veil of life that keeps us from remembering lifted, I knew he was afraid of what I could do, now that I had found the Church of Jesus Christ of Latter-day Saints.

I have no clue how old I truly am, but I am a really, really old soul. There were so many things going on during that experience. There was a realization of something in me that he knew and wanted, maybe needed. I knew I had a power, a gift to influence people and he was afraid of me using it to help them. He was trying to get me to use my gifts God gave me for evil, so as to keep families from uniting for eternity. His conversations went round and round always coming back to requesting I follow him. I would offer the same response that I am sure I gave him in the pre-mortal life, "I won't follow you, I am going to follow Jesus." That was repeated several times throughout the night.

Everything came back to me. It all made sense. The answer to the question everyone in the world wants to know was right in my face. The entire reason we are here on earth was so very simple. It is to use our freedom, our agency, to decide who we were going to follow, Jesus and our Father in Heaven, or Lucifer. Lucifer bet on the idea that if we had no memory and were away from our Father, we would lose our way and who we truly were. He thought we would become bad people and have no interest in God and what was light and truth. He was sure we would follow him. Father loves and believes in us and doesn't care what Lucifer thinks.

Father wants us to have experiences and make our own choices by using the gift of agency he gave us. He wants us to be like him. Father loves us all and knows us each individually. He believes in us and wants us to make our own choices without him being a helicopter parent. Not having the memory of being with him, we are free to choose as we like. He knew we would make mistakes and fall. That is why he has the perfect plan in place with our brother Jesus there, waiting to take our mistakes away, if we would only humble ourselves and repent.

A very unique thing was going on while Lucifer was with me. I am not sure what it was exactly but knew it was from God, at least Heaven. A little angel sat on my right shoulder the entire time Satan was in my room. It had a very soft female voice that sounded concerned. She whispered in my ear and spoke fast, "You better hurry! You don't have much time. Hurry! Hurry! You better hurry, time is running out. Hurry! Hurry"! I kept watching Lucifer to see if he knew she was there and realized he had no idea. I wasn't going to tell him. I kept wondering if I was going to die soon with that hurried rush in her sweet voice. What was I supposed to do and why was I to hurry?

As Lucifer spoke, I looked around my room at all of my worldly possessions that I had been so proud of and worked so hard for. These strange words came to my head, "It's all kindling." Who says that? I am so weird! How old am I to use that word, "kindling." I don't think I have ever said it on this earth. My soul must have remembered that this earth would be burned because I know that I meant it was kindling for the fire on the earth in the last days. Every worldly possession is just that, kindling. Everything was making sense.

Another curious thing is that Lucifer called me by a different name and I knew it and easily answered to it. It was much more comfortable than the earthly name I was given. I didn't realize until he left that he was calling me another name because it was so familiar and I knew it well. For years I have tried to remember it but cannot.

As night became morning I noticed Lucifer getting antsy. He kept looking at my blinds as the new morning light was coming in. He became more impatient with me, frustrated, and wiggly. I started to look at the blinds, too, and back at him, wondering if he was a vampire or something. He was more hurried in his request and started demanding I follow him. That just made me mad. Who was he to take away my agency anyway? Wait, he's the father of no agency. I remember now. He started to throw a five year olds tantrum, yelling at me to follow him. I almost started to laugh because he was such a big baby. I was even more firm now that he was making me mad and very confidently and sternly said, "I already told you: I will not follow you! I am following Jesus!" With that, he took another look at the sun that was now coming in pretty strong through the blinds and jumped to his feet. He had a red, angry face that wasn't so pretty anymore. He had his fists clenched and a very rigid stature. He yelled at me, "You'll be sorry! You'll be sorry! I'm going to make your life hell!" With that he took a step toward my bedroom door and vanished.

I had the most peaceful feeling. Fatigue was getting to me and finally I felt tired. I looked over at my clock and it was 6:00 am. Lying back on my bed I thought about going to sleep, but couldn't. I felt so strong! His threats were laughable at best. The scripture came to mind that states that he has power to bruise (our) heal, but we have power to crush his head. That is the truth! I completely knew that to be true and my soul remembered! As I lay on the bed I thought, "He can't touch me! He is nothing!"

I figured out a couple of things from this event. First, with the veil lifted, I remembered or knew that I was so incredibly stronger than he with my mortal body. He will never know or understand the things we do having a body. Second, this life was about choosing Jesus or Lucifer and backing up that choice. Third, there is nothing materialistic that matters. It is not going with us. Fourth, we don't have much time on the earth to back up our choice and prove to God that we are on his team. We don't know when our time is up. Fifth, we are all old souls, maybe billions of years old and knew God, Jesus, and even Lucifer totally and completely. Sixth, our relationship with God comes first, then our families. When priorities get out of balance, everything else starts to crumble. Last but not least, Lucifer stated that he would make my life "hell." Umm, has he seen my life? Just in case he hadn't noticed, I didn't need his help for that. It was running that course all by itself. Did he think I was on a picnic?

Many years after this experience I heard Elder Neil L Anderson perfectly express what I experienced and understood during my time spent with Lucifer. He said, "The choice between good and evil is at the very heart of our experience on earth. In the final review of our lives, it will not really matter if we were rich or poor, if we were athletic or not, if we had friends or were forgotten. We can work, study, laugh and have fun, dance, sing, and enjoy many different experiences. These are a wonderful part of life, but they are not central to why we are here. The opportunity to choose good over evil is precisely why we are here."

Tattle Tale

I heard my mom awake upstairs. She was in the kitchen. I heard some pans being moved around and thought I would go up and tell her what had just transpired. As I came out of my room, the extra bedroom door opened and another sister who had just been married walked out with her husband. I had forgotten that they were temporarily staying in the bedroom that shares a wall with mine. They followed me up the stairs to the kitchen. Before I could say anything, my sister pipes up, "Mom, Kayli had a guy in her room all night."

She was tattling on me. Her husband said, "Yes, it's true. They kept us awake with their talking all night." My mom was still washing dishes with her back to us. She said, "Kayli, who was in your room?"

"It was Lucifer." It went silent for a minute and my mom turned around and looked at me very seriously. She surprised me with her next remark.

"Don't you EVER talk to him again! How dare he come into my home!"

I think all three of us at the same time said, "What?" That was a surprise.

She then asked, "What did he want?"

"He wanted me to follow him and I told him no."

My mom turned to her new son-in-law and said, "What did you hear?"

"We could hear Kayli a lot better than him. His words were muffled and even sounded like it was maybe a different language. We couldn't really make out any actual word he said; we could just hear their talking going back and forth all night. They kept waking us up."

The experience with Lucifer was a turning point for me. I had to wonder why he came at this exact time in my life. With all of the years alone and so much time to critically and deeply think about life, who I am, why I was here, and many other deep thoughts, it was obvious to me why Lucifer came. He did not like me checking out those Mormons. My question was "Why?" Without talking to Mother about it, as to not excite her, or be the recipient of her pressure, I decided to start reading the Book of Mormon.

Desiring to know what was so important about this book, I would read a few pages every night before I went to sleep. It started out a bit slow but I kept on. Some parts were interesting, some boring, some violent, some sad, then the most interesting thing happened. A scripture came up that caught my interest.

> *Behold, I say unto you that whoso believeth in Christ, doubting nothing, whatsoever he shall ask the Father in the name of Christ it shall be granted him; and this promise is unto all, even unto the ends of the earth.* (Mormon 9:21)

I read that and thought, "Whoa, wait a minute. Read that again!" Again I read it and thought, "Did I just read that right? I just have to believe in Christ without doubt and I could ask anything and it will be given?" Okay, I like this scripture and I am going to test this out!

Around this same time I came across another scripture that supported the Mormon scripture:

> *I, the Lord, am bound when ye do what I say; but when ye do not what I say, ye have no promise.* (D&C 82:10)

The first scripture I read was kind of like a challenge, or an invitation from God to see if what I was reading was true. The second was Him telling me He would keep his promise, well more like He has to keep it. This was my chance to prove if there was a God who listened and if He indeed would keep his promises—so I went to work.

Darth Vader

My mother had always told me that her first husband and true love would be my father after I died. Wanting that so badly and wanting to believe her, I thought I would ask Heavenly Father. I did everything that I felt was required to get an answer to that request. There was no way I was telling my mother about what I was doing because I didn't want her to ask me about it, pray for it, or anything. This was going to be on my own terms. I really wanted to do this without someone with any spiritual ties. This was to be on my own, using my faith, if I had any.

I spent every day trying to do what was right. I began praying morning and night, keeping a prayer in my heart throughout the day, serving others, and reading the scriptures at night. Every night and morning when I would say my prayers I would ask for the same thing, to know if what my mother said was true. Again, I would read that scripture that I understood to mean if you ask for something and it be a righteous desire, and you are doing all that you are supposed to be doing to your ability, Heavenly Father would answer your prayer. I would say, "Okay God, it says right here that you have to answer, if it is a righteous desire. I want to know if Carl will be my father after this life. You are "bound" it says here. Is this book true? Is this scripture for real? I am doing everything I can that is righteous and want an answer."

After about a month of doing the same thing every day, and asking God in the same way, referring to the scripture, something wonderful happened. One night I went to sleep as usual, and was awakened by someone touching my shoulder softly. Last time that happened it was Lucifer who was there. This time I woke up and saw my mother's first husband, Carl, standing there next to my bed. I had only seen pictures of him. He was much taller and more handsome in person than the pictures showed. Mother always told me how handsome he was and what a great smile he had, but I hadn't noticed until now. He was dressed in street clothes, jeans and a red shirt. He nodded his head toward the door and said, "Come on, come and walk with me."

I got out of bed and followed him. As soon as we took the first step out of my bedroom, we were in the local chapel that was down the street from my home, walking through the halls. It was dark, just like it would be at that time of night. The corner streetlight was peering through the windows and double glass doors. It was a little bit creepy I thought, but felt very safe with Carl. We walked side by side together down the long dark hallway and he told me that he had been watching me throughout my entire life. He said, "Does this look familiar?" Just then, he turned towards me and made these very large eyes. It was a game that my half-brother and I used to play when we were young and trying to see who had bigger eyes, making them almost "pop" out of our heads. I would joke that my brother had cow eyes, but he would say mine were just as big.

Carl's action threw me off for just a moment and, startled, I started to run down the hall away from him. He loudly said, "I am sorry I didn't mean to frighten you." He then hurried down the hall to catch up with me. I realized that he was a really nice guy and was just trying to show me that he DID know me. I told him that I was okay and that he just threw me off.

He never used the Darth Vader line "I am your father", but the feeling around him was of great love and caring and I could feel this amazing priesthood power he held within. We talked about a few other things as we walked around the halls of the Church.

There was something very interesting I noticed about Carl. He had a limp coming from his left leg. It wasn't a huge limp, but definitely a prominent one. I thought it peculiar since I knew he was dead, that he would have a limp at all. We walked all of the way around the Church halls back to where we had begun. Those were doors leading to the outside parking lot. Carl started to get a little antsy and was looking at the door as if someone was talking to him. He told me that he needed to leave. I was so enjoying his company and wasn't ready for that yet. He became more anxious and became in quite a hurry and started to exit the doors. He paused for a moment and said "I have to go…but I will see you again!"

I yelled out, "Where are you going?" right at that moment, I was standing in the doorway of my bedroom facing the hall just as my little sister was passing my room. She looked at me very puzzled and stopped and said, "I am going to the bathroom!" I was a little thrown off and realized where I was and what had transpired and then stepped back into my bedroom and lay down. It made sense as I realized that Carl had to leave before my sister saw him and was frightened. Pondering the miracle of this answer, clearly I couldn't sleep. I got up and walked to my mother's room.

My mother is a very light sleeper so I didn't have to say much to wake her. All I could say was, "Mom, I saw Carl tonight." Mother, always seeming to surprise me more than I her replied, "I wondered what he was doing here tonight." She sat up with a big smile, motioned for me to sit down on her bed, and said, "Tell me everything!" I told her about the walk and what I had been praying about and then said, "Mom, there was something strange about Carl. He was limping." My mother was completely shocked as she put her hand over her mouth and said, "I can't believe he showed you the limp!" She then went on to explain, "Carl has one leg that is half an inch shorter than the other. He made me swear when we married to never reveal his secret to anybody, not even our children. He has always worn a lift inside his shoes so that the limp would not be obvious." As I asked mother why he would show me, she answered that he wanted me to know for sure that it wasn't a dream and that I really did see him. My prayer had been answered.

My mother called Carl's children the next day and told them about my experience. She then told them about the limp now that she could. They were so excited to hear about it and know he was paying attention to our lives. However, one of them said, "Why did she get to see the limp?" I should have said, "Because I'm his favorite."

This, I figured, is why he didn't appear to all four of his biological children. Truly I believe he didn't want to isolate the four older kids from the four younger ones, so he waited. Carl came and visited me to not only answer my prayer but with the intention of bonding this family as one and bring more unity instead of separating us.

Best (Boy) Friend Forever 1

It is not easy for me to meet new people from the experience of my youth and all of the many moves. There in Utah with this particular move, two relationships with two of my three best guy friends of this life came to be. There was Corbin, who I named my first born son after, and Christian who I first had as a boyfriend but later became what I call one of my best (boy) friends forever.

I don't know how Corbin and I met. I have thought about it for years and cannot remember. In asking him once he couldn't recall either. We clicked when we met as if we had known each other forever. He was probably the first person I shared the "Lucifer experience" with. Corbin was Mormon blood, good old-fashioned pioneer, plain-crossing Mormon blood. His great, great-grandfather was Joseph Fielding Smith, 6th prophet of the LDS Church.

Mormonism in its detail was not familiar to me, but he sure knew a lot. He was a stalwart example to not only his parents who had stepped away for a minute but many friends and peers. The only son of one of my favorite families in this world, he was fun and funny with a contagious laugh and a glass-is-always-full mentality. Many times I thought how he would make a great Santa Claus when he got old. The only things that ever seemed to get him down were girls and relationships.

His father had an amazing car collection with one being a red and white 1957 Corvette which Corbin always drove with the top off. So many memories with Corbin had to do with him picking me up in that car and us driving around town. He would tell me he only had it for a short time and "let's go for a ride." Everywhere we went people would yell out to us or give us a thumbs up for driving in such a cool car. (That car would pop up later in my life at a very important time).

The family Corbin came from was one of those that I would watch and yearn for in my heart to have for my own one day. His parents truly loved each other and seem to be best friends, even still. His sisters, Corbin loved dearly. One was Corbin's younger sister. She was so funny. In the old *Pink Panther* movies that I grew up with in the 70's, there was an Asian martial arts guy named Cato who the Inspector Clouseau paid to keep him on his toes. At any opportunity, he would jump out and attack or wrestle with Clouseau in a dual of one kind or another. That was her. We would be watching TV, lying on Corbin's couch when Ashley would pop up from behind it and pounce on Corbin. The attack would continue as they moved to the floor, seeing who could pin whom down. Corbin would sit on top of Ashley and act like he was going to spit in her mouth as she squirmed to get released and screamed with laughter and terror together. My stomach would hurt as I would be laughing so hard. I had no idea that this was how normal families were and I loved it! This is the family fun that was missing for me as a child.

Corbin was a great friend and example. We would later go to the temple together for our first time and go on missions at the same time, only to come home and marry (different people) within two weeks of each other.

One evening shortly after my "visit", Corbin drove me up to a very scenic view of the valley while I shared my experience. We must have talked about it for five hours. He had amazing insight as to what this meant and who I was. He explained a lot to me about the Church and had such a testimony about the truth of it. When he spoke about God and religion was the only time I would see him serious. He knew who he was and where he was going. He talked to me about missions and told me he was going to go one day. When Corbin received his patriarchal blessing, he shared it with me. He truly was loved and a very special spirit with big plans from God.

Best (Boy) Friend Forever 2

Christian was from another big Utah Mormon pioneer-heritage family. His last name is well known in the Mormon religion. That was one thing Christian told me later after we had dated for a while that he liked about me—how I didn't know about the Church. He said I got to know him for him and didn't date him for any other reason. His sister once told me the day he and I met was the day half of the valley's eligible girls cried. Christian was introduced to me after our mothers had met and talked about us being perfect for each other. As mothers are generally terrible at picking out people to date, I had zero interest in meeting this guy she was pushing on me. She assured me he was someone I would pick out, not someone she would. She begged me to accompany her to his family home one evening while I was sitting home by myself. Mother said she had to run by their house on an errand for Christian's mother and asked me to come along for the ride.

We pulled up to a huge gate and mom pushed the call button. The gate opened and the biggest house I had ever seen in my life was in front of me. Gasping, I then said, "If he lives here, he is a total snob and I won't like him anyway." Out of the many cars in the driveway there was my favorite car, a Saab. After admiring it for a minute we went inside. Christian's mother looked at me and smiled, "Oh yes, she is perfect." I felt like I was being sold or something, but then she called for Christian to come down. He walked in, our eyes met as she introduced us, and we both tried hard not to smile at each other. He was so handsome! He was also very quiet with a bit of wild boy look in him, right up my alley. His mother then said, "Will you go pick up your sister at her class and take Kayli with you?" We both nervously laughed and he said, "Okay." We went outside and of course, the Saab was his. As we drove, he said, "I want to apologize for my mother."

Chuckling, I said, "No, that's fine."

We immediately began dating. In fact we didn't leave each other's side except to sleep for six months after that night. He wasn't a snob at all. For the first time in my life, I was dating someone who treated me like a princess. He was one of the most kind, caring and gentle man I have ever come across. Chivalry is still in existence.

Not too long after we started dating, I was in my room, cleaning, when Christian walked in. It was the middle of the day with the sun coming through my basement window. Pleasantly surprised to see him and thinking my mother let him in I said, "Hi! What are you doing here? I thought you were at work." He gave me a quick excuse. He would scarcely look me in the eyes and something wasn't right. I know Christian and now he was freaking me out a bit. He came toward me looking down and then turned around quickly right in front of me. He said, "My back hurts will you rub it?" Just as I went to rub his back and right before I touched him, I stopped. I had a bad feeling. I don't know what inspired me to say this but I said, "You aren't really Christian, are you?" Right then he threw his head back and fast over his left shoulder and looked me right in the eyes and started to laugh the most evil, horrible laugh I had ever heard. His eyes were pure evil! This was out of a horror movie. It was Lucifer. He scared the life out of me, then disappeared. It is said that eyes are the mirror to the soul. Of course he wouldn't look at me. I would know who he was immediately so he turned himself away from me, attempting to fool me. I was so freaked out I had to leave my room and the house. Later that evening I told Christian about it and he was quite upset that Lucifer would transform into him to scare me. I assured him it didn't change anything. Lucifer wanted to corrupt things that were special to me. This was just the beginning of his torture. Neil L Anderson in 2005 General Conference said, "As we increase our understanding and love for the Savior, His light will illuminate everything around us. We will then see evil for what it is."

Happy Birthday?

It was Christian's 18th birthday and I decided to throw a huge bash at his good friend's home in Salt Lake City. After a fun and wild night with tons of people and loud music, we all decided to stay the night instead of driving all of the way back to Provo. We didn't want anyone to fall asleep at the wheel and it was past 3:00 am. With many guys and girls there, we all grabbed blankets and pillows or couch cushions and crashed on the floor or chair or anywhere. Morning came fast and I was awakened by what sounded like the house cat running around, playing. In the distance I heard this "ththump, ththump, ththump". I was so tired and trying to sleep. I thought to myself, "Dumb cat." Then it became a bit louder. I started to wake and notice the sun had come up and was peering through the blinds across the hardwood floor we were lying on. I could barely open my eyes but peered around. Christian was about a foot or two from me, asleep. There were two guys each sharing half of the couch above him. A couple of chairs were occupied as well with two or three others on the floor. We were all in the front room. I dropped my head and was falling back to sleep. I then heard the cat running around again getting closer and closer, louder and louder, "Ththump, ththump, ththump." I opened my eyes to see this creature like nothing I could even imagine. This "thing" ran right up my body starting from my big toe on my right foot. My eyes went wide, but I couldn't move. Completely frozen, I was like a marble statue. I tried to move anything, any part of my body to no avail. My mouth was partially open and I tried to scream, but nothing came out. Christian was right next to me and every muscle in my body was flexed, trying to reach to him. This creature was not a cat at all. It was the most horrifying beast I had ever seen. It was a partial squirrel, rat, rodent thing. It had a weird and ugly human-like pointed nose, skinny bony toothpick like legs and sharp claws. God makes such beautiful creatures and this was definitely Lucifer's work. It was absolutely hideous! It then came close to my left ear and began to talk. I could feel its frosty breath right into my ear. The hair on my neck was standing straight up and my eyes were about to pop out of my head as this thing said, "You know I'm here, but nobody else does." My spirit seemed to shrink to this tiny thing inside me, and my body seemed huge. I ran from one side of my body trying to get to the other on the inside. I started in my head at my right ear and ran all of the way down my neck into my right shoulder, then arm. I ran into each and every finger and headed for the leg and toes. There was a race going on to get to the other side to block that power it had over my body. It was trying to force me to listen to its message and although it had control of me physically for a minute, it did not have power over my soul. It seemed like I couldn't run fast enough, but I remember the "hurry, hurry" going on inside my soul as I raced through one leg, then the next, and up toward my left arm. I continued through every finger and up to my left ear. As it started to speak, inside my ear again, I rolled what seemed like a heavy rock over the entrance of my ear so I couldn't hear the message. I heard the mumbling but gladly couldn't make out the words. The cold, frosty breath bounced off of the "rock" I had rolled to block it. The creature somehow realized I couldn't hear its message so stopped talking, paused for a second, and took off down my body. The second it's creepy little last claw left my big toe, I was freed from the hold it had on me. With every muscle flexed trying to get away and the sound of my screaming held in bondage, the release was huge. A terrifying scream came out as I flew about two feet in the air and landed back on the floor with a "thud". Every person in the room about jumped out of their skins and was instantly awake. They were probably going to think I was crazy, but I told them what had just happened. Probably because I was out of breath and pretty shaken, everyone was very interested in what had transpired. They looked at me and each other pretty freaked out, as if I was telling ghost stories at camp in the darkness.

Scotty Dog

One evening I was sitting on my bed, writing nothing really important in a notebook. After seeing movement out of the corner of my eye, I glanced over at the bookshelf to see something quite disturbing. It was my little black Scotty dog, a stuffed animal Mother had purchased for me from the hospital gift shop after I had spent a day of blood testing when I was sixteen. The dog jumped off the shelf onto the floor and started walking across my room. Frozen in fear, again I couldn't move or scream, just watching it like a horror movie. It then stopped, turned its head to look at me, and smiled. It had a full set of human-like chompers. It was terrifying! I was then released and I screamed as loud as I could and ran at it, kicking it as hard as I could into the wall. It was back to its normal shape, but all I could do was to take that thing outside and throw it in the trash. This tormenting went off and on for months. It was difficult to go to sleep at night as I would see lights buzzing around me that I refer to as "bees" and would be frozen off and on. My many experiences would bring shame to horror movie writers. Many other terrible and terrifying things happened, but I will only share a few during this time period. Lucifer was making good on his word to make my life "hell." He was definitely showing parts and pieces of his world.

Every experience I have seems to make the veil just a bit lighter. I began to understand that every day on earth, every person alive has a daily battle with the adversary for their soul. I just have the dubious privilege of seeing it, feeling it, experiencing it. I have no idea why I was chosen to be a keeper of this kind of gift—except perhaps through my understanding a lot of what is going on around us, I can help my brothers and sisters on the earth. We have all forgotten almost everything about God and Heaven which gives Satan all of the advantage in the fight for our soul. He knows our weaknesses, shortcomings and insecurities. He is using those against us to make us doubt ourselves and then to weaken and destroy us. His goal is to keep us from returning to the happiest place in the universe, our home with Heavenly Father and Mother. His only desire is for us to be miserable like he is because he can NEVER go home.

I didn't talk much about my experiences at the time, as I felt people would think I was crazy, but it came to a point in which I wasn't sleeping at all. Every time I closed my eyes something horrible would happen. My mother noticed how tired I was, but I was afraid to talk about it. I didn't want to give Lucifer power by looking like a victim or like he was winning. I started to tell her about a few of the incidents and why I was afraid to go to sleep.

It was after 9:00 pm and the doorbell rang. I went toward the door, but mother beat me to it. It was her bishop who apologized for it being so late but said, "I don't know why I am here, I just know that I am supposed to be. Is there something I can do?"

Mother looked at me and said, "Come on in, Bishop."

Totally blown away at his random appearance I said, "Yes, you are here for me."

I barely mentioned a thing or two of what had been going on and that was enough for him. He said "Let me bless this house." He said a special prayer on the house that night and left. That was the best sleep I had in months. I had been completely exhausted. Nothing molested my soul that night and peace reigned for several more. This experience gave me a testimony of the power of the priesthood that he held. It also amazed me at how God is so aware of what is going on.

Due to the number of events going on in my life, I requested a personal blessing from a priesthood holder in the Church to comfort me. What came from the blessing was a bit of a surprise. After telling me how much God loved me and was aware of me, he went on to say that in my life I would "be given the trials of Job." *What? Who was Job?* I grabbed my Bible and looked him up. Are you kidding me? This man lost his family. He lost everything! Haven't I had enough trials and lost enough already? I thought I had. It should be easy now that I was older. I had survived my youth so now what? Was my whole family going to die somehow? What in the world does that mean?

GPS Set To Home

These many different experiences were just a beginning to what would lay ahead for me. In analyzing what was going on past the veil, a world I could get a glimpse of but not yet perfectly see, I knew that the LDS Church was true. I didn't know how or what or why I knew, but it was true. It was only after I started to look into this particular religion that all of these spiritual experiences truly began. It was as if Satan was trying to scare me to death to back me away from what I had just found. If this church really was a bad place to be, he would have left me alone.

When we all lived among each other with our brothers Lucifer and Jesus, as well as our Father in Heaven for millions of years, Satan knew everything about every one of us. He knew I was stubborn and opinionated, and most importantly, a seeker of truth. If I believed in something 100% to my core, I would share it with everyone I knew in hopes that they would partake in that same truth to better themselves and their lives. I would want them to understand who they are so that they would be on the right path in this world to make it back to God, our Father.

Satan has the upper hand in remembering who we are with all of our unique talents, strengths and weaknesses, while we don't get to remember anything. All of us are born with the "Light of Christ", a gift from God, something like a little tracker or GPS to help us know right from wrong and find our way home. It is that particular little voice or light inside us that tells us that something is true or that the path we are on is the correct one. When we are alone or lonely and have that feeling of homesickness, but there is no home to go to, it is our Heavenly home that the light is trying to help us find. Most of my life has been spent trying to find a home and safety only to finally realize that home is back with our Heavenly parents. The homes here on earth are "kindling" and just temporary. We don't realize our souls are trying hard to imitate what we had before this life and establish the same home and security we had prior to the "GPS" within us. Innumerable nights throughout my life, I have cried to the heavens saying, "I just want to come home!"

We were not sent to the earth by accident. We were all preordained to come down at our own particular time for specific purposes, in circumstances that help us gain the most that we can out of this brief mortal journey. We have the greatest opportunity for happiness and success at each of our exact times on the earth. We have come to "school" to learn and grow. We are here to find our own unique talents that God has already placed within us. We are to polish and make them worthy of all acceptation before our Heavenly Father as we use them to serve others. There may be rainstorms and lightening on our way, maybe bullies and mean kids, but like our own earthly parents still send us to school in spite of those things, so does our Father above. He knows that in the long run it is for our good. There comes a graduation at the end if we endure and keep doing that homework and taking those tests. We will fail some tests, maybe many, but Jesus is there so that we may try again. We cannot grow, if we give up.

No one can possibly know what happiness truly is if they don't understand sorrow and pain. There is no appreciation for sweet if we have never tasted bitter. Can we appreciate how wonderful light is without seeing and feeling darkness? The most important thing with this earthly school is to keep trying, keep plugging away every day. We are to do the best that we can. There are so many tests and quizzes for so many years for our benefit so that we may grow. If it seems we are failing, just continue forward, studying harder. Trials are for our growth, not our hindrance. They show us our weaknesses so we can know what things we have to work on and they can become our strengths. These are our individual missions. There is no giving up. We cannot just drop out of school. Our own parents wouldn't let us and neither will Heavenly Father. He will not test us with more than we can handle. Remember that every trial is to help us grow in some way, a way that we may not understand right at that time but have faith in Him.

Our Father will not forsake us. If he expects us as imperfect humans to be kind, loving, and understanding parents, what kind of Father would He be, knowing all and being perfect, to just abandon us? He has not. He is, just for a time, like loving parents watching their toddlers pull themselves up, letting us fall down so that we may learn to walk by picking ourselves up and trying again. He knows what he is doing and we have to trust in that.

The experiences I had were the beginning of my heavier attendance in the Mormon Church. It was shortly after that my boyfriend Christian stated he was going on a mission. He turned in papers to the Church and received a calling to Chicago, Illinois. When he was entering into the Missionary Training Center in Provo, Utah, I went with his family for the day to drop him off and hear the mission president speak. Upon entering, the strongest, most incredible feeling came over me. It was the first time I felt a light inside turn on and tell me I was a little closer to home. Right then and there I knew I needed to go on a mission, too. When Christian and the many other new missionaries separated from their families and left, I cried. There wasn't a few tears shed, more like Niagara Falls. The thought of not seeing him for two years seemed an eternity. As in the past, I retreated to my room and spent days, then weeks in mourning. I even made a Christian shrine.

Corbin to the Rescue

Thank goodness for my dear Corbin. He came over, more and more, to pull me out of the coffin I had been building for myself. He was an amazing distraction. My mother was so grateful for him, too. He and I went to movies, dance clubs, singles wards on Sunday for church, and many drives in that '57 Corvette. Corbin was always on and off with a girl that did not appreciate him and tore him down a lot. He, being a positive person, would just shake it off or come to me while licking his wounds. All I had to do was tell him how awesome he was and that she was just stupid for not noticing. He would perk right up into the Corbin I knew and loved. He was too good for her anyway. How could anyone not appreciate perfection! Corbin and I would just laugh all of the time. We would poke fun at ourselves and then everyone else. He taught me it was okay to really laugh at myself and not take things so seriously. There was no show with Corbin; he was the real deal.

One night we had driven to one of his favorite views of the valley—really a make-out spot for others, but we just enjoyed the view. We had one of our several hour talks and he told me that he was going to go on a mission. I think I wanted to die, again. Corbin said that he wanted to help his family and had faith that a mission would bring them closer to the Church. He also wanted to help others find God and understand their relationship with Jesus. I just cried when I knew I would lose him to the mission field as well.

Corbin knew what he wanted and had thought about it for a long time. He had a very powerful testimony of the Church and an even more powerful patriarchal blessing that talked about the kind of spirit he is, was, and would become. I knew I would have to support him. He was going either way.

The following Sunday I attended my singles ward. The bishop asked if he could speak with me. He told me that he felt very strongly I needed to go on a mission. I replied that I was too new and didn't know much about the Church.

"Well then, there is no better way for you to learn than jumping right in."

"Shouldn't I take missionary lessons and get baptized?"

"Weren't you baptized at eight years old?"

"Yes" I replied, "But I didn't know what it meant, and after was baptized by another church."

"Your baptism at age eight still stands."

"Okay, I will do it."

My mother was thrilled with the thought of her daughter going on a mission. Corbin was also super excited about my mission. He and I were able to plan together and get our papers submitted close to the same time. Our mission calls came back with Corbin going to Scotland and me to Japan. We were both elated! Both of us needed to go to the temple so we made appointments to take out our own endowments and were able to schedule those at the same time.

The temple day came and Corbin and his grandfather were together as well as me with my mother. There was no time for me to meet Corbin's grandfather before the session. Throughout the endowment proceeding I kept looking over at Corbin but had to peer past his grandfather who was sitting on a chair closer to me. His grandfather kept seriously looking at me in quite a strange manner. At the end of the session, Corbin told me that his grandfather had pointed me out and remarked about a young woman that kept looking at him the whole time. He said, "Doesn't she figure that I am probably married and unavailable?" Corbin was hysterical, trying to tell me the story. He said, "No, Grandpa, she is looking at me, not you!" We had a good laugh about it, over and over. I said, "Your grandpa has great self-esteem!" It is one of those funny memories that never get old. Corbin left on his mission before I did, so we didn't get to be in the training center together, like I had hoped.

With my older brothers going on missions and all of the missionaries I had seen in pairs around in my life, I had previously wondered why in the world these young men and women would spend their own money and two years of their lives going around teaching people about Jesus Christ and God. I had heard many missionaries would spend all of that time and maybe only have one baptism and sometimes none. Wasn't their whole mission a waste of time and money? I came across a story from an unknown author that changed that thought process completely for me so I had to add it here:

> *A man was walking along a beach when he saw a young boy. Along the shore were many starfish that had been washed up by the tide and were sure to die before the tide returned. The boy was walking slowly along the*

> *shore and occasionally reached down and tossed the beached starfish back into the ocean.*
>
> *The man, hoping to teach the boy a lesson in common sense, walked up to the boy and said, "I have been watching what you are doing, son. You have a good heart, and I know you mean well, but do you realize how many beaches there are around here and how many starfish are dying on every beach every day. Surely such an industrious and kind hearted boy such as yourself could find something better to do with your time. Do you really think that what you are doing is going to make a difference?"*
>
> *The boy looked up at the man, and then he looked down at a starfish by his feet. He picked up the starfish, and as he gently tossed it back into the ocean, he said, "It made a difference to that one."*

I realized that the work for the few people out of thousands these missionaries came across truly mattered. It changed their lives, that of their family and of eternity. One of my favorite little sayings about missionaries is really the best definition: A missionary is someone who leaves their family for a short time, so that others may be with their families for eternity. Now that, my friends, is the truth. My challenge to you is to feed the missionaries so that the missionaries can feed you!

Distractions, Distractions

Distractions! That is what happened about eight weeks before my mission would begin. A nice young man, Ashton, popped into my life. He had just come home from a very successful mission in Europe and met me in the singles ward at Church. We clicked instantly and sparks were flying. There was no way I was going to let myself get serious because my mission was closing in, so I thought. It didn't take but a few weeks and we were in love, together every moment. Now what? He pleaded for me not to leave on a mission and proposed. My heart was so torn as to what to do. Corbin was a bit disappointed that I was considering marriage and wanted me to go on my mission. Christian was like, "Get on your mission now, please!" Ashton told me that in the Church, if given the opportunity to marry, girls were supposed to do that rather than go on their mission. I was so new I didn't know what to do but wanted to make the correct choice. What did Heavenly Father want me to do? The mission was two weeks away when Ashton told me that a special speaker was coming to the Marriott Center and we should go listen to him. He thought that maybe we could meet him after. Ashton said he was the presiding bishop in the Church and his name was Henry B. Eyring. I didn't understand why so many thousands of people would fill a conference center to hear a bishop speak when every ward has one, but okay.

To this day I don't remember anything about the topic spoken but it was good. After, Ashton said, "Let's go meet and talk to him. We will ask him what you should do." We stood in line to shake his hand and as soon as we were up, Ashton said, "My girlfriend is new to the Church and has a mission call. I want us to get married and she doesn't know what to do. I was telling her that girls usually get married when that opportunity..." The Bishop cut him off, grabbed my hand with a tight grip as if to shake it, pulled me closer to him, looked me square in the eyes, and said, "Go on your mission!" I said, "OK!" That was my answer. Ashton wasn't too happy.

I had no idea at the time what an amazing experience that was. A presiding bishop is not just a bishop but a general authority of the Church, serving under the prophet and first presidency of the Church. Wow! I wish I could have appreciated that incredible experience back then instead of years later.

CHAPTER 4

Mission Mayem and Miracles

The Mission

It was my time to finally go to the Missionary Training Center. I was so excited, had bags packed, and was totally ready. There was a huge concern about leaving my mother who had recently been diagnosed with breast cancer, but she wouldn't hear anything about me staying home. She kept saying that if she died, "Let the dead bury the dead." I still don't understand that, but she meant for me to go.

Some crazy things happened on my mission. I went into the Missionary Training Center on Halloween. Our room was dormitory style with huge cinder block walls, military-style heavy metal beds that were meant to last a hundred years and metal desks to match. Showers were out in the hall. My companion was a typical California girl and super cool. We had been in one of the many classes learning how to teach others about the church. There were easily two hundred missionaries in the class. The teacher briefly spoke about Joseph Smith and then went on to other topics. After about twenty minutes I leaned over to my companion and said, "Sister, who is this Joseph Smith guy?"

She about fell out of her chair as her mouth fell open. "Oh sister, we need to talk!" she replied. After the class and dinner we went back to our room where she taught me all about Joseph Smith and his experience seeing God and Jesus and how the LDS church began.

Umm, kind of important! My Bishop maybe should have had me take the missionary lessons or clued me in on this Joseph Smith guy. I didn't have any questions for her; it all made sense to me. I just needed to know the information.

I was only there a few weeks, learning about being a missionary and practicing my language, when my appendix ruptured. Thanks to my companion not listening to excuses of my abdominal pain being related to gas from too much food, but calling for help, I had a successful surgery and survived. After spending a few days in the hospital, I returned back to my mission companion at the training center. I slept on the bottom bunk of the one set of bunk beds while she slept on the top bunk of the opposing beds. We should have had four sisters in our room but there weren't any others but us. That was the first time I had ever been in surgery and was extremely weak, on pain medication that made me nauseous, and still in a lot of pain.

One night, something very intense happened. I was asleep on my bed when I felt a dark and heavy presence enter the room. I don't remember there being windows in this cinderblock room and I couldn't see anything. All of the sudden, I felt as if there were a thousand evil spirits trying to invade my weak body. The weight on top of me felt like a thousand pounds. I couldn't move, scream, or get any kind of help. These spirits where diving at me and I could feel them bouncing off of my body. It's as if I was a steak and a thousand starving dogs were all fighting for it. I had every muscle flexed and my stitches hurt so badly, but I had to keep the spirits from their possession or invasion into my body. I had thought of the story of Joseph Smith and his similar experience my companion had just told me and I tried to call out to her for help to no avail. It felt as if I would have to give into the darkness because of my lack of physical strength, but my spirit refused. Instead, inside my head I prayed for God to help me. I then thought of how my mother taught me to cast evil out and, thinking it, I said, "In the name of Jesus Christ, I command you to leave." God must have heard my prayer, and forced the spirits to release me. For just a few seconds, I could breathe again. My stitches hurt so bad from flexing to keep them out and my muscles were exhausted.

As I began to relax, they hit again. This time it felt as if five hundred spirits were attacking me. There wasn't as much power. This time was different because I could whisper. They were trying so hard to get inside of me, looking for any opening or weakness, bouncing off of each other and myself, like popcorn in a hot pan. Every muscle was flexed again and I felt like I was lifting 500 pounds of weight at the gym, grunting and flexing with everything I had. As I flexed my body to keep them out, again I commanded them in a whisper to leave. They released me and I fell back into my bed, completely exhausted.

A third time I was hit, but by about fifty spirits. This time I was able to vocally command them to leave, in the name of Jesus Christ. They left for good. While they were present, I didn't smell, hear, or see anything. I could only feel the evil and cold feeling mixed with the weight of a thousand desperate souls. Having things under control, I had hoped that I hadn't awakened my companion. I lay there for a minute, breathing hard from the workout and catching my breath. Just then from the other set of bunk beds I heard a little voice that said, "Sister, please don't tell me what just happened until morning." I said, "Okay."

It was so dark I didn't even know it was morning until the light popped on in our room. My companion sat Indian style right next to my bed on the ground. She said, "OK, what happened last night?" After apologizing for waking her, I told her what I had experienced and then asked her what she heard. She told me that I did not wake her at all but that she awoke at what she felt was a wall of darkness and evil coming into our room. She was so afraid that she went under her covers to pray. She then heard horrible sounds coming from my bed. She knew I was being attacked and could only hear my one ton metal bunk bed crashing repeatedly into the wall, floor, and maybe ceiling, as if it was being slammed. She was crying and praying for me the whole time, terrified at what I was going through in my weakened state. We pretty much kept the experience to ourselves. It was terrifying.

I left the training center and went to Japan. My first area was in Hirosaki. It was the farthest northern Japanese city in the mission. It was freezing cold and had tons of snow on the ground. All missionaries had only bikes to ride everywhere. My seasoned companion was very used to riding in the snow. It was very difficult for me to speak the language (which would continue as my main mission trial) and I certainly could not read the signs. On a twenty-five minute bike ride home, my Tour de France companion lost me. She never would look back to see how far I was and I could not call out to her in that cold, snowy wind. Wearing a dress and heels while traveling fast on a bike in the snow was just unnatural and something only time and experience could quicken. I came to a corner and was stopped at a red light. When looking all three ways to find her, I didn't see her anywhere. The light changed and I rode as fast as I could, deciding to turn right. There was a panic in my heart as I hoped to see her ahead, but after traveling a distance, never did. "Lord," I said, "help me find my companion. Where is she? I've got to find her!" At that very moment, a male voice came into my head and said, "Turn around and go back." I said, "Okay." Knowing that wasn't my voice or thinking, I turned around. Traveling a small distance back, and turning right to go up a hill, I saw my companion on her way down, looking for me. I was so happy! We would have never found each other in that city. I was sure the police would have found me frozen to my bike somewhere, dead, with a Book of Mormon in my hand.

I Think I'm Turning Japanese

In the book of Alma 26:37, I love where it reads: *God is mindful of every people whatsoever land they may be in: yea, he numbereth his people, and his bowels of mercy are over all the earth.*

The Elders were teaching a girl, Ito in her early 20's, about the Church. She started having a terrible time with evil spirits harassing her. Terrified, she came to the missionaries for help. They taught her how to cast them out but other than that didn't know what to do or say and she thought she was losing her mind. The Elders were asking us what we thought. Quickly, I jumped in. Not able to speak the language, I sat down with her and asked them to translate for the two of us.

She said that when she was introduced to the Mormon religion, she felt in her heart that it was true. She felt so grateful to find it. Her father told her that he would disown her if she joined. She said that she wanted to join anyway, but after that decision, all of these terrifying things kept happening to her in her apartment at night. Buzzing yellow lights would fly around her room and at her (the "bees", I thought) and other times, it would feel like her apartment would fill with a dark and cold evil, scaring her under her covers. She said sometimes she would be so frozen in fear that she wouldn't be able to move or speak. She asked if I thought she was "crazy." Oh, I've got this!

After telling her she wasn't, I told her my story about Lucifer and how he didn't want me to follow Christ and join this church. The Elders kept stopping and would look at me really funny. I would say, "Go on, say it!" They would tell her my experiences and she covered her mouth in surprise and began to cry. She kept saying, "You understand me! You understand and nobody else does!" She had tried to tell others about this and they thought she was crazy or the Church was evil. "That is what Satan wants you to think as he scares you away from the Church and its truth," I said. She went on to tell me that she thought the girl in the apartment above her was possessed. She said that every time she went to pray, the neighbor girl will start screaming as if she is in pain. She said it also happened when she commands the evil spirits to leave her apartment. It is as if they were going into, or being forced out of, her neighbor. In relaying some of the things that happened to me when joining the Church, she became very serious, looked into my eyes in tears, and said, "I am the reason you came to Japan." It blew my mind.

I was only in Hirosaki for seven weeks when I was transferred. Ito became a dear friend. She was still wrestling with a few spirits and was devastated I was leaving. She wouldn't stop sobbing when I was talking to her on the phone. I told her to keep her chin up and to come visit me in America one day. She said she would.

I never have seen Ito again, but I have always thought about her. We didn't have the technology in the early 90's that exists today and we lost touch. She did call me in Utah once after I came home and we spoke for an hour. She said that she continued with joining the Church and her father had disowned her, but she knew it was right. Two weeks after that, he died in a car accident. This was truly sad as I know she wanted to have the time to reconcile with him.

Steel-toed Boots

My next area was Morioka. Companions come in all shapes, sizes, and colors. This companion was a little blonde with a short "bob" haircut. She was an American who spoke perfect Japanese and seemed to come out of a military magazine. Affectionately, I called her the "sister with the steel-toed boots." She was very serious, especially about missionary work. Many sisters were worried about becoming her companion, that they may be worked to death. She had extended her mission and would only be there for two more months. I was thrilled to get an opportunity to work with her. Not feeling the love from my first Canadian companion, anything was going to be better. Truly, I was there to work. Out of several companions throughout my Japanese journey, she is the one I learned the most from.

One evening on our way home, my companion said, “Let’s just stop at one last apartment. It’s always that last one that is the golden ticket.” We rode into a complex. The minute we did, I said, “Sister, I have a really bad feeling about this place.” She said, “Let’s just go and see what’s here.” We walked to the bottom of the stairs of one apartment. The feeling I had grew stronger. Again I said, “Sister, I don’t like this.” She wasn’t worried and said, “Stay right here at the bottom then, and I will knock.” She went upstairs and my feeling became intense. Lights were on and she knocked one time. Exactly when she knocked I spoke more aggressively and said, “Shimai (Sister), I have a REALLY BAD FEELING!” She looked at me with fear and said, “Let’s get out of here, NOW!” Never had she moved so fast as she took about two jumps to come down that flight of stairs. As I was running for my bike, she jumped on hers and yelled, “Go, NOW! Don’t look back!” We pedaled so fast it was unbelievable. The evil that we felt coming at us was so strong. We got back to the apartment and were pretty spooked. Shimai said, “I have never had an experience like that in my life and I am really sorry I didn’t listen to you. From now on, if you have that feeling again, tell me and we will leave right then. I don’t know what was on the other side of that door but the second I knocked, I felt pure evil there.” It was really cool to see a very experienced and successful missionary be so humble and teachable from her very new, inexperienced greenie.

One day my sister with the steel-toed boots and I got into a deep discussion about our missions. I confessed my frustration with my prior companion and what I felt was a dislike and lack of respect towards me. The language was not coming to me as I had hoped, and with my 100% obedient effort and hard work I put in, I was not feeling like there was any success except for talking with my friend, Ito. She could feel my frustration as I vented.

My companion said some things I really needed to hear. “Shimai,” she said, “You have been so blessed. If you work the rest of your life doing nothing else but being 100% obedient to God, teaching people about him, and praying constantly to ask him what you should do next to serve him, you have given him 1% back of what he has given you. Don’t expect anything! Don’t feel you are deserving of anything! You deserve nothing, just like I deserve nothing. He already gave us everything!” She woke me up. I knew she was right. We have had such minor persecution, trials and difficulties compared to Jesus. I was truly blessed to have such an amazing companion.

Chest X-rays for Everyone

There were several health problems that I was having, starting in the training center with my appendix rupture. I didn't know what was going on with my body. I was sick all over, all of the time. On top of that, my energy was zapped. It was as if any energy created was being immediately sucked out of me no matter what I did, how much I rested, what I ate, it didn't make a difference. The doctors are a bit different in Japan. There is a strong draw to the Caucasians. Any blonds are like movie stars and my companion and I would get touched a lot, our pictures taken, our hair touched—it's different. There is pornography everywhere and usually the advertisement shows American women. We are seen as sex symbols. They even make their cartoons with large American eyes.

When my previous companion had to go to the hospital for ulcers, they had her remove everything on top for a chest x-ray. Then still without a top, 6 doctors consulted in that same room along with one other male assistant taking pictures. I told her she would be on the cover of next month's Playboy. She said, "Thanks a lot! That helps!" I told her it was only a problem if the mission president saw it on display.

Even though I swore I would never go to the hospital there, I had to for a severe sore throat that needed antibiotics. Instead of looking at just my throat, the doctor decided I needed a chest x-ray, too. They asked me to remove everything on top and then wanted me to walk out of the room, and a quarter mile down the hall, topless, to the x-ray room. Let me repeat that—topless. Hello! Let me remind everyone I am a Mormon missionary, and quite a bit conservative.

Word spread quickly about the topless American and there were twenty guys waiting in the hall to get a glimpse. Some were out of breath, obviously in a hurry to not miss the show. I thought to myself, "Word travels fast." Loudly I proclaimed, "This is not going to happen!" I requested, well, more like demanded a robe and they were… shocked. Seriously, do they think American women just walk around showing everyone their goods? They must watch a lot of fantasy movies. It took them quite a while to find me a robe. This is a hospital, people! It shouldn't be that hard to find me one, unless they were purposely trying not to. I would have waited all day just fine. As I assumed, my diagnosis was tonsillitis. I am so glad they have a chest x-ray of me.

Bad Dog

My companion and I got another companion. The mission was waiting for a sister to come from the Japanese Training Center so put us as a threesome for a couple of weeks until she arrived. When we met, she shook my hand and said, "I am really excited to meet you, Shimai, but am also afraid. I have heard the stories." That was a bit puzzling as I wondered who knew what stories. We went tracting on a very active road, kind of like their main street where tons of people walk and shop outdoors all day. It is a great place to meet people to teach about Jesus. As you get to the end of the shops, there is a bridge going over a river that has grass-lined banks. People picnic on the green strip on either side of the river, watching the water go by.

As we came to the end of the road, I glanced over the bridge to see a dog on a small island in the middle of the river. Looking back, my two companions were getting to know each other just chit-chatting away, following about twenty paces behind me. It was evening now and there weren't that many people left to talk to, and nobody down on the grass. Being a huge animal lover and saving those in distress, I felt my duty to help this dog. It was a very large, very fluffy white dog. I have never seen that kind before—in fact in Japan there are very few dog breeds that you see at all. This was not one of them.

The dog appeared very stressed as it paced the tiny island it was trapped on. The water was moving fast and I tried to figure out how it ended up there in the first place. This wasn't the kind of river that would be dry earlier and fill up due to rain. It always had a lot of water running in it.

Calling down to the dog did nothing. Usually a dog will look up at you when you are calling out and whistling to get its attention, but this one wouldn't look. My companions reached me and I told them that we had to save that poor, stranded dog. They were having a good time talking and were just kind of "whatever" so I started heading to the stairs that go to the river. To get to the stairs, you cross over the bridge and walk down a path parallel to the water which is lined with tall bushes blocking your view of the grassy park and river area below. You then come to the first set of stairs that face the river.

Those stairs bring you to a landing where the stairs then turn for flight two which runs parallel to the water, leading to the grass, and pointing toward the bridge. As the sisters had basically just fallen back, I pushed forward toward my mission to save the dog. I knew that we aren't supposed to get near the river, but this was a lifesaving reason so I felt the rules didn't apply. At a swift, dedicated pace I crossed the bridge and headed towards the stairs, passing the tall bushes. Reaching the top of the first flight of stairs, I glanced to see my companions following behind, quite a bit slower but laughing and singing as they came. Missionaries are not supposed to be out of the others sight, ever! The fact I saw them coming I felt was good enough. They were right behind me, I rationalized while pressing forward. The sisters couldn't see me as I started the stairs. I turned as I began the second set to see them finally pass the bushes and study the long staircase while at the top of the stairs. They began down.

Hurrying, I cruised down the second stairs onto the grass and toward the bridge. Apparently I was just navigating my course there without looking for roadblocks or danger that may be in my way. I looked up ahead toward the bridge and lo and behold, there was the dog. Not only was he 10 feet in front of me on the grass staring and waiting for me, he wasn't even wet. His eyes were glowing red.

My heart sank. I couldn't believe Lucifer had lured me with the old "help the puppy" trick. I was angry at myself, so disappointed. This time, Lucifer had won! I thought I was strong enough, smart enough but he is just too conniving and has the advantage of knowing everything about us. I exhaled loudly, knowing I had been beat. I looked over my shoulder to see my two companions running as fast as I have ever seen, hopping two stairs at a time, up the second set of stairs and around the corner of the bushes where they couldn't see me any longer. They were gone. At that moment, I knew I was dead, defeated. I remember thinking, "This is it. He is going to attack and kill me and I will be dead in a minute." I was so angry at myself. I was so disappointed. He had lured me like a lamb to slaughter. I had no idea what was coming.

Just as I was ready to give in, an amazing event occurred. Two very large angels appeared, one on either side of me, grasping my arms above the elbow. They were huge, like seven feet tall. One second I was facing the dog and a second later I was opposite, facing the stairs. I heard a voice that said, "Walk!" As

I began to walk, it said, "Slower." I slowed down but wanted to run. "Slower!" it commanded. I began to look back to see where the dog was and a loud voice commanded, "Don't look back. Walk slower." Then again I turned my head, "Don't look back!" I wanted to scream. That story in the Bible came to me about Lot's wife being told not to look back and when she did, she was turned to a pillar of salt. The last thing I wanted was for my mom to find out I was turned into a pillar of salt. That is worse than the dog killing me. I had to obey! As much as I wanted to see if that dog was behind me, I had to obey the voice. One of the angels, I call them my "Stripling Warriors," then released my arm and dropped back behind me. I assumed he was going after the dog. When I accidentally tried to see where he went, the voice of the other angel sounded the same as the first, "Don't look back." It felt like eternity had passed when I finally got to the bottom of the first set of stairs. As my foot went to touch it, the voice then yelled, "RUN!" I had been waiting for this! This was music to my ears. I think I hopped twice before I was at the top of both sets of stairs, rounded the bushes, down the path and actually passed my two companions on the bridge, still running. When I passed them, they started to scream really loud. They assumed the dog was chasing me and now would get them since I was faster.

We ran back into the safety of the main street with people and shops. I started yelling at them, "You guys left me! You cannot leave me!"

"That was no dog, sister! That was NOT a dog!"

"I know! Thanks for leaving me with it!" They then told me that they were minding their own business, following me when on the second set of stairs going down, almost to the grass, they heard a very loud, commanding voice yell, "Get out of here!"

"We are so sorry! What were we supposed to do?"

I was calm and said, "Obey the voice."

We were walking through town to get to our bikes on the other end of the main street when the "warriors" returned together. They followed us, protecting our path on our way home, just a small distance behind us. I wondered what they did to the "dog." We were all totally freaked out so went straight home.

Our newest companion was a comedian and would knock on her wooden desk really loud every day after that and say, "Sister, there is a wolf at the door asking for you!" I would say, "So NOT funny sister" but it was.

Coming to America

I was sick so much on my mission that Salt Lake had requested that I come home and see American doctors. I was sad to leave the country I loved, although the language was still difficult. I had been in the mission home for weeks with no energy to even eat. The kitchen help maid would come to my room and force me on small walks outside, then to eat small bowls of rice or curry. Sleeping more than seventeen hours a day with continued exhaustion was enough concern for our mission president and his wife that home I went.

Being diagnosed with chronic fatigue syndrome in 1992 was difficult. It was a new diagnosis at the time with many doctors not even believing it was an actual condition. They certainly didn't know what to do with it. I was put on medications and antibiotics, off and on, for a year.

Finally, one doctor told me that I would have to work out every day on a stair stepper machine for twenty minutes. He said he didn't care if I was laying on it as long as I did my twenty minutes. That is actually the only thing that began to work.

During my health struggles, Mother had hers. She had a successful run of chemotherapy and radiation for her breast cancer prior to my mission, but it was back, and worse. It had spread to her lymph nodes and colon now. Thirty-two lymph nodes were removed along with 2/3 of her colon. She had to do chemotherapy and radiation again. She just cried. I know she begged God to please not make her do this. The cancer was eating her up from the inside and, similar to when I was a child, there was nothing I could do to help her.

Mom had moved into my sister's home. When I returned to America, that is where I went also. It was a bit awkward with her family so as fast as I could, I got a job to afford my own place. There was a room I found near the university that would be shared with two roommates.

CHAPTER 5

Losses and Love

Ryan, My Brother

My younger brother had been living with some friends since his teens for several years out of state. One of those roommates was Ryan. Speaking to him on the phone several times and hearing all about him from my brother was as if I already knew him well. Now that he and my brother moved to Utah, hanging out together was in order. Instantly we clicked but in a brother and sisterly way, not because he wasn't attractive.

Ryan was incredibly good looking, blond, greenish-blue eyes, super tall and had a perfect washboard stomach that I loved to rub because it felt like a rock. I had my own relationships and he had his. We were friends, good friends, family. Ryan came from a home of all boys which usually isn't my favorite thing from my dating experiences since (here goes my stereotype) they don't understand women or emotions very well. However, Ryan was different. The love and respect for his mom ran deep and he certainly treated me well. I think he would have been a great brother to a bunch of sisters. His parents taught him well. Ryan understood me. A few years older than I, he watched out for me. We went to clubs, restaurants, anything to spend time together.

At a restaurant specializing in 'down-home' cooking and fresh pies, Ryan had ordered and was eating meatloaf. We were talking when he interrupted me for a second and said, "Hold that thought." Grabbing his phone and dialing I heard, "Mom, I just want you to know you make the best meatloaf. Yes...That's it, just wanted you to know. Love you, bye." He then said, "Sorry, continue." I just started laughing.

"Did you just call your mom for that? That is the cutest thing I have ever seen! Oh my gosh, you are so cute!"

"Stop embarrassing me," he said, blushing. "This meatloaf just isn't as good as my mom's. I thought she should know." That was the kind of son Ryan was.

No matter what was going on in my world, Ryan was there. He was extremely protective of me. At one point I had a stalker that was becoming more frightening, aggressive, and dangerous. Stalking wasn't taken as seriously by police even ten years ago like nowadays. I was used to lots of guys chasing me, even a stalker in California once and always handled it well and by myself, but this one was different. No matter what I said to this guy to make him leave me alone seemed to make him want me more. Finally it was at a point where he was everywhere I was, completely hunting me, and saying what he was going to do to me.

Not sure how to handle this escalated situation anymore, I finally told Ryan. He blew a gasket. He made me tell him who he was, where he lived, his name and telephone number. He wouldn't tell me what he was going to do, but I never heard from that guy again. Ryan's only response was, "I laid the hammer down for my sister." Ryan and I remained brother and sister tight for the rest of his life.

Destruction and Nihon

Never do I dream without it meaning something. This was a very unusual dream I had of the country I love. One night, I dreamt I was standing on the beach in Japan, looking out over the vast ocean. I had done this before on my mission, but it was beautiful then. This time looking out there was nothing but garbage as far as the eye could see. It seemed like this was the dumping ground for everything. There were couches, garbage bags, all kinds of trash, and furniture. The water was not visible due to the amount of trash. The only way to tell there was water was by watching the movement of the filth bobbing slowly up and down. The smell of death and fish consumed the air. No people were present on the beach; in fact there weren't people at all. Looking at my feet, there were only dead fish and creatures everywhere. They just kept washing up, thousands of fish. In the distance I saw movement. Surfacing, a large whale pushed through the debris and was choking on sludge as I watched his desperate gasp for survival through its blowhole. I wanted to help the whale but as usual, I was helpless. Tears poured down my face as I ached for the land of my heart. Crying, I yelled out, "What happened to this beautiful land? Why?"

I woke up in bed with true tears streaming down my face and my pillow was wet. I was wondering how long I had cried in that dream before I awoke. What does this all mean? I don't know. Possibly it was something that happens in the future. Twenty or more years have passed since then and I am starting to believe it was a tsunami or some kind of global disaster that I saw ahead of time. I guess we shall see.

Vegas, Baby!

On a quick Vegas weekend run with a friend, I met a great guy, Kent. He came to Vegas from Newport Beach with a large group of friends. He stood out like a sore thumb. Kent was nothing like the guys he was with. They were womanizers and partiers. Kent was classy, debonair. My friend began a conversation with their group as we were all lying by the pool at one of the casino hotels. They invited us to meet up for dinner and a concert. We accepted and Kent and I had such a great time. We ended up spending the entire three-day weekend together, having a blast. He was definitely a diamond in the rough. We began to see each other after the weekend was over with one of us flying to see the other in Utah or California. I told him I had just returned from a mission. He was curious about religion, death, and the purpose of life. At the time, his mother was dying of cancer as was mine. He started seeing the missionaries and learning about the LDS religion in Newport.

One night late, I received a call from Kent. He was clearly terrified. He told me that there were evil spirits or something in his house. He said he heard something strange and as he went to check it out, these yellow lights (I call them bees) were buzzing around trying to get him. I knew exactly what these were. I told him to put his hand to the square and cast them out. He did and they left. The next night, same thing happened. He was so terrified he couldn't remember the words to cast them out. On the phone call I said, "In the name of Jesus Christ, I command you to leave." They left. Kent told me he couldn't take it, but we talked a lot that night as I shared my similar experience when I looked at the Church. He received my warning that they would continue to try to run him away from the Church by bothering him. They attacked him repeatedly all the way until his baptism. This reminded me of my friend, Ito, in Japan who was also a very sweet and kind spirit with similar trials leading towards baptism. Kent finished the lessons in California and flew to Utah where he was baptized. After his baptism, he didn't have any other experiences like the prior.

It is just amazing to me the great lengths Lucifer will go to keep people from finding God, Jesus, or the truth that will bind families after this life forever. He will do anything and everything in his power. I have always felt that my friends on the earth were all very strong and special spirits in the pre-existence and that is why we gravitated towards one another here. Our minds may have forgotten who we are, but our souls remember everything, including the close friendship that we shared.

The Truth Shall Set You Free

My mother's cancer was spreading quickly, now to her pancreas. She wasn't given much time to live. It was Mother's Day and according to doctors, it would be her last. As a gift, I asked her out to lunch. While talking about life and trials it came to me that I had to ask a big question of my own. "Mom, why did Dad hate me?" I asked.

"Oh, he didn't hate you dear. It had nothing to do with you," she said.

Right then, I remembered my first grade teacher Mrs. Jensen calling in my mother to the school and telling her that I had said my father was moving out of the house because he hated me. I don't remember saying that in class but clearly at six years old, I knew what was up. Mother had brought me with her to the classroom and together with my teacher they told me that with separation the parents both loved the children, it was the parents that were trying to work out some issues. Mrs. Jensen had no idea that I was telling exactly the truth. Under normal circumstances, she would be correct, but my father did hate me.

"Seriously, Mom, I know he hated me, just tell me the truth," I pressed.

"No sweetie, it was me he had the problem with, not you," she repeated. This was unacceptable and making me mad.

"Mom," I raised my voice now, "Please, cut the crap! I know he hated me! I have always known. Please, tell me the truth! I need the truth!" One more time she gave me a lame answer.

"Mom! You are dying!" I said harshly. "I have always known Frank hated me and I need to process this. I need to know why. I have known since I was a little girl. I'm a big girl now, I can take it! Please, please tell me the truth as to why? Please!"

Mother began to cry. Shaking softly she said, "Because you reminded him of me!"

I nodded my head and said, "Thank you!"

That answer was so freeing to me. Children always know. Maybe kids don't know the exact answer but they know the question. I wasn't crazy. My feelings that he hated me were real and correct; I just didn't know why. With the answer, finally, I could begin to heal. I could trust my own feelings. I needed to hear this, the truth, not the protected answer.

Here Comes the Bride

For some reason, I didn't really believe Mom would die. Maybe it was denial or that she was too young. A miracle of some kind was going to occur because she couldn't end her misery yet. She has been there for me my whole life. She has suffered through much more than illness in her own life. No matter what the doctors said, I thought she would get better. My sister and I always joked about how no one in our family could get off of the earth and away from this cursed life if they tried. Even if a plane we were on crashed, we would survive—in fact would be the only survivors. We would walk away from that plane alive but, of course, maimed in some horrible way, burned on half our body. We knew this to be true and it is still our joke and so at the time I absolutely believed Mom was somehow going to survive, never escaping one second of the misery and pain that was our family's portion.

I had met a guy in a neighboring apartment building who hung out at my place a lot and became a friend to see movies or grab a bite to eat with. My roommate Kate was very serious about him…for me! He wasn't exactly my type, but my mother had always told me that you should marry your friend because romance and looks come and go but friends are solid. I had always dated pretty hot guys but knew several of them were players and not the marrying type. What did I know? There were a few great relationships I had seen with my own eyes, but usually girls grow up to marry someone like their father and that was my biggest fear.

Thinking it would be best to marry someone I wouldn't normally choose, a nice looking friend, when my neighbor and suitor proposed, I said, "yes." There was a lot of opposition from his family about me not being from "Mormon" blood. Some terrible judgement was made about my family and the relationship I had with my fiancé. It was very difficult for us both.

I had so much hope to be adopted into a family that adored and wanted me in it, hoping they would see my goodness and worth. All I wanted was to be appreciated and loved, desperately! That was my greatest desire in life. My heart ached to be accepted and loved for just being me. Clearly that would not be the case.

We married anyway with not much emotional support from my new husband's side of the family, but mine was supportive. Mother was so weak she had to be pushed around in a wheel chair. Walking into the temple, I hesitated for a moment with the clear thought: *His name DOES NOT MATCH mine like the angel had told me.* I married him anyway.

The day passed fast and we left for the night only to return in the morning to talk together as a family one last time. Mother couldn't even open her eyes as she spoke. She had given every ounce of strength to be there for my wedding. We talked for the last time before I left on my honeymoon. She told me how much she loved me and how proud she was that I was her daughter. She said she realized the potential I had and that I was big-hearted and tender on the inside but tried so hard to protect myself from more pain and she understood. She hoped that one day I would be able to let my guard down, opening my heart to trust and love. She was very sorry about my father and expressed gratitude that she was my mother. My "happy spirit, even when things were hard at home" she admired and she wanted me to always be a good friend to others.

I told her she couldn't die because I always planned that after growing up, I would work really hard so that she could come live with me and my family so that she would never have to work again. She could play with her grandkids all day, her favorite thing in the world! She could cook if she wanted to, sleep in and never have to worry about bills, food, and money. Maybe one time in her life she would experience what a manicure was like or even a pedicure. I wanted so much to give her some nice things. At twenty-three, finally I was getting to where I could help Mother. She had always worked and tried so hard, not always successfully, but definitely tried to take care of us kids. There was nothing of value that Mom possessed but she said, "Wealth has nothing to do with money. It's our precious relationships that make us rich."

I remembered how Mom loved the old Mercedes convertibles from the late 70's and would joke and say "Someday, when I find my pot of gold..." and she would laugh. I wanted to buy her one as a surprise one day, just so she could ride around and feel free. Even the license plate I had planned to personalize as "FORMOM." Never did she get a break. She never got out of poverty and she had experienced so much emotional and physical pain, heartache, and heart break. I had plans for her and us. I wanted to take her for one time in her life on a vacation, maybe to Hawaii. She HAD to live! What would I do without her?

Mom said she wouldn't know how to enjoy those nice things anyway and they were, after all, just things. I argued that life was not fair and her life was so "crappy." She said, "I would do it all over again to have you children." Mom said she had no fear of dying and that Carl was waiting for her. (My siblings told me later that she kept talking and waving at him in an empty chair sitting in the room, right before she died.) Her heart just ached because of our tears for her. She said we would never be alone and she would always watch over us. Then she told me her life was over now, and that she loved me and was so, so tired.

Wanting my new husband to be happy, I had to leave on that honeymoon, knowing I would never, ever in this life see her again. My heart was breaking open, I was bleeding out. It was horrible.

The Other Side

The dreaded phone call came at midnight, the tenth day of my marriage. Mom had passed. I felt numb and tried to wake my new spouse to talk about it, but he wouldn't wake from his deep sleep and just rolled away from me. Beginning to cry, I fell to my knees next to the bed and prayed. Not feeling any relief or anything at all but incredible grief, I lay in bed and finally dozed off in the darkness of my room and heart.

As soon as I fell asleep, I was standing in the afterlife behind my mother. She was on this stage-like area, one that I would see again. Carl was standing right next to her with his left arm around her waist. He had the biggest smile I have ever seen anyone wearing. There was a crowd of people facing mother which also meant facing me. They had smiles similar to Carl's. There was what looked like thousands of people or more. There wasn't an end as far as I could see. It is definitely what I would call a multitude.

The people farther back in the crowd were on their tip-toes, all trying to get a peek at my mother. It was as if she was a rock star, this was a concert, and she was signing autographs or getting to know her fans. Everyone was trying to get closer but in a much more polite and organized manner. The multitude had gathered just for her. All of these people were dressed in regular clothing, street clothes. Even mother was wearing the cotton floral patterned stretchy comfortable dress she wore in the wheel chair at my wedding. Carl was wearing jeans and a short sleeved t-shirt with his right arm gesturing from mother to different people in the crowd in front of her as if he were introducing her. It seemed like he had told people about how wonderful she was and they were there to finally meet her. Mother nodded politely but looked a bit uncomfortable and had her arms tightly secured at her side. She looked as if she were a bit confused, trying to understand and attempting to comprehend where she was and everything going on. I'm sure she felt like she was in a dream, standing there with Carl. It looked to me as if it seemed all surreal for her. Did she even know she was dead? I felt like I was looking through a window into someone's home, watching everything going on and they had no clue about my presence. The dream was a comfort to me, but I thought it only to be a lovely and comforting dream.

My new spouse and I had barely unpacked our things when we were repacking for the flight to the funeral. We arrived at my sister's home and I saw my eldest brother and his wife. Mickey had joined our family in her teen years and Mother became like an adopted mom to her. They were very close. I started talking to my brother and decided I would tell him about the interesting dream.

Shortly after I began the story, he looked puzzled, and then called for his wife to come over. He said, "Mickey, listen to this dream." As I started the story over again, she interrupted my details with, "Did Mom look really uncomfortable to you?"

"Yes" I said.

"And was there like this huge multitude of people there trying to greet her?"

"Yes" I said.

"Was Carl's arm around her waist and did he have the biggest smile you have ever seen on a face as he introduced her to people?"

"Yes" I again replied.

"I saw all of that, too, but I wasn't asleep! After the family called you, we had to wait for a couple of people to get to the house. We then all gathered around Mom's bed and said a family prayer. Everyone then went downstairs to talk and wait for the morgue to pick up her body. I stayed with Mom. I couldn't leave her! I began to cry and said, 'Mom, I am just not ready to let you go.' Just then this vision opened up in front of me and showed me exactly the same thing that you saw. I knew she was with Carl and that she was going to be okay and happy. That was the only way I could let her go."

I realized it wasn't a dream that I saw, but the actual place that my mother was exactly when it happened and precisely what was happening with her at that moment. It all made sense to me now. When a spirit leaves Heaven and becomes a baby that is born on earth, multitudes of friends and family members gather in Heaven to see that spirit off on his journey on the earth. It is difficult to see that person go. There are tears and some sadness mixed with excitement for his earthly experience. On the earth, family and friends gather and celebrate that spirit coming to earth. We have baby showers, infant blessings or christenings at Church, and other parties or family celebrations and reunions.

When the beloved spirit leaves the earth to go back home, everything flip-flops. The sadness is here on the earth and the welcome home party is in Heaven with thousands of friends and loved ones there to greet you home. Jesus is also present for the righteous to hug them or hold their hand. What an amazing thing to realize! Nobody is ever, ever alone! There are loved ones on both sides of the veil, waiting and celebrating their arrival. Nobody ever has to be afraid of dying! You are always walking with a loved one that you hold dear whether on this side or the other. What an amazing experience and a loving God! (Of course that is not how I felt at twenty-three years old).

In spite of seeing the many things I saw, at twenty-three, losing my only parent, my beloved mother, was unbearable. I would wait for my husband to be out of the house for a period of time and I would fall apart. My grief brought me to my knees. In despair, all I could do was call on God to relieve my suffering and keep my heart from crumbling. How is it that I was only given one parent to begin with and God could take her away! That was so unfair! I was hurt. I was angry. Most people have these families and extended families. Ours was so small and broken with only one very old and tough grandfather who was months from passing himself. We then would have none. Why would God take all that we have?

Someone suggested I take a grief class. It was once a week. My husband agreed it would be a good idea. The first thing I learned was the instructor's definition of grief that she created after losing her husband. She taught, "Grief is the process of putting back together the pieces of a broken heart. A hole so deep in the middle of your heart that it aches and it hurts and you think it will never stop hurting." I thought that was pretty good and summed up my feelings. Everyone in our group shared their losses. It didn't matter who or what was lost, the pain was the same. The emptiness and sadness seemed endless.

Happy Birthday to Me

Three and a half months after mom had passed away I woke up to a familiar song. It was Mother's voice singing, "Happy Birthday to you, happy birthday to you, happy birthday dear Kayli Sue, happy birthday to you!" I shot straight up in bed. "Mom!" I yelled out. I had been in a horrible nightmare of losing Mother and it was all a bad dream. Mom was here, everything was okay! I looked around the room. The sun was coming through the blinds of our bedroom window. My spouse was still asleep. Nobody was there. I was devastated! I was so sure I heard her voice, just like every year before, in fact, I knew it.

This whole thing must have been wishful thinking or dreaming, I thought. I was twenty-four years old today. The loneliness and emptiness of Mom being gone swept over me. The many times I had run to the phone to call Mom in the last few months to tell her something that happened, only to realize she was gone, came back to me. My heart sank and I started to cry. Trying not to wake my husband, I walked into the bathroom and closed the door quietly. With tissue I looked in the mirror and started drying my many tears running down my cheeks. Just then I heard someone familiar say, "I am so sorry! I didn't mean to make you cry!" It was Mother's voice I heard, soft as always but clear as day. She was standing right next to me. She wasn't visible but I knew she truly was standing right there. I could feel her and definitely heard her. "It's okay," I said, loudly. "I just miss you so much." At that point there was no way to contain the waterfall of tears that came pouring out of my eyes.

I felt terrible that I cried and have told her several times I was sorry for making her feel sad because I treasure that experience so much. Poor Mother just wanted to make me happy and smile on my first birthday away from her but instead it backfired for her and brought me to tears. There is nothing like the comforting voice of a mother. What better gift than to hear her voice again. I missed her terribly. She never sang on my birthday again. Sometimes on that day, I close my eyes and try to listen really early in the morning but "Happy Birthday" has never been heard since.

I did hear Mother's voice one other time in my life, though. I was dreaming. Mother came to me in the dream, but it was like I was looking at a picture of her and not her alive. We talked and I could hear her voice perfectly as if she were sitting right next to me. After she told me she was happy and not to mourn her, I asked if she could visit one of my sisters who really were having a terrible time. She told me sadly, "No, I cannot. I can only visit those who are pure and faithful."

Did I hear that right? I have never in my life used those words to describe myself. It was pretty shocking actually. She said that was why she could come to me. My sister was living with someone at the time and apparently she was not allowed to go into that situation. I have thought about that many times when people have passed away, "Am I pure and faithful so that I am worthy for them if they wanted to come to me?" This was an interesting thing to think about.

CHAPTER 6

Angels and My Angels

Encounter with an Angel

A very interesting thing happened to me one day. I was working while my husband went to school and every day walked with coworkers to the exact same place to eat for lunch. One day as we approached there was what appeared to be a homeless man sitting right outside the door against the building. He was truly in rags—one of the worst cases of homelessness I had ever seen. He was so incredibly thin he had to have bones showing. He wore no shoes, was completely filthy, his hair was in knots, and the rags he wore would hardly be considered clothing. The lunch place, however, was busy and bustling with tons of professional people going in and out. The line was almost outside as many people paused right next to the bum and waited for room to step inside the building.

I watched as everyone treated him as invisible, ignoring the needy man. I had never seen him there before and wondered where he came from. A male coworker walking with us, fearing the man, told me to be careful and walk on the other side of him. I said I was fine and continued closer. He wasn't begging or asking for anything. He just sat there. As we were about to go in, I reached into my purse, pulled out money, and handed it to the man for lunch. He reached and lightly grabbed my hand as to hold it, looked up into my face and said, "Thank you." As he looked into my eyes, I saw the Savior. His eyes were the most beautiful I have ever seen in my life. I fell into them. I could see

Heaven and angels in them. The color of what looked to be blue was radiant as if he had swallowed the sun. I gasped as I stepped back, pulling my hand away in complete unworthiness to be in his presence. He was so incredibly beautiful.

My coworkers missed the whole experience. One scolded me for giving him money and another thought he had hurt me and asked if I was okay. I couldn't tell them what I had just witnessed, thinking they would think I was crazy. I never saw him again nor have I stopped thinking about him twenty years later.

Since that experience I believe, truly believe, the Savior comes to every single one of us somewhere and sometime in our life. I also believe we will be responsible for the handling of that situation. *Verily I say unto you, Inasmuch as ye have done it unto one of the least of these my brethren, ye have done it unto me.* (Matthew 25:40)

My Own Angels

As I suffered through my grieving process alone, I was also dealing with my first pregnancy. The doctor said I was allergic to it. Of course I was! My therapist always said, "Success in life is learning to deal with plan B." My whole life is always plan B or C or sometimes Z. Never would I get the easy way through something. It wasn't my calling.

I was insanely ill and vomiting the entire nine months. The bright side was I had a washboard stomach at six months pregnant. The down side was I had only gained nine pounds and was still wearing my same jeans. The doctor was very concerned. I couldn't help it. Everything eaten came right back up. There was no opening the fridge or the smell would do me in. My husband couldn't even warm up soup or the smell would make me lose my lunch, literally. Mother would be there to help me if she were here. My husband couldn't understand anything I was going through; I wanted my mom. He had not only his parents still alive, but three of his grandparents too. His attitude was "You know where she is so it shouldn't be a big deal." I had to cry in secret and felt so alone.

The worst experience of childbirth ever, happened. Of course it would happen to me. My son became stuck and wedged in the birth canal for an extended period of time. This was due in part to an ignorant, tree-hugging nurse that turned off my epidural by rationalizing that "Women have done this for centuries without pain relief and so can you." The back pain felt like the Texas Chain Saw Massacre and went on for hours with a doctor that used every possible means except Caesarian to get him out. He said the damage of pulling the baby backwards after him being stuck would cause even more complications for the both of us. After most of the day, finally my son was born.

Completely torn apart, I had lost so much blood I was in need of a blood transfusion. After begging and pleading with my doctor because of the AIDS scare, he agreed with me but said I would have to stay in the hospital in observation for a few more days and take iron for a year to make up blood. That bittersweet day ended with a darling, perfectly healthy 8 lbs., 12 oz. son I named after my best boy-friend Corbin. The day had been so full of chaos and concern that I was exhausted like I've never felt before.

I woke up in the middle of the night. It was dark except the lights from all of the machines around me. Looking down at my hands on top of my belly were my mother's hands, right on top of mine. I was not expecting that. There was an empty chair next to the bed and I knew she was sitting there. She would never miss the birth of my first child; it made sense. I am sure she was there as I was screaming in pain, rolling back and forth in back labor, begging for the doctor to help me. She had been with me throughout that whole traumatic day and now that I was resting, she put her hands on top of mine as a gesture of love that she would never leave me when I needed her.

God gave me the perfect baby, one that I really needed at this place in my life full of grief—hope of the future. Corbin never cried. He fussed if he was hungry or wet, but besides that he just didn't cry like normal babies. When I would hold him and look into his eyes, he would connect and look right through me and into my soul. It was overwhelming and tears would come down my face as I would look away. I felt unworthy in some way to care for such a valiant spirit. God knew exactly what I needed right then in my life. There was never stress with him, ever. He was an unrealistic but true to life doll. Truly, I felt joy in being his mother.

My mother didn't leave me alone that year. This was evident when Corbin was alone in his crib. My husband and I would hear him start laughing that darling little baby laugh. He would laugh and then do this sweet little "Ahhhh…" as if waiting for someone else to say "Boo" and then his big laugh would happen again and again. My husband one morning said, "Who is in there with him?"

This event happened several different times. We tried spying on him a couple of times. As soon as we looked in, he would be looking toward the ceiling as if someone was standing over him looking into the crib. They must have looked over at us because he then would immediately do the same thing and catch us.

One night as we listened to this game again going on with him and whomever in his room, I said, "I wish we knew for sure who it was playing with him. I bet it's my mom. She LOVES her grandbabies more than anything in this world." Right then we heard this loud "bang" in the living room. We both jump up to check it out. We found the framed picture of my mother and me at our wedding on our bookshelf had fallen over. It had never fallen over before. I said, "Yep, she just answered our question."

A second precious and darling son joined us two years later. Chandler Ray was named after my grandfather William Raymond. He was a large baby, too, which my doctor induced two weeks prior to the due date as to not repeat the earlier experience with his older brother. This time I banned the previous nurses from my room. They were a bit offended, but they were indeed banned! Chandler, weighing in at 8 lbs., 8 oz., still tore me up, but I didn't feel the pain this time; my doctor made sure of that. Chandler was opposite of Corbin. I called him a colic baby, but he wasn't. He wanted to do what his big brother could do and wasn't at all happy in his little body. He was our little Hercules and was trying to stand up at six weeks old. Yes, that's right—six weeks! Never have I seen a baby with calf muscles. He's always been strong like his great-grandpa. Chandler followed Corbin from Heaven. I knew that from day one. Corbin is the only person that could make him smile, even in the middle of crying. The sun rose and set on his big brother.

Grandpa

Grandpa was very old. Knowing he would be leaving us soon, we made the trek to California where he had moved for warmer weather. He held Chandler and said, "Be careful with this one, he's very sensitive." Grandpa was right, Chan was sensitive. Grandpa passed away not long after we visited. He had worked outside with the sheep, cow, chickens, and the garden as usual. It was lunch time and he came in, hung up his cowboy hat and washed up. After lying back in his lazy boy, cowboy boots still on, for a quick nap, waiting for Grandma to finish lunch preparations, he died. Grandma couldn't wake him.

That has got to be the best way to leave this earth. Grandpa had on his favorite boots, napping in his favorite chair, was at home, smelling lunch cooking, and had finished all of the morning chores. I love my grandpa!

The Empress of Soul

My husband finished his schooling and it was time for us to get settled somewhere. Looking for the best possible chance of success, we chose Las Vegas. There were great memories of Vegas still held from years earlier with my friend Kent. I was excited and loved that town. We packed our little family and made the move right before the 4th of July. Already having closed on the sale of a small house, we moved right in. It was the first time since Grandpa built our house that I wasn't in a temporary home and it felt so good! There wasn't anything I wanted for my children more than stability and love. Finally for a moment, everything was perfect.

When you unpack your things in a new house, at some point a grocery store visit is necessary to fill your cupboards and fridge. After getting my angels off to bed one evening, and leaving my spouse to more unpacking, off to the supermarket I went with a large list of things to get. I had only begun my shopping when walking down an aisle with my empty cart I saw a familiar face. Where did I know her from? I walked up to this lady. It was after 9:00 pm and hardly anyone was in the store. She had on shorts, a t-shirt, baseball cap, and sunglasses. I said, "Gladys?" She turned around and said, "Hi." It was Gladys Knight, the "Empress of soul." She was just reading labels, shopping at the supermarket. Yes, stars shop just like us! I recognized her from my mother's vinyl records. She was so very friendly and must have been bored or very kind to spend the time she did with me. We just started shooting the breeze. Her mother had just died as had mine so there was a lot to talk about there. After about half an hour, I thanked her and said I had better get to my shopping.

"What are you doing for the Fourth of July?" she asked.

"I am sure there is a park or something we will go to."

"Well, you are coming to my house."

"You are so kind and thank you, but no, we will be fine. Thanks though."

"You said you just moved here and don't have family or friends living here, right?" she pressed. "You are coming to my house. I am having a party and am expecting you to come."

"Umm, wow, are you sure?" I said. Quickly she pulled out a pen and paper to give me her address. "I will put your name with the guard at the entrance and he will let you in," she insisted. After me asking what to bring and us working out that I would bring a dessert, she requested the ages of my boys. Then she said, "You need to meet my daughter. She has a beautiful daughter, and a son the same age as yours. She will be there tomorrow."

"Great, thank you so much!" I said, thinking *Oh, my gosh! This is Vegas? My first friend is Gladys Knight?!*

When I got home and was questioned as to why I took so long, I told my husband that we were invited to Gladys's house for the 4th.

"Gladys Knight? We are personally invited to just go hang out at Gladys Knight's house for the 4th of July?"

"Yes, I said."

"She is just being nice" he scoffed.

"She is nice for sure, but truly she insisted! We have no other plans so we ARE going!" I wasn't about to miss out on this adventure.

We drove up to the gated community in the early afternoon and sure enough my name was on the guard's list. We drove in and there was a second gate through which we got in. My husband had doubted that she would remember her invitation, so I was pleased to look at him smugly and do a little "Um-hum." I was a little nervous ringing her doorbell, but she was amazing and welcoming as if we had known her for years. We walked through the beautiful, food-filled kitchen and dropped my dessert off before being directed to the backyard where the pool, music, and party was going on. It looked very "Los Angeles" to me with what seemed like record producers, backup singers, all kinds of entertainment industry folks. My husband leaned over and said, "Did you notice we are the only white people here?"

I said, "No, but isn't it great?" My high school in California had stripped my eyes from noticing color by the end of that year. We are all just people.

Gladys walked out to where we were with an arm full of supplies. She said, "I bought a couple of life jackets for your boys so they can swim and you won't have to worry about them. Also, here are some pool toys they might like." Gladys handed us a bag of pool toys and things from a sporting goods store she bought for the kids. Unbelievable! The prior night I had been with her until late talking, so that meant she went out that morning specifically to get our kids their size of life vests and toys? Seriously? I believe she is the nicest human being ever! I was a complete stranger and she took me in, just like Jesus would do!

About an hour later, Gladys introduced me to her daughter, Kenya, who showed up with her family. Kenya would become one of my "besties." Her son and my son hit it off like brothers. They just swam around together, talking like they already knew each other. I also met other members of the family who were just as friendly and wonderful. Kenya and I went into a small business together, traveled together, and then she was my visiting teacher for several years. We had fun. Really, a great family! Kenya surprised me later that week when I saw her, her mom and her sister-in-law all at the same church I attended. What a treat! So far, loving Vegas and it's been three days.

The Children Always Pay

I am not going to blame anyone for the falling apart of our marriage. I have been over it for a long time. In fact, he with his new wife and me with my new husband are all friends and have been for years. I will say that it happened and was very painful at the time. We were young and dumb and luckily have both grown up since.

Because of my father, or lack of, I swore I would never divorce, yet here I was. We tried, but it didn't work out and I was not happy about it. Court was ugly, custody uglier. It doesn't matter who did this or that or who's right or wrong; the kids always pay the price. My dear son, Corbin, four when we split up, inhaled this whole thing. Once a happy, outgoing and care-free child, he became quiet, sad, and introverted.

Because of my childhood and the monsters in my closet, I was terrified of going back to being single. A small investment was made in a security system and I felt a little safer going to bed at night with the boys tucked in and the house armed. I still hated being alone. One very early morning the alarm went off, and it was loud! Flying from my bed and racing down the stairs, I found Corbin. The back door was open and he wasn't sure of what to do with that alarm screaming. He had on his Elmo backpack over his blue and red zip-up pajamas with the slipper-feet and held his favorite pal, Sam, his sock monkey. He looked as if he was ready for a long trip.

I ran to put in the code and turn off the alarm. The security company called and I gave them the password to not dispatch police. I was so grateful

I had that alarm to wake me. At this point I dropped to my knees, eye to eye with my little guy.

"Corbin, where are you going?"

"I'm going looking for my dad!" he, firmly and assuredly, said. I just broke down. My little boy couldn't sleep with all of this. The pain and longing for his family to be together kept him up. He was going out in the cold with a pack on his back, knowing he was going to be gone for a long time to find his daddy and bring him home. It was heart-wrenching! It still is. He was in so much pain because of our adult choices. Not just me, but WE were ruining our perfect baby. This horrible pain and suffering had to stop and it had to start with me, no matter who thought who was at fault.

I decided then and there that I could not hate my soon-to-be ex-husband. Somehow and some way I was going to have to forgive him. It was not about me anymore. That relationship was over. Now it was about the children. I needed to get over myself and my pain.

No matter if I wanted things or not, I could not change someone or take away their choices or agency—just as they couldn't change mine. That is Satan's plan. In my mind he should have done this or that, could have tried harder, didn't do certain things. My heart was screaming out, "It's not fair! I'm the good person here. Why does he seem to just move on without a problem and I'm falling apart? How does he get out of this responsibility or that situation?" IT DOESN'T MATTER! IT IS OVER!

If it's possible to learn from the mistakes of others, know this: Get the counseling you and your children need. Drop to your knees every night after you have tucked those kids in and pour out your soul to our Father above. Tell him what is really bothering you. Tell him about your concerns. Tell him your fears of being alone or not providing for your children. Plead for strength and for him to help you be the parent those kids need. Beg to let your heart forgive your partner. Really, tell him everything like he is sitting *right there* because he really is *right there*! I know that from experience, but we will get to that later.

When you roll out of bed in the morning, roll right onto your knees first and say a prayer to be able to smile for those kids. Let them see your strength and know that your little family is going to be okay. Tell them that sometimes parents make mistakes, but it has nothing to do with them. (My father notwithstanding, most people really do love their kids, so it really doesn't have anything to do with the children.)

Tell your kids how much you BOTH love them! This will be really hard to do in the beginning. You want to tell them how bad the other parent is. You want them to know you are the one sacrificing for them (so somehow you love them more?) Do not do that! You will only hurt your children. I was young and learned this all from experience with my precious and perfect Corbin being the sacrificial lamb. It was very hard on his sweet soul. The pain he endured due to our stupidity hurts me to this day.

Of all people in this world, that rejection hurts, I know from experience! The dreams of growing old together were now gone. The fear that you have to be a single parent, realized. The dream of keeping your family together forever, shattered, well temporarily only. Know that things will get better. Think of it this way: why do you want to be with someone who doesn't think you are the cat's meow? Would you want to force someone to stay with you? We have to get past all of these mixed feelings and still be strong and loving parents.

My little boy's stress and sadness through those sleepless nights breaks my heart to this day. I am so sorry! I didn't think he was old enough to understand. He was grieving, truly suffering in silence until he had to find his daddy to put our family back the way he knew and thought it should be. I was so caught up in the divorce and my grief that I didn't see my baby suffering.

Suck it up, parents! Our first responsibility from this point on is our children. We have to secure their world again which starts in the home and with us. Pull yourself together! Know that you are worth so much more than that spouse gave you credit for. They didn't see your immense value. So sad for them! You are a prince or princess to a Father who is a Heavenly King. Give yourself some credit. You do not want to be with someone who doesn't feel that you are all that and a bag of cinnamon bears. I promise you. Wait. Let me repeat that one more time: *I promise you God has it worked out.* Just keep reading.

The Start of Something New

I named this section what I did for a reason. We, as a society, need to start something new. A few have caught on, but it needs to be widespread. First, we need to forgive our exes and try to be friends with them and their new loves. Right now you are saying I am nuts. I will explain.

When I realized the pain my son was suffering, I couldn't just change overnight. There needed to be a real change, though, and I had to figure out how to do it. I was still angry and hurt. I am sure my ex-spouse was, too. We said terrible things about each other in court. We did anything and everything to hurt each other or make the other look like the worst person on the earth. At this point we hated each other. As my therapist always said, "Anger is a secondary emotion to pain." As my mother always said, "Kindness begins with me." My ex was on his second girlfriend, but this one serious, when I was able to implement my plan.

To begin with, I just wanted us not to hate each other. At first it was hard but I had to stop giving nasty glares, blaming, and mumbling naughty things during kid exchanges. The kids see this and it hurts them. Start with your kids by saying to them, "Oh, I am so excited for your fun weekend you get to spend with daddy." I know at first my smart little five-year-old boy looked at me and said, "Mom, give me a break." Hang in there when that happens. "Really, I know daddy is excited to spend time with you." Our three-year-old didn't care where he was as long as Corbin was there, he had a sippy cup with apple juice, and his "Ee-hee" horsey blanket Grandma made. This was a fun adventure for him. Corbin was going to take more effort and convincing.

When his dad dropped him back off to me, I made it more like a party.

"Hi, my sweet boys, I bet you had so much fun this weekend! Did you tell daddy thank you?"

Then it was my ex saying, "Give me a break." When you keep using your words, your actions tend to follow. I started joking around with my ex. He would give me the child support check and I would say, "Thank you, wow, an early birthday present?" or "Thank you, you still care." He would get a weird look and say, "No, it's for child support." Like I didn't know, but his answer would change later to a nicer, "Yeah, right."

This truly did start to leave an impression on my Corbin that things were a new normal, a good normal. I was finally at a point to speak to the new girlfriend. We were at some event for Corbin, like a soccer game or something and I said, "I am sorry I seem like a witch. This has nothing to do with you. I am actually a really nice person. I am just trying to get over my anger at the situation right now. Please just bear with me." She looked at me, really surprised, and an awkward situation turned into an okay one. She said, "Thank you for saying that." That experience started the ball rolling. She and I became friends before my ex and I did. It wasn't long before my future husband and ex-husband became friends, too.

Long story short, we all hang out together now. They come to our home for parties, and our kids have had no serious effects from our divorce. Corbin at sixteen once mentioned he wished we had stayed together, because it's ideal, but went on to say that he really loves his step-mom and his step-dad so it was okay. People have commented for years how strange it was that we all hang out together and get along, but most add a "Wow, I've never seen that, that is cool" or "I wish my ex and I could do that." You can! Kindness begins with you! Our boys love it! They have been so happy, growing up with their moms talking and planning who picks up and where the birthday party was going to be. We began to work together, co-parenting. Talks with the boys became, "You have four parents who love you…" and "Don't think you are going to get out of that by going to your dad's house. We have all already talked and you are going to have to spend more time studying at either place." Both houses are different, of course, but when they know the four of us, especially the two moms are talking almost daily about their well-being, and working together, their life is very, very stable. It is called "co-parenting" for a reason. This should be everyone's new normal.

VIPs

Don't get me wrong, this enlightened state didn't come easily to me. As I grieved on my own after my divorce, I knew I had to find my own new normal. It would not be easy on me. My beloved mother and grandfather were gone and I didn't feel close to my siblings. In fact I felt quite alone in the world. My loneliness and grief were unbearable. I would put on my smile with the boys around, but when they would leave for their dad's, I didn't know what to do. All of my friends were married and had kids and lives. I must have worn out my carpet with the lack of sleep and the pacing I would do around my house. I would clean like crazy and then I would go to the gym. A word to the wise—turn anxiety and restless energy toward running, biking, or going to the gym, not eating. Of all things when you are divorced and starting over, the last thing you want to do is gain a bunch of weight. Luckily, working out was exactly what I did. Some days I would spend up to four hours in the gym. Was it excessive? Yes! Did I look amazing? Absolutely! You are already a bit beaten down, depressed enough. Give yourself something you don't have to worry about, something to make you feel good. When others start noticing, it is such a compliment to you. You are finally doing something for you and your self-esteem. You are date-ready, but only on the outside.

Thank goodness for the LDS Church in my life. Wherever you go, anywhere in this world, there is an instant "adopted" family waiting and ready to help and love you. When I first moved to Las Vegas and after going to Church the first time, I met the bishopric. There was Bishop Camp and his two counselors Brother Richardson and Chad Lee. They were the first men we met, ready for this new little family. Shortly after that, the Relief Society presidency came by the house with open arms—and a mixing bowl and hand beater which I still have. I met Hope Walton, Becci Hadfield and Heidi Lee, Chad's wife. Little did I realize the significance of these exact people and their place in my life at that perfect time.

Chad Lee was assigned to be my home teacher and would come visit perfectly every month with one of his three sons or wife, Heidi. He always had a prepared message to share, but we never really got to it. I had so many things I was struggling with such as self-esteem and my new single life. He spent more time talking to me like a brother about options and choices I could make. Countless hours were spent listening and watching me cry as he counseled and lifted me up. There were many times at my home when he would pick up my bills and take them with him to pay. Who does that? Bishop Camp had encouraged me to go to counseling and even found a counselor which was incredibly helpful. After the Church had assisted and paid for a good portion of the weekly bill, Chad insisted on picking up the rest. When talking to him later in life, he didn't even remember that he did that. He is so incredibly good and Christ-like that it was perfectly natural for him. He didn't do it for any recognition or praise but because he wanted to help his "sister." No strings attached. I certainly wouldn't forget his kindness and generosity.

Chad and Heidi invited me numerous times out to dinner or to bring the kids for a swim at their home. I remember going over to spend time with them and their family for family night. Talk about magnifying your calling! Little did Chad know he would be my home teacher for more than ten years! I know I contributed to many of his gray hairs. Exactly like a caring older brother, sometimes he would be very concerned or a little upset with me about choices I had made. He wasn't afraid to tell me what he thought of my poor decision but would then lovingly counsel me how to fix it. Heidi was so sweet and supportive and gave me sisterly advice as well.

The Hadfield's played another significant role in my life. They were my go-to family any time I needed help with the kids or a break for myself. If I had worn poor Chad and Heidi out, I would give them some time to recuperate and talk to Bart and Becci. The Hadfields had a son and three daughters with one set of twins that were all fantastic babysitters. If the girls weren't available they would say, "We are home tonight, bring the kids over anyway."

One Christmas, knowing I would be home alone, they invited the kids and me to spend time with their family at a cabin in Utah. The true concern and love they had for me were unbelievable. If I wasn't in this Church, there is no telling how I would have survived not knowing these amazing people.

The Dunfords were another incredibly special family to me. They would call out of the blue with "Can we take those babies overnight?" or "We are coming to pick up you and all of the kids. We are going to dinner." People outside the church don't usually do that, at least not from my experience. My kids had several sleepovers at their home. Again, I don't know how I would have survived without that amazing friendship! These were truly Christ-like attributes being magnified.

CHAPTER 7

Angels Among Us

Marie Callender

The great room in my house was my favorite room of any house I had ever lived. It was two stories high and had several large windows on the first floor area, plus two large windows up high on what would be the second floor. A smell of new carpet still lingered, mixed with a very slight paint smell. At 1,800 square feet, our house wasn't big by American standards, but I loved it. It was the best house ever to me. I would lie on the couch and stare up at the twenty foot ceilings for what seemed like hours sometime just in disbelief and appreciation that I lived in such a beautiful house. It was better than my childhood dreams, but the best thing was that I would never have to move again. It was mine. However, inside my heart, I was still dying. Getting past the feeling I had no value and was forgotten was my new challenge.

The boys were gone for another weekend, an extra-long holiday weekend with their dad. So many people had gone out of town. I had paced, worked out, hardly slept, hardly ate, cleaned the house until every corner sparkled and there I was. Despite the goodness of friends, there were times when I felt completely and utterly alone, my worst fear in the world. When the house felt empty, I couldn't take it.

Standing in my front living room, I saw the sun shining through the closed thick wooden white blinds. I dropped to my knees right there in the openness of this great room, closed my eyes and began to pray. I said, "Heavenly Father, does ANYONE even know that I'm alive?" As soon as I said that I opened my eyes, looked around the empty room and said to myself, *This is stupid! I guess I should close the prayer.*

Still on my knees, I put one foot up to stand and the doorbell rang. *That's weird*, I thought. Hurrying to the door I opened it and saw the Phelps family from my ward at church. There the family stood with a Marie Callender pie. I didn't even say hello due to my shock. Handing me the pie, they said, "We were thinking of you and thought you might like a pie." I still couldn't speak. I stood there frozen in total shock just staring at them with a pie in my arms. They looked at me kindly and said, "Okay, hope you like it," as they turned and got back into their car. Still I didn't move—just watched them drive away. They must have thought I was on crack. I would have loved to hear their conversation on the way home. "Wow she's weird" or "What is her deal?" I found myself just standing there, alone, so walked back into the house and to the kitchen. The second the pie was placed on the countertop, I burst into tears. *Unbelievable!*

After regaining my composure I called them to say thank you. The mom, Leesa, answered the phone.

"Leesa, I'm sorry I was so rude and didn't even thank your family for the pie, but let me tell you what happened. The boys are with their dad this weekend and I was on my knees in prayer feeling very alone, asking God if ANYONE knew I was alive. I just finished and hadn't even stood up when the doorbell rang. I hadn't even stood up! I just couldn't believe it! There you all were. There was your beautiful family with those kids and the excited faces and I was so overwhelmed and in shock, speechless. I am sorry I was seemed so rude. Please tell them thank you! You all just answered my prayer. I still can't believe it!"

"Kayli, we just had family night and I had bought us a pie earlier for dessert and one extra to take to a family. Our family prayed together to find out who we should give it to and your name was what came up. Can I share what you just told me with my family?"

"Of course, thank you so much. I just still can't believe it," I repeated.

Several times after that, I received Krispy Kreme doughnuts by the dozen just sitting on my porch, pies, brownies, and other sweets. I know many of those anonymous gifts were from the Phelps, even though I don't have proof. Thank you, wonderful families and friends! They did not go uncherished.

The amazing thing here is that God knew how I felt and what I needed before I had even asked Him. The answer to the Phelps question in prayer was given to them and they were in the car and on their way to my house before

I even hit the floor on my knees to ask my question. Again, that prayer was being answered before I asked. There is a God and he knows us personally, knows when we really need him and loves us!

Hope

The dictionary definition of hope is to believe, desire, or trust. This section isn't about the noun or verb of hope but a special person named Hope. She was my Relief Society President at church when we moved to Vegas and while the divorce came down on me. Some people truly magnify their calling, using the gift of discernment. Every one of my Relief Society presidents I ever had surprised me with this. Several times during the worst possible days I could have, Hope would unexpectedly ring my doorbell.

"Hi, I was at the store and thought, Kayli needs some cookie dough ice cream. I'm just here to drop it off—how is your day going?" Another time it was, "Who doesn't like mint chocolate chip ice cream? I just wanted to sweeten your day."

Oh my goodness, people like this really exist? Miraculously, each time she did this, I had just had a bad day in court or was extra discouraged. She truly gave me hope!

"I cannot believe how you always know what's going on and how inspired your parents were to name you Hope, because that is what you give me," I told her. I had hoped that God really was listening to my prayers.

Clearly, I had to thank the ward before I moved out of state for keeping weight on my bones with all of the sweets delivered to my house counteracting the million miles I ran on the treadmill.

Life Goes On

Seeing a therapist every week was healing and helpful. Terry had that plaque that I have spoken about behind his head during our sessions—the one that read, "Success is learning to deal with plan B." He doesn't understand how much that little phrase has been said and thought about in my life. Probably a million times! I looked forward to unloading from the week.

However, with the rejection from my father and now a divorce, it would take three years before I truly felt better. The loneliness and sadness was intense from the loss of my future dreams and eternal family. The fear of not being able to provide for my children like my own mother was horrifying. Being a convert to the church eight years earlier mixed with the difficulties I was going through didn't help my anger that I "deserve" better than this. I had worked so hard to be a good person. Why couldn't I just get past the marriage crap and get on with my life? After all, I had only ever asked for a normal life, not anything spectacular, just normal. Normal looked so good to me! I decided I was too angry at God to go to church. I wanted my boys raised in it so I would go every other Sunday when they were with me. It was hard for me to sit and see all of those perfect families and yet I was totally alone. I didn't go for months which concerned my friends, but clearly, I didn't fit in. From what I could see, there were the few that judged me, like a girl we will call Megan and her friends, but God will take care of them. The majority of the people from Church did not judge me but were loving and supportive. Still, why am I the black sheep? Even in God's family, I am the odd sheep out. I felt like He knew me and cared, because He is God, but not as much as He cared for everyone else. Why would He want me to feel like this? It felt as if there was something that no men in this, my world, could stand about me. I was angry that God gave me whatever that trait was. This was proof that I was at the bottom of His list just like my own father, and then my husband's. Why me? What did I do? Why would he put these people in my life?

Once, standing in my great room at home, again alone in the house, I looked up at the tall ceiling and threw my hands up yelling, "Whatever I did to tick you off, *I am sorry*!"

Our Brother Jesus

There I was in a dream, not an ordinary dream. All of my senses were alive. I was in a great big gymnasium or warehouse-looking place. I realized I was on a cot, like a camping cot. Trying to move, I couldn't. It was as if I was glued to it. Looking about there were rows of cots, everywhere. Thousands of cots in perfect line order as far as I could see in every direction and covered with people "stuck" to them.

There was a door, almost standing alone that appeared to me like a closet or something similar. I could smell the lacquer of the shiny floor our uncomfortable cots were on. People were softly talking in their cots and I realized this was my life, the cot. I realized we were all sick. It was everyone in the world. Everyone was sick, stuck to these cots in this huge room with a tall ceiling but no walls.

Jesus always teaches in parables. Throughout the New Testament in the Bible are parables. He never just comes out and gives you an answer. That would be too easy. Take for example, the parable of the ten virgins. What did the oil in the lamp represent? Who was the bridegroom? This was not a literal story. He wants those he teaches to think about what it all means. I want you to think about what this means.

There I was on my cot. From off to the lower left I hear people yelling out, "He's coming, Jesus is coming!" I lift my head like everyone else, trying to get a glimpse of the Savior. There he was in a beautiful white robe to his feet, the way I would expect him to look. He had shoulder length, dark brown hair. His white robe and goodness seemed to radiate. He went from one bed to the next blessing people, healing them. He didn't go to everyone. People would call out, "Over here, Lord!" or "Jesus, save me!" or "Lord, heal me." I was intrigued as I was watching all of these people call for him and how busily he would go through the rows of sick people like a bee to flowers, going about his healing and blessings. During this experience, I knew he was keenly aware of me. In fact, he was watching me through his peripheral vision. *Why was he focused on me?* I thought. *Was it because I was ignoring him, God, and the Church?*

Jesus was getting closer and closer. I was watching him, watch me. He finally made it to the bed at my left and healed that person. I was thinking, *Good, he can heal me now.* Instead, he watched me through the corner of his eye and went completely around my bed to the person on the other side and blessed them. I was so shocked! Actually, I was mad. Then he had the nerve to attend to the person directly in front of me, then in front of him. *How dare him,* I thought. He continued to watch me as he got farther and farther away. I had gone through so many emotions, including stubbornness, anger, hurt, and now I was starting to panic. He was almost out of earshot distance. It was my last chance. He was just about to put his hands on someone when I yelled out, "Lord, forgive me!" I don't know why I said those words instead of "heal me" or "bless me" but I did. As if I had just said the magic words, he stopped. Not even finishing the person he was with, he stood straight up and did a quick "about face" towards me and put on the biggest smile I have ever seen. He was GLORIOUS—not a word I have ever used in this life but the perfect word for him. He was so beautiful. I had never seen that in pictures of him. I saw love and kindness and so many other traits but not beauty, handsomeness. "WOW!" That is all I could say. He kept that smile and it seemed like he had swallowed the sun with a brilliance that radiated through him. There was Jesus, our loving brother, completely (and always was) aware of me, coming to bless and heal me.

What is the symbolism here? What I got from it was that we are all in need of healing—whether physical, spiritual, psychological, or whatever it may be. Also, he went to those that believed and called out to him. He was very aware of everyone though. The scriptures say "Ask and ye shall receive." He knew, and I knew, I needed healing. I had my agency to accept it or not have it at all. He knew I wanted it but was going to wait until I was humble enough to ask. As soon as I called on him, that very moment, he dropped everything and so happily came to me. The dream was real. I know that perfectly in my soul. I saw him and he was real. I love that guy!

Life Boats

Here I was in another symbolic dream. In fact this dream occurred three times, continuing on the dream each time. There was this huge winding river with inlets and branches going off to several smaller rivers. Boats were everywhere and each one had the name of the family on it. I saw Hadfield, Reid, Camp, Lee, Jackson, Dunford, Walton, Smith, Phelps and many others. You get the picture; it was a busy river. Some people had faster boats and zoomed by, breaking from the main river to a destination of a smaller one, wherever that led to. Many boats just casually cruised along; everyone at their own pace. There I was in the middle of this big river, but I didn't have a boat. Even though I could see the bank, it was impossible to get to it, like those never ending hallways in movies. So, I am stuck in the middle of this river and all I can do is swim. I realize that this was what I have been doing my whole life, swimming. There has never been a boat for me. Sometimes I would stop where I was and tread water for a while, not sure which way to go. It was exhausting until one of the boats would come along and stop for me. I would grab on to the side of the boat to rest for a bit. The family of the boat would feed me, but I never saw food, and then encourage me to continue my journey and keep swimming. This happened with many families taking time to stop when I needed rest or was completely exhausted. The same pattern ensued of me grabbing on, them somehow feeding me, and, after I was ready, I would have to let go. The boat families were very patient and never hurried me off from my rest. They waited each time until I let go, then they would continue themselves. I became so tired and so discouraged, realizing that I would never get to stop swimming. That was my destiny in this life. There would never be true rest; always would I be dependent on someone else's boat for a break. There was nobody else like me in the water, at least not near me. Very far away once in a while I would see another swimmer but never near me. Mostly many boats with names crowded the river.

Why do I have to be different? How come I don't get a boat of my own? Again I am the black sheep, the odd one. I began to struggle because I was so tired. Coming up for air seemed to be getting harder and harder. I was treading water, then trying to rest by floating on my back. There were all of these different waterways in front of me and I didn't know which one to choose and where to go anymore. I had lost my way. My inner GPS was gone or at least not working. There was a lump in my throat. The tears inside were welling up, making it more difficult to swim. I was unable to breathe. I wanted to yell and cry out but would sink under the water every time. That was it! I decided to give up and just sink. That was never on my mind before to just give in to the pull of gravity in that river. Fighting for my life and destination had always pushed me to keep swimming. Not today, not any more. I was done. The tears running down my face kept being swallowed by the river. Desperate and alone, I gave up. Nobody knew I was drowning. I let myself go for the first time and the water quickly sucked me up. Watching with eyes open wide, the surface started to move away. With one last desperate attempt, I saw my left arm reach up towards the surface, but I was far enough under water it wouldn't reach the top. Nobody knew I was under. Nobody knew I was drowning. I had given in and was floating calmly downward, holding my breath for the moment, knowing it was my last. Right then, I saw a man's arm reach down through the water and grab that left arm that was completely relaxed but still pointing toward the surface. He forcefully pulled me up and not to hold on to the side but actually for some reason could pull me completely into his boat. I had never seen the inside of a boat, but I just collapsed in exhaustion.

What did this whole dream mean? Well, it was very symbolic so, again, a dream brought to you today by our sponsor, the Savior. The river was life with all of its twists and turns. Nobody is going the same way. Each person has their own path. My lot in life was that I never got to have a real family, thus no family boat. I was completely dependent on these other families to give me rest or share their family love with me, thus the food I never saw. No one that stopped for me ever pushed me away. They would stay until sufficient rest and encouragement was received and I had to let go to move forward. My boys weren't in the water possibly because they had a family boat to rest in through their father and his family. Plus, this was my life, not theirs. Maybe they start out with their own boat. I didn't know anything but survival, in other words, the swimming. More than anything I wanted to have a boat. It just wasn't my lot to have one for whatever reason. There were very few others that came through life like me, thus the few swimmers, most had a boat. Who was the man that saved me in the boat? You tell me.

Months later I entered into another dream. I had been in this boat for months and had to continue my journey so had to get back into the water which I really did not want to do. This kind man had taken me in until I was completely rested this time, unlike the hanging off the side I had been doing to catch my breath. Not happy about it, I had to get back into the water. Oh how I wanted to stay in the boat. My heart sank as I climbed back into that cold, heartless water. As I let go of the boat, the man grabbed my arm again and this time, put a life vest around my neck before letting go. I never had seen or even thought of a life vest. Why hadn't I ever seen them in the water or on the boats? Why could nobody else give me one? Whatever the case, this "vest" I got to keep for the rest of my journey on the earth. I knew it was there for good and nobody was ever allowed to take it from me. My life, still difficult and still swimming, would be just a bit easier now.

CHAPTER 8

What Goes Up...

Club C2K

Randomly, I met this clothing designer who just happened to be a single, LDS, awesome girl. It had been four months since my divorce had finalized and I was a bit of a man hater. Not really, just wasn't feeling there was that much out there for picky me. She had convinced me to go to a few church single events that ended up totally lame. The one or two cute, eligible guys were surrounded by girls and quite arrogant and full of themselves. The rest were too quiet, shy, loud, socially-retarded, boring, tons of other adjectives but not marriage material. If I could ask God one thing, it would be to work on the singles program, it sucks!

My new friend, clearly inspired, asked me to go out with her Halloween weekend to check out some clubs since I didn't have my boys. She said there was a new club opening called C2K in the recently finished Venetian Hotel and Casino. Really, I didn't want to go, but she begged, telling me it would be good for me and I really needed to get out. Even though it had been four months since the divorce, court had gone over a year prior to that so I wasn't really jumping into things. I agreed to go, but before leaving the house on my first real man-searching outing, I got on my knees to pray.

"Heavenly Father," I said," I am so sick of these disappointing men. I don't even want to ever look again. I don't think there is anyone, but if there is someone you want me with, you are going to have to throw him in my face. Amen." That was my prayer. My friend and I set out for club number one.

When we arrived at the Rio Hotel club, we discovered they were having a special engagement requiring prepaid tickets. A bit bummed out, my friend said, "There is a Church Halloween dance." We decided there was nothing to lose so went there only to be disappointed again with the man selection. The only guy that was the slightest bit attractive to me was a player that thought he was doing me a favor by handing me his number.

"I know you will call me sometime."

My answer to that was, "Barf, no." I tossed his number in the garbage. Arrogance is uglier than even ugly on a man, yuck! I was ready to go home, but my sidekick insisted we go to just one more place, that grand opening at the Venetian she had told me about. She begged one more time and said we would leave immediately but that she just wanted to see what it looked like. "Fine" I said.

We got there and the line was huge. I didn't mind waiting an hour or more, because the people-watching was phenomenal. Good music was blaring and I felt like I was eighteen again. There were really good looking guys and girls going in. Finally, our turn came and we walked in. At this private table straight in front of me as I entered the club was a guy. The white lights that were whizzing around to the music set exactly on him right as I looked at him. I swear I heard angels in heaven singing, "Laaaaaaa", as the white lights shone, resembling a halo on his blond head. I said out loud, "Wow, he's beautiful." As soon as I said that, my newly negative realism set in and I said, "He's probably an arrogant jerk if he is that good looking." Seriously I didn't think of him again as we walked around the entire club, checking out every corner and watching people. It was probably twenty minutes total until we finished our tour. Knowing I had been anxious to get home, my friend and I felt we had seen enough and headed toward the door. Right then, a guy seeming to come out of nowhere jumped right in front of me and said, "Hi. Do you want to dance?" He was right in my face so much that I had to step backwards to focus on him. It was that gorgeous guy I saw as we entered. My friend and I said at the same time, "Yes," as she shoved me towards him.

This hot guy had a super sexy Canadian accent with a lot of "Ayyy?" in his speech. It was difficult to contain my smile as we danced. I was trying to play it cool, but it wasn't working out. I just kept smiling at him and then all of the sudden, while staring at each other, dancing to a fast song; very forwardly, I went in for a kiss. That was shocking, even for me. It had been many years since I had been in a club and for me to kiss a complete stranger was weird. He just smiled at me. I told him I really wasn't like that. Whether or not he believed that, I didn't know.

After probably an hour, he asked if I wanted to get a drink and sit down. "Water would be perfect" I replied. Sitting down he asked me a hundred questions. I then asked him a hundred. I found out he was a waiter at a steak house restaurant and lived with his brother. He was from Vancouver, British Columbia. It made sense with his super cute accent. He looked like a Canadian snowboarder with his spiky blond hair, green eyes, and shy smile. We seemed to really hit it off. The reason why he was at that club was that his father was the project manager for the construction of the casino. He had just come to see the new club.

Realizing I didn't come to the club with him, I panicked for a moment to find my friend. She was on the dance floor with someone and gave me the thumbs up that she was good, I was fine, and to continue. There was such a strong connection with him and me, even she felt it. I started thinking that maybe he is "the one." That would be nuts to happen so fast like that; I don't like very many guys instantly. However, being a very, very, extremely very picky person about my men, this was definitely something.

After one hour of dancing, I was already asking myself if he was or could be "it?" I must be insane. Well, maybe not. Really badly I wanted to find out his name so I asked and he replied, "Steve." Well, that doesn't match my name. A bit surprised that it didn't match I began wondering about his last name but thought it was strange to randomly ask. He had walked up to the bar to get himself another drink so I decided to come along and try to look off his credit card when he pulled it out. It was so dumb that I just wouldn't ask. Certainly I didn't want to seem desperate and too curious. The lights were still whizzing too fast around and I couldn't read the last name as he held the card in his hand. That was it, the defining moment, no more waiting, I had to know. "What is your last name?" He leaned over with the loud music and said, "Coffman." Right at that moment, I knew we would be married. I had known him for barely 1 hour.

My friend came over to me and said we should probably get home. It was then 5:00am. The time had flown by. Steve pulled out his new cell phone (since he had just moved here from Canada) and was trying to get my number entered. We said a quick goodbye while he said he would call me later that day, and we left for home. It seemed like the stars had aligned for us to meet at that club. He lived exactly on the opposite and farthest side of Vegas from me.

There is no way our paths would ever cross had we not both been there that night. We lived at least an hour from each other.

Anxiously I awaited his call. One day passed, then two, three. Okay, I can understand not wanting to seem desperate by waiting a day or so, but now I was kind of bummed. Maybe he wasn't going to call. My intuitions are usually right about people and I thought we truly had a connection; I know we did. Why wasn't he calling? My heart kind of hardened and I thought, *That figures, he was a jerk. Of course that was too good to be true.*

On the fourth day, I was trying to forget about him and our "connection." The phone rang. I picked it up and heard a soft, "Kayli?" It was him and that darling accent.

"Yes" I said.

"Oh, my gosh, okay. Uhm, your number didn't save. Oh, this is Steve by the way. I met you at.."

"I know who you are," I interrupted, happily.

"Your number didn't save on my phone and I panicked. I have been trying to find you for four days. I remembered that your phone number had consecutive numbers in it with its 45678 but not knowing how American phone numbers are here, I didn't know where they were in the number. I have just been calling all of these people and trying all sorts of combinations. I can't believe I found you!" He sounded so happy, excited and mainly relieved. Oh my, that was the sweetest thing I had ever heard. Knowing we would never run into each other again, he searched for me for four days? That was so romantic!

"I was kind of bummed because I thought you just didn't want to call me."

"No, no. I am sorry. I, I couldn't find you." Brownie points for Mr. Wonderful. How many guys would have given up? I was already in love!

The Whirlwind

That is a joke. Ideally, after Steve finding me we should have dated like crazy, been engaged at six months and married at a year. Nothing EVER happens like I want. Again, as my therapist kept reminding me, "Success is learning to deal with plan B." There never has been, nor will there ever be, success with plan A in my world. Who am I kidding? Plan B never works out either. I'm a bit plan Z.

Steve didn't believe in marriage. "It is just a piece of paper" was his motto. That is a bad motto when you are dating a Mormon girl with kids who would like to have a daughter or two added on. In fact, he had three brothers who were also not married, nor dating anyone. With all of the boys in their mid-twenties, I thought that strange. Steve told me he had two uncles. When I asked about them, the same answer repeated, "They aren't married."

"Are they all gay?"

"No, not at all, he said.

"Well, are they ugly? What is wrong with them?" He seemed surprised at that question, like that was normal. Seriously? Why do I have to find the perfect guy and then after I am sold on him find out that marriage was not going to happen, ever! Why God? Why dangle a carrot in front of me that will never, ever be eaten. It is like trying on the perfect little summer dress that you are completely in love with only to find out that its price tag reads $500, oh, and it is not on sale even though it was on the clearance rack. Frustrating! Can't anything work out for once, the way I want it to?

Steve and I were so meant to be together, so drawn to each other, it didn't make sense. Even when we had our first kiss, you know the real yummy ones? It was as if we had kissed each other a thousand times before. We kissed the exact same way. We even talked about how familiar that was. He finally agreed to negotiate with me. His negotiation? Four years! What? I could be dead in four years. He said we could marry but not for four years. I was starting to better understand the Bible story in Genesis 29 of Jacob serving Laban for seven years to marry Rachel, but then he gets Leah. That bites! Didn't they live to be like 200 years old back then? That is probably equal to four years in my life span. I mean I am already thirty at this point. I am running out of eggs! Well, at least the good ones with no dust on them.

First Comes Love, Then Comes Twins?

Steve is probably the most stubborn person I have met on the earth. Without a doubt, I had to accept the fact that we wouldn't be marrying anytime soon. Waiting would be difficult, but his love was worth it. We spent every minute together. We were completely in love! Our chemistry ran deep. When your chemistry is perfectly matched, without marriage, it's a ticking time bomb.

I had doubled over in pain one night clearly having what I knew to be a kidney attack to my only remaining kidney. I called one of my best friends, Beverly, who rushed me to the hospital emergency room. As I had recently found out I was pregnant and Steve not believing in marriage or wanting fatherhood, I told Beverly that I needed to give the baby up for adoption so that it can be raised in a family with both parents. As we spoke, there was a sonographer looking over my kidney and internal organs. He piped into our conversation, "It is a shame that you would give both of those babies away." Beverly and I looked at each other confused and then started to laugh. I said, "That is funny! I bet you scare the life out of expectant moms with that one!" He then turned the monitor toward Beverly and me and showed us two embryos in their sacs as he counted, "One, two." Our mouths fell open and Beverly said, "Uhm, I'm going to call Steve."

I knew God had a sense of humor when I found out I was pregnant with twins. It had been almost a year and a half after Steve and I met that the twins joined my brood. One boy and one girl, weighing in at 4 lbs., 14oz. and 4 lbs., 11oz.—how perfect is that for twins? (Thanks Beverly and Michelle A. for being my birth coaches and Pammy for the school help, emotional support, and forcing me on ski vacations to clear my head. You really are the best). It was the first girl in Steve's family and the first grandkids, so one would think it kind of a big deal.

I am going to spare the excitement of the ups and downs of a high risk pregnancy for twins, extreme illness and vomiting, no marriage proposal while hormones are everywhere, caring for two little boys and having both my "boyfriend" and me in school. All of that drama was so graciously saved for our close friends and family who helped us through it. There was no smooth sailing ship here; it was a barrel of monkeys.

Giving Up

There will be no blaming of who was right or wrong, again. Another failed relationship, two more kids—in the end it doesn't matter what either of us should have or could have said or done differently. It was some of the worst pain in my life, but we ended our relationship. Steve didn't want marriage and I didn't want the twins to grow up like this. The older boys already had divorced parents, the twins were newborns. To have to give up a child in any way is hands down the most difficult thing anyone can go through. Whether it is through adoption or through death, it is still a deep, aching loss. Where there was once love and promise in Steve's and my relationship was now just a painful, empty hole of what could have been. I couldn't see myself with anyone else at that time. He was supposed to be my soulmate. I was so in love with him; how could I give up our beautiful babies? Why wouldn't he want this relationship, this family? My heart felt like it was dying. As much as I loved these babies, it wasn't fair to raise them in a single parent home with a struggling mom who had no education and a father that may or may not be involved. As much as I tried to do things differently, it was a repeat of my mothers' life. Here I was a thirty-one year old woman who was supposed to have it all together, to have known better. I was humiliated. Why did I feel my relationship would make it and was the exception to the rule? Maybe because everything about me is the exception so why couldn't it go the other way, a positive exception? It clearly didn't.

Raised in a single parent home myself, I swore I wouldn't do that to my kids. I swore I would do everything to make sure they had a normal life with both parents involved, preferably together in the home. That was so incredibly important to me! It felt like I was in front of King Solomon, splitting the baby. Do I want my babies because they are mine and I love them so much or do I make the choice that saves them from pain and grief and gives them the best opportunity to succeed in this life? I had to do what I didn't want to do, what was best for them, put them up for adoption.

Looking for a Family

Nursing school had been put on hold that year for the twin pregnancy. Again I had been allergic to the babies and extremely ill. When all was said and done, I had only gained 22 pounds total for two babies. They had stayed almost that whole first week in the hospital for some lung growth issues and monitoring.

Prior to their birth and knowing things were headed this way, I contacted LDS Social Services about the possibility of placing the babies with a family. They had large books that contained a confidential letter from the hopeful adoptee parents with only their first names. A picture was attached of their own family, extended family, home, all sorts of varied things, to each letter. Since school had forced me to take time off due to illness so many of those hours were spent pouring over hundreds of possible families. Crying to and from these meetings was a normal thing, but I was serious about them not having to grow up like I did. The suffering and self-esteem issues I had endured alone were enough to keep me on track, looking for their new parents. I realized my love for them and their future outweighed what I wanted or felt I needed. Parenting isn't about the parents; it's about what is best for the kids. Steve and I being "rocky" was an understatement and with no promises, I wasn't gambling with their lives.

There were many great families I read about but not the perfect one. Nothing at all jumped out at me. Being very specific about what I was looking for, more and more books were piled in front of me. There had to be a family that would be just like Steve and me, had we married. What would our lives together have been like and were there people like us? Steve and I were huge gym rats. It would be nice to find people who took care of themselves, had healthy lifestyles, and loved the outdoors.

Snow—I had to find skiers. Steve and I loved to ski and our kids would have grown up on the mountain in winter months. And water—hopefully they had access to a boat or pool. Our kids would be big water babies. The families kept coming and still nothing.

I had almost given up and then something bittersweet happened. I found them. I found the perfect family. They had adopted one child who was now two years old. Dad was some kind of doctor like Steve would be, and mom would be at home but now worked. They had been together since high school and very solid. You could see the fun they had together. There was admiration, respect, and love for each other in each and every snapshot. I wanted that so badly in my own relationship. It was vital to me for my babies to be in that environment. There were pictures of them skiing, a house with a pool, camping and other outdoor pictures. They were the ones! I remember their names, Dean and Deb. After telling social services, who were thrilled because they were running out of books to look at, I drove home.

All in the Family

When I got home, the phone rang. One of my best friends, Kate, who knew what I was going through sounded a bit desperate. "Whatever you do, don't sign anything for those babies. My aunt and uncle are looking to adopt and you can keep those babies in my family. Then you can see them and always know how they are doing. Kayli, you are going to love them. They are the most awesome people."

"I already told family services my choice," I said. "I found a really great family."

"Just meet them, you will love them! You already know most of my family and Deb is my dad's youngest sister," she insisted.

"What? Did you say Deb? That's funny. What is her husbands' name?" I asked.

"Dean," she answered.

"Do they have a profile through LDS Services?" I questioned.

"Here in Texas they do."

"I saw them! They are here in Vegas too. I picked them! They are the couple I picked," I gasped. Before I knew it, Dean and Deb were flying to Vegas.

I called Steve and told him I had found the perfect family for the twins. He said he wouldn't sign any papers unless he met them. "Perfect, because they are flying here and will be at my house tomorrow," I said.

Dean and Deb came to the house. My new babies were home from the hospital. It was hard to keep from falling in love with them, but knowing adoption was best, I tried not to get too attached. Of course I would feed, bathe, and care for them but tried to not kiss or hug them, at least, too much. The twins were sleeping so this gave us time to visit and talk about things.

They were everything I had hoped they would be. There were no surprises. We talked about how I already knew the whole family so would occasionally see them and I already knew the kids would be raised in an extended family of love and support. They even brought presents for my two boys. The goodness and love that they carried shone from the inside and was real. The pictures were not posed or fake. What an amazing couple.

They were so antsy for those babies to wake up and as soon as they started to stir and we heard them, the excitement and smiles on their faces magnified. Both babies I brought down the stairs in my arms and handed them each one. Dean had the little girl and started to kiss her little face with the biggest, proudest smile. You would have thought this was already his daughter. He was the most perfect and amazing father I could ever ask for. Deb was so tender and loving, playing with my baby boy and checking out all of his little fingers and toes. She seemed so happy. For once in my life I had good fortune.

That comment alone brings a pain back into my heart. I had believed Steve and I would be that fantastic couple and those would be our babies, yet here I was giving up babies from the man I loved most. His name was tattooed deep inside my heart and it could never be removed. The dreams of us happy, caring for our own little family were shattered. But I remembered why I was doing this. Those babies would have exactly the life they deserve and would have had if Steve and I married. I was happy for them and for their future home of love and laughter. They would thank me one day for giving them to such wonderful parents. They would be so grateful I hadn't been selfish and kept them. I knew they would be right. There was no way I would be able to provide what this couple could.

Steve got to the house and we all went out for lunch. With two babies and carriers we had to take two cars. At lunch it was Steve that had all of the questions for them. I had already read about them, spoke to them and chose them. I was sold. Steve seemed more interested than I had ever seen him. Question after question arose as to how the kids would live, where they would go to school and what they would eat. We must have spent at least two hours at the table talking before we decided to go back to the house.

Back at the house, Steve continued talking and questioning. They wanted to make sure we knew there was no pressure on us from them. They understood there were tons of emotions between us and this situation. So graciously they thanked us, kissed the babies, then left. Steve and I took a deep breath and each fell back on one of the couches to refresh ourselves. That was exhausting! Finally, I piped up and said, "Well, what do you think? I did a good job, huh? Aren't they just perfect?" He sat there spacing off for a minute, somewhere in the universe. He then quietly said, "I want to be just like them."

It would have been nice if Steve had meant that about he and I being a great couple like them, but he meant it about them as a whole and his future life being like them, not including me. He decided to not sign the adoption papers. He would pay child support and I would be forced to keep the babies in a situation I didn't want them to grow up in. I was devastated. Not about Steve and me, but what lifestyle the kids would be forced to grow up in. I had been there and it is not fun.

The Worst Phone Call

I had been overwhelmed, feeling like I had a lot on my plate but thank goodness my "brother" Ryan had weekly or at least bi-weekly business in Las Vegas so we could get together and talk. It was a ritual on Tuesdays for him to come over and let Corbin and Chandler wrestle and jump all over him as if they were truly his nephews. He called them "my boys" every time he spoke about them. We would then go out for dinner or I would make something at the house. After the boys went to bed, we would talk until late. It was so comforting because I knew he cared and always gave me his big brother thoughts of how I should handle events in my life. Ryan always made me feel special since I knew he truly loved and believed in me.

Sometimes in life, everyone gets their worst phone call. It was a beautiful Saturday morning. The babies had just come home from the hospital and Steve was over. My brother called on the phone and sounded shook up. I asked what was wrong and he said, "Ryan's dead."

"What did you say?" I hoped so badly I heard him wrong.

"Ryan is dead," he repeated, breaking into sobs.

"What? What are you saying? What?"

"He died in a car accident on an icy road."

"No he didn't! NO! NO! NO!" My legs buckled as I fell to my knees and started screaming at the top of my lungs. They were deep anguished sobs from my broken soul. "Not Ryan! No! No! Not Ryan!" My brother was sobbing, as I was hysterical.

"Nobody wanted to tell you because we knew you would die. I'm so sorry. He's my best friend; I loved him too. I'm so sorry!" I was sobbing, dropped the phone, and kept screaming, "No! No!"

Steve came running from the babies' room, not knowing anything and just dropped to the floor and started rubbing my back. I was sure my heart would stop. I couldn't breathe. I think Steve hung up the phone; I don't remember. He stayed right there in the same spot on the ground, rubbing my back for probably three hours, I think. I was rocking back and forth, trying to not lose my mind completely, but I couldn't stop crying. How was I going to live without my Ryan, my brother?

Ryan was thirty-three years old when he died. I flew out for the viewing the night before the funeral. My plane was late so no one was at the mortuary anymore which was better for me. They had fixed him up pretty well for an open casket. His right ear wasn't perfect like I knew it to be. Ryan's right arm was broken and wrapped well in gauze. His body was just a shell; there was no spirit there. Sitting for a while and stroking his hair, I talked to him about the babies he was supposed to have seen three days after he died. Ryan was more excited for those babies to come than anyone I knew. He had met Steve and liked him a lot. He had plans to come out that Tuesday but died on Saturday. Bringing a picture with me I placed it in his casket of my babies. I'm sure Ryan was standing right there, trying to comfort me while I spoke, but I couldn't feel him. My heart had died and I was too numb.

At the funeral, I couldn't speak. Still in so much shock and completely broken-hearted, I couldn't even get up to speak so didn't. Several of our friends were a little surprised but understood. Still barely breathing, there would be no sleeping or eating. The grief was all consuming. Usually, I can pull myself together but not this time. Even at my mother's funeral I was able to speak. Maybe because her death was expected, I don't really know. The loss was the same. What I did know is that I was furious with God! There are few things I have in life and even fewer loved ones. Those few are so precious to me, yet he takes them, one by one. There are billions of other people, why take mine? I already have a crappy hand of cards, only have a couple of aces and he steals those from me? Seriously?

Suicide

This section is very difficult for me to write, as I can still feel the pain I was going through at that time. I cried to the Lord saying, "I don't believe people can die of a broken heart or I would have died a hundred deaths by now! Please just let me come home! I can't take the pain any longer!" I had decided this time to not get back up when the rug was pulled out.

There is one thing I cannot stand hearing. It is when people say that those who die due to suicide are selfish. First of all, judge not, lest ye be judged. Second, weep with those that weep and comfort those who stand in need of comfort. Third, have you ever been there? Have you truly felt real suffering, broken-hearted, complete and utter despair, the feeling of total loss, the loss of your hope, faith, or light of any kind feeling? Add in the pull-you-to-your-knees emptiness? Have you been to that place where the suffering is so intense your heart hurts to take another beat and you wish you were an injured horse so that someone would shoot you in the head to remove you from the misery you can't escape from yourself? If you have ever been there, you would never say that about those that cannot take the pain any longer. It is a horrible, dark place to be. I have been there a few times in my life. My heart breaks every time I hear of a suicide whether it be a bullied teenager, a father's job loss and ability to support his family, someone within a family unit due to divorce, abuse, any shattering of a relationship where those involved can't take the pain, failure, or heartache. It has nothing to do with whether others around love them. It is that person's own personal pain and heartache. You can't sleep, eat, or breathe because that hurts, too. This had nothing to do with Steve or my previous divorce. Neither of those things even crossed my mind. It was much deeper than that. This was about my children, their future, and my heartache due to the many shortcomings I possessed. All of my mother's difficulties seemed to be repeating. The words of my father telling me I couldn't do anything right. The heartache that I promised myself my children would have things different than I. There were so many fears and rivers of past tears swallowing me now.

Three months after the week the twins were born and Ryan was buried, there I was in that very dark place. I had been there before but it was much darker this time. There was no way I could get back into nursing school, caring for new twin babies with opposite sleep schedules that needed constant care and have the ability to pass my classes. Because of that, I wouldn't have a way to support them. I had my two little boys that also needed my love and attention. It was my responsibility to raise them but how would that happen without being educated to gain employment? There were no parents for me to fall back on or family to call for help, although a few wonderful families, the Hadfields, Lees, and Dunfords from church would take the babies as often as possible so I could get a little bit of rest. Several times I would call Dean and Deb in tears, so frustrated that I couldn't give these babies to the most wonderful couple I knew who had the biggest perfect extended family with tons of support. They were sad but would encourage me to continue on. Yet, there I was and I had nothing to give. My childhood was repeating itself and there was no way I was going to let that happen to my children.

Still reeling from the loss of Ryan— mixed with some post-partum depression and my sense of having utterly failed my children—I felt there was only one way out. It wasn't like I felt completely unloved or anything like that. My children loved me, people from church, and friends too. Would my friends be upset and heart-broken? I knew they would, but this had nothing to do with them. I rationalized that the boys were so young they wouldn't remember me after a few years. They loved and worshipped their new step-mom anyway, and with their dad as a professional and from a big family, they would have all of the things they wanted and needed in life. If I were gone, I knew Steve would not keep those babies. He had professional school ahead and his parents wanted to retire in a few years. There was no extended family or friends there for support on his side. They certainly would not take the twins. Chances were that the wonderful Hadfield family in our ward who absolutely loved those babies to pieces and had them at their house more than anyone else would adopt them. They would be close by so Steve would sign off his rights but could see them when he wanted and not have the responsibility of raising them. Eventually, he would let them go.

The best case scenario would be that Deb and Dean would be contacted and the twins would be given to them after all. My children would all have a great life if I wasn't there. They would all have happy, loving homes with both parents—not a stressed out, working single mother who couldn't spend time with them, was broke and had no family. What I had to give was pathetic. If I stayed here, they would suffer as I did. My many, many misfortunes and failures were not going to be passed on to my children. There were no options for me. I had thought this out. For the benefit of my children, this was the most unselfish thing I could do so that they would flourish.

My suicide was thought out and planned. It was the beginning of a long holiday weekend. Corbin and Chandler were picked up by their dad and step-mom. I kissed and hugged them for a minute longer and said good-bye. They happily raced to their daddy's truck, excited for the weekend. I watched them drive away, thinking how I loved those little boys with my whole heart and soul, hoping they knew how much I loved them and praying that they would forgive me one day. I went inside and called the Hadfields. That was one of the safest, most loving places on earth I could take those babies. They were, as always, happy to take them and said they would for the weekend. I knew they would keep them for much longer, if not forever, when I dropped them off. Kissing the babies goodbye, I handed them off and went home.

After I got home from dropping the twins off, I sat down and wrote letters to the kids, telling them how much I loved them and that I knew they would have a nice life. I took all of the blame for not being there for them and said how sorry I was for that. This all had nothing to do with me not wanting to be with them.

When I was done writing my letters to the kids, I went into the kitchen and took a bottle of prescription pain pills I had prepared and hadn't used from the twins' childbirth three months prior. Upstairs to my bedroom I went and lay down on the bed to take a nap. I was thinking about the children and how happy they all were, right at that moment, being loved and having fun. That would give me peace to fall asleep. Knowing this was a long weekend, I planned to try to die on Saturday so that in case I was unconscious, there would be nobody to find or "save" me for a few days so for sure I would be gone by that time.

Everything was hazy after that. A flash and I saw police, another flash and I was in the back of an ambulance. One more and I woke up in the hospital. All I knew was that I was incredibly sick but didn't know how I got there. My close friends, Jenny and Nicole from out of state, flew out to be with me and help with the babies when I got out of the hospital with the Dunford family picking them up. Then the story came together.

Jenny, Nicole, and I are good friends and met when our husbands were in professional school years earlier. The three of us were almost always together. We survived the widowhood of school, working as apartment managers and meeting for lunch regularly at a park so our kids could play while we hung out and talked. We are the type of friends, like most of my friends, that can go a year or much longer without talking, then pick up right where we left off in five minutes.

Jenny told me she had a very strong feeling to call me. It had been a year since we had spoken. I guess she was the one listening when the still small voice was talking. She said she called my house and (I have no idea how) I answered the phone next to my bed. She said I sounded totally "not right, out of it." She asked if I was sick and I answered "No." Jenny then asked if everything was ok and I again said, "No." She didn't hear anything more from me and called 911. The police broke down my door and an ambulance took me away.

God wanted me preserved for something, but I didn't know what or why for that matter. There was nothing left of me to give.

The Blessing

Time had passed since the divorce, Ryan's death and my attempt to die. Not surprising I was still angry and bitter. Why was I forgotten by God? Where was he? Was he so far out in the universe and so busy that he didn't have time to answer prayers, help me out or just check in once in a while? Why is it fair that my ex seems to be able to move on so easily? Why do I have to be so lonely? Why did Ryan, so full of life, have to die in that accident? Why did I have to live when I wanted to die so badly? I was not feeling like the whole church thing was for me. It seems I tried, really tried to be a good member of the Church, and it all fell apart anyway.

Nobody teaches the doctrine that if you repent and do everything you are supposed to do, it can all still be taken away from you. Where was that in the Sunday school lesson or the LDS handbook? I thought we were supposed to live happily ever after! I found the Church, married in the temple, had kids, was a good wife and mother, prayed daily, read my scriptures, did my visiting teaching and my church calling. I want my happily ever after! That is how it is supposed to be! That is why I try so hard! What a total rip-off for me! No matter how hard I tried to be the perfect wife, mother, and member, it collapsed. Why try anymore? There wasn't a point. What I needed to remind myself of is that they say God loves everyone, yet I didn't believe that. He didn't seem to care what hardships I went through. How is this considered "love"? Obviously He didn't care about me. I will never understand why, but it is just that way. Although I carried a small bit of hope for my future, I could not continue to have faith in God or His church. There were no plans of happiness included for me in this life, and no blessings coming.

I started doing some "deep therapy" my counselor encouraged me to do. At the beginning of it, I received this poem:

> Whenever I start to hang my head in front of failure's face,
> my downward fall is broken by the memory of a race.
> A children's race, young boys, young men; how I remember well,
> excitement sure, but also fear, it wasn't hard to tell.
> They all lined up so full of hope, each thought to win that race
> or tie for first, or if not that, at least take second place.

Their parents watched from off the side, each cheering for their son,
and each boy hoped to show his folks that he would be the one.
The whistle blew and off they flew, like chariots of fire,
to win, to be the hero there, was each young boy's desire.
One boy in particular, whose dad was in the crowd,
was running in the lead and thought "My dad will be so proud."
But as he speeded down the field and crossed a shallow dip,
the little boy who thought he'd win, lost his step and slipped.
Trying hard to catch himself, his arms flew everyplace,
and midst the laughter of the crowd he fell flat on his face.
As he fell, his hope fell too; he couldn't win it now.
Humiliated, he just wished to disappear somehow.
But as he fell his dad stood up and showed his anxious face,
which to the boy so clearly said, "Get up and win that race!"
He quickly rose, no damage done, behind a bit that's all,
and ran with all his mind and might to make up for his fall.
So anxious to restore himself, to catch up and to win,
his mind went faster than his legs. He slipped and fell again.
He wished that he had quit before with only one disgrace.
"I'm hopeless as a runner now, I shouldn't try to race."
But through the laughing crowd he searched and found his father's face
with a steady look that said again, "Get up and win that race!"
So he jumped up to try again, ten yards behind the last.
"If I'm to gain those yards," he thought, "I've got to run real fast!"
Exceeding everything he had, he regained eight, then ten...
but trying hard to catch the lead, he slipped and fell again.
Defeat! He lay there silently. A tear dropped from his eye.
"There's no sense running anymore! Three strikes I'm out! Why try?
I've lost, so what's the use?" he thought. "I'll live with my disgrace."
But then he thought about his dad, who soon he'd have to face.
"Get up," an echo sounded low, "you haven't lost at all,
for all you have to do to win is rise each time you fall.
Get up!" the echo urged him on, "Get up and take your place!
You were not meant for failure here! Get up and win that race!"
So, up he rose to run once more, refusing to forfeit,
and he resolved that win or lose, at least he wouldn't quit.

So far behind the others now, the most he'd ever been,
still he gave it all he had and ran like he could win.
Three times he'd fallen stumbling, three times he rose again.
Too far behind to hope to win, he still ran to the end.
They cheered another boy who crossed the line and won first place,
head high and proud and happy -- no falling, no disgrace.
But, when the fallen youngster crossed the line, in last place,
the crowd gave him a greater cheer for finishing the race.
And even though he came in last with head bowed low, un-proud,
you would have thought he'd won the race, to listen to the crowd.
And to his dad he sadly said, "I didn't do so well."
"To me, you won," his father said. "You rose each time you fell."
And now when things seem dark and bleak and difficult to face,
the memory of that little boy helps me in my own race.
For all of life is like that race, with ups and downs and all.
And all you have to do to win is rise each time you fall.
And when depression and despair shout loudly in my face,
another voice within me says, "Get up and win that race!"

My therapist knows me well. To this day I can't ever read that poem without crying. It is so completely my life!

A dear friend of mine, Tammy, told me that I needed a priesthood blessing. Having many friends at this point, she was the only single friend I had, well she, me, and Gladys. The three of us were the only singles I knew. I guess I wasn't in bad company. So, Tammy set up an appointment for me to meet with Brother S.

Brother S. was a very calm and gentle man. He reminded me a little bit of all the good characteristics in Mr. Rogers but in a really good way. He was not fake, but truly good, inside and out. Very much like a child's innocence, his goodness radiated. Jesus wants us all to become as a little child—meek, humble, patient, full of love, etc. That was Ron.

For not knowing me, Ron gave the most amazing blessing. It was shocking. After explaining that Heavenly Father was aware of my trials and tribulations and hadn't forgotten me, he said that my own mother had been assigned to be my guardian on the other side. That she would be able to better help me than others due to our relationship. He then said something shocking. It was as if God was getting after me for all of my murmuring about life. Abruptly and with some chastisement in his voice (as if I remembered something from the pre-existence), he continued, "You KNEW about the divorce before you came to the earth and it was so disturbing to you that you went and spoke to Heavenly Father and Heavenly Mother about it. When they explained why things had to be this way, you agreed to continue with your mission on the earth." That was interesting.

Thinking he was done, my mind started to wander and think about what was just said, but he continued to surprise me with more. Ron went on, "Corbin and Chandler had to be born at their particular times for their own particular missions on the earth."

Okay, a preordained marriage and divorce for a preordained family order? It was all in my mission call to the earth.

Mission Call to the Earth

Another night, another dream. Actually, I hardly ever dream. If so they are very detailed and I remember them vividly. There is meaning behind each one. They are clues to my life, whether past, present, or future. They are experiences, memories or visions, and they are always true. This one was from my past.

It was the preexistence in which my memory was wiped clean when coming to the earth. There I was, standing on a stage, kind of a platform. I had seen this stage before when my mother passed so I know this was not a dream but a past experience I was watching happen right in front of me. Looking around twenty-five years of age by earth standards, I stood in front of a multitude of people, again like when my mother returned to heaven, a multitude. There was no end to the amount of people. They were everywhere. Quiet and in perfect order they awaited the reading of my mission call to the earth. The smiles and excitement on everyone's faces were apparent as there were big hopes and wonder of where I may be going and what kind of life I would have. Just like when Latter-day Saint missionaries open their mission calls in front of a room of excited guests for some adventure teaching about Jesus, somewhere in the world, it is exactly the same pattern coming to the earth. Truly God is the same yesterday, today and forever.

There I was on that stage with the multitude of smiling people. I was standing at the same place I had been when watching my mother, almost like a window but a little bit behind and to the left. The people facing me I could see perfectly, but whoever is on the stage like my mother and Carl had been, I could only see their faces if they turned their head to the side. Watching myself from behind, I (my spirit) began to read my mission call.

I was not privileged to listen to my reading of the call. My ears were blocked from hearing what was being read but I know what it said, especially now since I have lived it. The more I read those in the multitude began to lose their smile. My body language said it all. As my head began to droop and my shoulders slump, the look on many faces turned to sadness, concern, and tears. Previously holding the calling with both hands excitedly in front of me, now one hand held it and dropped to my side as my head fell back as if to look into heaven asking "WHY?"

The sound came back to my ears so I could hear what was going on at that moment. The despair was present in my body language. You could have heard a pin drop, even with thousands of people there. It was perfectly silent as all grieved for me. At that point I spoke and said in complete agony, choking on tears as if preparing to sob, "I will NEVER make it back!" As I wallowed in grief for a moment and thousands with me, the silence continued. All of the sudden, halfway to the back of what I could see and on the left a hand went up as if to ask a question. A voice said, "You can do it! I will be there for you." Looking up I saw Chad Lee, my current home teacher from church for ten years. (I was so surprised that I knew him then, in the pre mortal life). There he was like the best brother in the world, telling me he would be there on the earth to help me on my journey back home.

Now, I was no longer watching this memory but was now inside myself experiencing it, remembering it. As I sat in silence feeling tears running down my face, amazed at the love for me held by this brother of mine and the concern for my safety back home, I was astounded! Two more hands went up right in front of the stage, right side, front row. It was the Hadfields, both of them, there together before this life just like they are on the earth. I heard Becci say, "You can do it! We will be there too!" As Bart said, "You'll be okay, we will be there!" Different hands came up and then I heard many voices rooting for me that I could do it, I would make it back, I am strong enough, that they would help me. It was overwhelming as a river of tears poured down. This multitude was cheering me on. In shock and amazement, I just stood there so appreciative of their love and confidence in me.

The amazing thing about this memory is that those people were 'there' for me on the earth, like they had said they would be. They didn't even remember why they wanted to help me in this life, but they did. The little GPS in their souls knew what it was doing and where to go. It was amazing that they all kept their promise to help me while on the earth and did it all without even remembering a thing.

How many people did we make promises to? That little GPS inside telling us to call this person, drop off cookies, visit in the hospital, anything. All of those things meant everything to me! The only way for me to survive this life and my trials was through the love and service of others.

CHAPTER 9

Guardian Angels and the Priesthood

Marriage Number Two

As I went on to nursing school, my wonderful ward family rallied around me and organized the kid care between different families. They had a schedule of people picking up the boys from school and where they would go, along with who took the babies, even if one went to one family and one to another. I knew they were always safe and loved.

The Lees gave me an amazing gift during all of this craziness. Knowing I was neurotic about my house, they had a cleaning lady come to my home every other Friday from when the twins were born until they were three years old! Holy cow! Talk about the best gift ever! This kept me sane.

Eventually, Steve came around. He wanted to be like these wonderful examples of families he had seen. This time he wanted it with me and finally proposed. The best thing here for everyone would be to keep this little family together. After all, we had been through a lot and had grown, each in our own way. Besides, I had known he was my soulmate back when we met.

Steve lied. It was four and a half years until we were married. The Hadfields had graciously let us use their gorgeous back yard, complete with pool, gazebo and flower gardens. Hope's husband had become our bishop and married us. The twins were a little older than three and cute as can be. My son, Corbin was adamant about being the ring bearer and involved. He was now ten and Chandler, eight. All of the men sported tuxedos, even little Chase. Kenya was my matron of honor, while Steve had all of his best friends from Canada fly in for the occasion. As an added surprise and bonus for Steve and the guests, Kenya, my friend, Mich, and our friend Joni decided to be back-up-singers for my rendition of "I Say a Little Prayer." The day was perfectly beautiful and sunny. That night instead of retreating as a couple, we decided to go dancing with all of our friends visiting Vegas from Canada for the first time. Finally with Steve, I felt like a family.

Mother Loves Her Grandkids

It is true that our loved ones never leave us. Again I witnessed this with our precious Savannah. Steve and I would hear her at three years old having a tea party in her bedroom. We would peek in as she clearly would be talking to someone and would see one open chair along with her own and tea for two set up. She would say, "Is that enough tea for you, Grandma?" She would continue on in her conversation with Grandma. Steve and I would look at each other funny. Once, we let her see us and questioned, "What are you doing?"

"Having tea with Grandma," she said with a funny look like we were dummies.

"Daddy's mom grandma?" I asked. She shook her head as if to say no. "My mom, Grandma B?" I asked. She nodded yes with a big smile. Steve and I thought that strange since they never met and I only have one picture displayed of her. Savannah was very young so it wasn't like we had all of these conversations about Grandma.

One night while playing late, we went in and said, "Savannah, you can't play anymore. It's time for bed." She immediately looked between Steve and me, as if she saw someone perfectly standing there and said, "I go to bed now, Grandma. We play tomorrow, ok?" Steve and I looked between us and then at each other and did this, "creepy" look at each other. We went to bed talking about it. Many times this happened. When she was four, she was in tears one day. We asked what was wrong and she said, "I don't see Grandma anymore." I have heard as children get more into the world the veil for them tends to close and they don't see spirits like they do so easily as babies. I don't believe my mom ever left, Savannah just outgrew seeing her.

The Last Supper

Corbin was in middle school and had just started the football team. He was at practice when a tackle went very bad. His ankle was severely twisted and broken, requiring surgery. His ankle was stabilized, but we had to wait a few days for surgery. I took Corbin out for a burger lunch and jokingly called it the last supper. Dr. Camp, our surgeon, performed a successful surgery but explained Corbin would have problems with metal detectors from now on.

Three days after surgery Corbin became very ill. He was cramping up so badly one night I took him to a local hospital. They couldn't find anything and wrote it off as a stomach bug and sent us home. Corbin was worse the next day. He had severe abdominal pain, was nauseous, vomiting but mainly was rolled into a ball in tears. He already had fresh surgery with a leg that was hurting and healing as well as being sick. Corbin refused to eat or drink anything and wouldn't take his pain pills for his ankle even though he was in so much pain. I was so worried and returned to the hospital that again sent him home, telling me I was an overly concerned parent, infuriating me. A couple of days passed and Corbin was either sleeping or moaning in pain with no food or drink. He seemed to be losing weight quickly and was awfully pale. Now the little urination he had was bloody and there was a lot of blood in his stool. I freaked out. We went to a third hospital that again sent us home. The frustration led to tears and terror as I called Dr. Camp who was very concerned and requested we come in and he break open his cast to look at the surgery site. Dr. Camp looked at the site and it was clean so casted him again but said, "Kayli, you know something is wrong and as a Mother, trust that. Don't stop looking."

I took Corbin home in tears. I had begun fasting that day for help and still nothing. Corbin said, "Mom, it is okay to let me die."

"No Corbin, it is not. I won't let you! I can't!"

I got him settled in bed, went to my room and fell to my knees. "Dear God" I pleaded "Please don't take Corbin! You can't do that! I can't handle it! My heart can't take it! He's my angel! But please, don't make him suffer! Let me keep him. Please heal him. Help me find the doctors who know what is wrong with him."

The cast and pain made it so difficult for Corbin to get up I was constantly helping him to the bathroom which became more and more often. I moved Corbin to the floor next to the bathroom in my room and called Chad Lee for help. He came over, put his hands on Corbin's head right there on the ground in my bathroom and gave a beautiful priesthood blessing. I don't remember a lot of it but he did say that Corbin had great faith and although this illness would stay with him, he would use this experience in the future to help others. I was so relieved to hear there was a future for him. Corbin was so pale and ill and looked as if he had lost at least 15lbs. I don't know that he heard any of that blessing. I believe he was at death's door.

I was up and down all night with Corbin, still fasting and begging with God for healing. The next morning Corbin was in excruciating abdominal pain and while helping him to the toilet, his bowels began bleeding profusely. It was like a horror movie. He was scared and I was terrified! All of the sudden, in my head came the thought, "take him to his pediatrician." I called the office and they said to bring him right in.

We couldn't even get Corbin to the room before he needed to use the toilet that was next to it. I helped him in and stood outside the door when the profuse bleeding began. Corbin called for me to help just as the doctor came looking for us, took one look at Corbin and said, "I will be right back."

I watched him run into his office, pull out a very large medical book and flip through pages very fast. He then picked up the phone. I couldn't hear what was said but a minute later he came back and said, "Take him as fast as you can to the children's hospital. I already talked to them in the emergency room and they are expecting him. Don't stop anywhere! Go as fast as you can."

That is exactly what I did. When I got there, four staff members were waiting for him. They helped him get into a gown and gave us about 10 minutes while they were waiting for a certain doctor to arrive. Corbin's best friend's family had called while I was driving to the ER and met us there. His best friend Ryan, from childhood, walked in, took one look at his pale, thin, weakened body and burst into tears. Corbin was about twenty pounds less than when he had seen him a week earlier before the surgery. He was terrified to even touch his buddy. His dad said, "C'mon, it's okay." Ryan gave Corbin a hug before they wheeled him away. This little family asked "What can we do?"

I answered, "Just pray."

At this point several families and friends had called, asking about him and members of so many different churches and religions, complete strangers started praying and fasting for him as well. His name was put on LDS temple prayer rolls in several temples around the United States. All of the kids from the middle school signed a huge card wishing him well.

Corbin had a severe and rare case of E-Coli in which he should have died. It was so frightening that the state went in and did an inspection in the restaurant we had visited. We had not eaten the same menu items which is why I didn't get sick. To this day I don't know if anyone else was sick because I was too busy. He was in the Children's Hospital for about a week and I slept in the room with him. I was so afraid something would happen if I left and I wouldn't be there. Corbin was the talk of the hospital and there were at least fifty doctors and residents that came in to see the 'boy that had survived' E-Coli to ask him questions. Corbin still has some lasting effects, but all thanks goes to God as we are so happy that he survived.

Steve's Baby

As much as I wasn't interested in another pregnancy (love the babies, hate the pregnancies), Steve wanted one more baby. It took about four months and I was pregnant. How I hate pregnancy and this one was the worst ever. So completely awful and sick, I had to quit working and stay home, attached to an IV pole and PICC line with fluids running 24/7. My doctor exclaimed I was the sickest patient he had in twenty-five years. I'm telling you, I'm always the exception to the rule. The pregnancy and vomiting, mixed with the massive amount of drugs and fluid trying to keep me hydrated and from nausea, was exhausting. The medication side effect was to make me sleep most of the day. I even had a spit cup since I couldn't swallow my own saliva.

Every time I fell asleep on my bed, something would run past the foot of the bed and slap one of my feet. It would startle and wake me. Wondering who did it, I would realize I was alone. Back to sleep I would go and be fine. It happened almost every day, at least one time. Becoming more aware of whatever "gift" this was, I began to cover my feet with a blanket. That was the trick. It wouldn't happen if they were covered.

One morning I awoke, feeling like someone, possibly one of the kids, was watching me. As I opened my eyes, there was a middle-aged gentleman kneeling right next to the bed not even a foot from me, staring right into my face. It's as if he was studying every movement, mole, freckle, counting my eyelashes—I don't know, but he was seriously studying me. He had salt and pepper hair that was not quite to his shoulders. He had his arms folded on the edge of the bed next to me and his chin resting on top of the folded arms, like he had been there for a while, just watching me sleep. The angel or spirit was wearing a white top, kind of like a scrub shirt with a V-neck and loose. He looked about fifty years old. As soon as I saw him, he quickly disappeared. Never had I seen him in my life, or since. I have no idea who he was or what he wanted.

Knocking on Heaven's Door

My pregnancies are always terrible, each topping the last. This one had to be the whip cream and cherry. Almost every day I was extremely ill, but something now was different. Some kind of bug had been added to the mess of my normal nausea and vomiting as it came on fast with a fever and flu-like symptoms.

One morning I felt like I was in an ice cube bath, just freezing. Scooting closer to Steve for warmth, he said, "You are burning up." With my teeth completely chattering, I said, "Something is wrong with me, I am so cold. I am just so cold." He bundled me up and added more blankets, swaddling me tight. My whole body was shaking, more like convulsing on the bed. Steve called the doctor. He said, "Just a minute" as he took my temperature. "101.5," he said. Steve hung up and gave me Motrin for my temperature. He left for school.

Super sick, I stayed in bed sleeping and shaking all day. Steve was back when I woke up and on the phone with the hospital this time. "103.5," he said. He double dosed me with Motrin as I drifted back to sleep. In the morning on the phone I heard Steve talking, "She still has a fever." The hospital thought I had the flu so weren't overly concerned, but I had never felt like this.

At six months pregnant and on a permanent IV, getting around wasn't easy. Steve was gone to school and the twins were home with me. Something was wrong, seriously wrong. I needed help and my doctor. With no appointment scheduled, I went anyway. Doing my best to pack up the twins in the car with an IV and on medications, I headed towards my doctor's office. I knew driving was not what I should be doing but felt like this was crucial, like my body was shutting down. The twins were fussing and trying to talk to me. I kept repeating, "Mommy is sick, mommy is very sick. Just give me a few minutes please. Let me focus for just a few more minutes."

Thinking my heart was trying to stop and I would crash, I hurried on, trying to focus, praying out loud as I went, "Please God, let me get to my doctor. Don't let me pass out. Help me drive this car. Don't let my babies get hurt." Speaking to my body over and over I kept saying, "We are almost there, stay awake, keep going, please stay with me. Come on, please God, we are almost there."

Pulling into the first spot, I jumped out and grabbed the twins by their arms and dizzily hobbled as fast as I could with my big belly and all into the doctor. As I walked in the door, a nurse just came out to call one of the many women waiting in that full room. She took one look at me with a very concerned and strange look on her face, as if I were pink and purple, and said, "Mrs. Coffman, please come in. Right then I took two steps toward her and collapsed on the ground. It was over, I was out. All I could hear were people calling out and hustle bustle, yelling for a doctor, an ambulance, and my name several times. Everything was black and I felt like I was dying.

Unbearable pain woke me up as I came to in the hospital with two nurses attempting to take my blood pressure. "Her pressure is so low it's not registering," one said.

"Get it off of her, the blood is pooling in her arm."

I was screaming at that point. Looking towards the direction of the pain in my arm, it was blue. The color was a true blue. The blood had stopped moving and you could see it all sitting as if I already was dead. I felt like I could barely move. The rigor mortis was setting in but I was still alive. The nurses looked at me like I was the walking dead. I saw their uneasy glances as they said a few things back and forth. Trying to stay calm and not alarm me they said, "Umm, we will be back in a minute with the doctor."

What they didn't know was that I was a nurse, too. Their little secrets and codes were known to me. I knew I was in a lot of trouble. Those nurses were pretty sure I was going to die. The blood tests had come back negative, but my temperature was now 106 degrees. My baby hadn't moved since the fever started. As the day went on, my temperature moved to 106.5. I knew my body couldn't hold out like this. All of the things that should be happening to me kept racing through my head. Day turned to night and everything was being done to see what was wrong with me. More labs were done, again and again. Nothing was found. Now they were sent to outside labs. My doctor, I could tell, was panicking and told me he had a rare disease specialist flying in the next morning. The temperature remained at 106.5, no matter what was attempted to bring it down.

As a nurse in school we were told if a patient tells you they are dying, believe them. They know their body. Now, I understood that. My body was dying and I could feel it preparing to shut down. Calling Steve on the phone at 11:00pm, I wanted to tell him goodbye. I said, "Babe, I'm dying."

"No, they will find out what's going on in the morning," he said.

Starting to cry I said, "Really, I am dying Steve. It sucks because I have been waiting for us to get married and to be happy. Now that everything is going well for once in my life, it figures, I die!"

Steve said he was going to miss school in the morning and come in after getting kids off to care, and that I would be okay. I told him I loved him and we hung up. Inside I knew I would be dead by morning.

Dr. K to the Rescue

At 2:00am, my doctor, with a team behind him, came running into my room. They were literally running. The lights flipped on, all sorts of equipment, drugs, you name it were hauled in and being setup. If I were a beehive, they were the bees busily working all around me. The doctor said that an outside lab found that I had severe sepsis. From the start of that illness you have 72 hours to discover it and start treatment because after that window, you have organ failure and die. It is very serious. The doctor said I had to be running right around 70-72 hours at that point and every minute mattered a lot. I told him I felt like I was dying.

"You are," he responded. "We are going to save you right now."

"What about the baby?"

"You are our top priority, then we will see about the baby."

The team pulled my PICC line that was fed to the opening of my heart from one arm and painfully started a new one on the other arm while IVs of heavy antibiotics were pushed through me, one after another. If a vein collapsed due to the powerful drug going through it, they would start on another. They rushed to work on me for what seemed like a long time, but I felt so sick it didn't matter. All of the scary, last resort antibiotics were used, ones you only want to use once in your life. *They are going to kill my baby,* I kept thinking.

Dr. K. literally saved my life that night. I will be forever grateful. Steve came in early in the morning and the doctor informed him of the seriousness of what went on. Steve smiled and said, "See, I told you you'd be okay."

We were informed the baby could be damaged from the long-term 106 degree fever and sepsis or the heavy drugs they shoved through my veins that are a huge no-no for expectant moms. We wouldn't know until she was born. This would not be a fun waiting game. After another day passed, she started to move again.

Unfortunately, the heavy drugs pushed through my system may have saved my life, but there was a price to pay. My left ear began to loudly ring (called tinnitus), like crickets at night when you are camping, and has never stopped. It used to wake me up and make me crazy, but I am used to it now.

Baby Ella

As with all of my pregnancies, this one had to be induced as well. We, along with the doctor and some specialty nurses and our pediatrician, were concerned how this birth would play out. The baby had been through a lot, but we did not know the long term damage. Dr. K. was LDS as well as myself and said after my sepsis incident, "We can do testing to see how she is and what, if any damage she has, but I don't know if you want to go through all of that since I'm assuming you still would want to keep her no matter what the result."

"Dr. K, you are right and I'll wait to find out when she is born." He was correct. She was mine no matter what damage had occurred. There was no terminating this pregnancy and certainly I would not give her away.

Two years prior to my pregnancy with Ella, I lost a baby. It was a deeply stressful and difficult time in my life. There was so much going on with school and the twins were two years old. Steve and I were up and down with our relationship prior to the loss. I sadly apologized to the baby for the extreme stress placed on it and promised one day I would try to have a baby again and hoped he would be able to return and try to grow that little body. Not knowing if it was a boy or girl and four months pregnant when the loss occurred, I named it Taylor. It has been twelve years and I still think about Taylor. I do not believe it was Ella, but that was the only opportunity he had to get a body. I will see Taylor and raise him/her after this life. That experience solidified that this baby and her survival was very special.

When Ella was born, she had her cord wrapped like a noose several times around her neck. All I could think about was my body being 106.5 and her stuck in a Jacuzzi, trying to get away from the heat, rolling around and getting tied up. Dr. K. quickly removed it, but it was really tight. After cutting the cord, he grabbed her and with the nurses left me to work on the baby. She didn't make a peep. The whole medical team surrounded her and was quite busy working her over. Steve had the camera out but didn't take pictures right then. He couldn't see anything anyway. I kept looking at him, concerned, and mouthing, "What's going on?"

"I don't know, I can't tell,"

Minutes went by and we kept looking at each other a little more concerned every time.

It probably was shorter but seemed like a good 5-10 minutes of just doctor and nurses whispering amongst each other. My mind was preparing for the loss and then I heard a gurgled little peep. Dr. K loudly said, "There she is!" Without a doubt I knew there was a whole other team of angels working on her as well. This baby was supposed to live. They handed her finally to me for about a minute, then Dr. K. said, "The baby needs to go to testing for a bit. She will be in good hands. I know you understand." Knowing exactly what tests they were doing, I handed her off and she left. It must have been five hours later, at least it seemed, when they brought my baby girl back. The nurse handed her to me and said, "She is perfect. Honestly, we are kind of surprised so did some additional testing, but we can't find anything wrong with her. She passed our tests with flying colors."

Ella was a fat little bouncy nine pound baby. All of that sugar water running through my IV during the pregnancy put some plump on her. I was just thrilled we both made it through those terrible nine months.

A year after Ella was born I had another pregnancy that looked to be a repeat set of twins. By three months I was as big as my normal six months. Going into the doctor for an appointment, he told me I had lost that pregnancy as well. My body refused to terminate it and kept holding on so we had to go in and remove everything. It was all I could take physically and emotionally. We made the decision and Steve had a vasectomy.

NASCAR

Ella was one and a half years old and I was back working at the hospital. After finishing my shift and heading home one evening, I had stopped at a light on a big street that had three lanes going each way. I was in the farthest inside lane closest to the island/median. As the light turned green, I accelerated to the limit of 40 mph when a small car came darting from my right. The cars to my right hit their brakes, but I didn't see her until she was a foot from my car. There wasn't even time to hit my brakes and I remember saying, "You have got to be kidding me!"

The driver hit a perfect T-bone to my side. You would think I would be safe in my huge SUV, but her tiny car went under me. My back tires pretty much ripped off her whole front end as my car began to spiral through the air. I was thinking, "Oh, no, no, no!" Then I was knocked out. I woke up with rain splashing against my face. It took me a second to realize I was sliding upside down about 35 mph and it was glass fragments hitting my face, not rain. The car was sliding down this very busy street, completely out of control. Because my eyes were inches from the ground, I couldn't see anything in front of me.

"Please, God, don't let me hurt anyone! Oh, God, I don't want to hurt people; please don't let me hit anyone!" I could only imagine a family walking across the street or kids on bikes and I was helpless to steer away from them. To my left I saw the concrete median inches from my head, whipping past me. If the car drifted just a little to the left and rolled to its side due to the "step up", I would break my neck. Hanging upside down with a very tight seatbelt holding me, I started to pray, "Please God, don't let it hurt. I don't want to feel my neck break." I was sure this would be the end.

As if I had hit a brick wall at a high speed, the steering wheel airbag deployed, scaring me to death as the car suddenly stopped the pace forward. I felt like I was on a roller coaster as the car then cork-screwed through the air. I could hear myself screaming as loud as I could. Flying through the air, I was going right into oncoming traffic. There must have been thirty cars coming my way and I saw faces looking at me in terror. As my SUV landed perfectly on its tires in the middle of the three opposing lanes, the cars all swerved around me. Crazily, nobody hit me or each other. It was unbelievable!

As the car began to roll forward, I pushed the brakes but my foot basically went through the floor. There were no brakes. It came to a slow stop. Just then a couple of guys came running up and tried to pull my door open. It was difficult, but they got it.

"Let's get you out of here! Are you okay?"

Like I was used to doing nursing assessments at the hospital, I began at the top of my head and started feeling down my body for what was hurting. My head, back, and neck hurt a little, but I seemed okay. As they helped me to the curb they were almost laughing.

"Holy cow! That was CRAZY! Like a Hollywood stunt movie! WOW!" they said. They told me they were driving behind me and saw the whole thing. With big smiles they said it was an "incredible show." I then said I was going into shock and to find me a blanket which they did.

There isn't a lot I remember about the rest of that night, but I do remember waking in the night coughing up pieces of glass, screaming and holding my head. I have never been a person to get headaches; in fact, this was my first. I felt like someone had hit me in the head with a hammer. The pain was excruciating. To make a long story short, I was diagnosed with TBI or Traumatic Brain Injury. Not only was my brain injured, the ringing began in my right ear as well. Now, I had crickets in both of my ears. Did I mention I hate camping?

Just Call Me Dory

After my terrible head injury, my friend Kate nicknamed me Dory. I could not remember anything from the previous two years, unless it was a traumatic event. In fact, because the injury was severe and fresh, some of my long-term memory was also affected. This made life very difficult. The previous year we had moved homes due to a new baby which meant kids schools, sporting locations, etc. It was very random which things I could or could not remember. Ella, I knew was my baby, but could not remember the birth or that first year of her life. Picking up a prescription for her, the pharmacist asked me her date of birth. I had no idea! He must have thought me the worst mom on the planet,

"You don't know your baby's birthday?"

Scratching my head, I just kept saying, "Uhm, hmmm." It would not come to me.

"Is this your baby?"

"Yes" I said.

"Well, she looks at least a year old."

"Yes, she is!" I blurted out, excited to know that much.

"So, is her birthday maybe May or June?" he hinted.

"Ummm, YES! June!" I yelled.

He gave me the prescription and didn't call the police, thank goodness. That night in tears I recounted the traumatic event to Steve who so matter-of-factly said, "Why didn't you just tell him you had a head injury?"

"Because I didn't remember that I did!!" There should have been one of those information necklaces around my neck to help people around me realize what my problem was. The problem with that idea is that it would cause me to implement a plan, create, and multi-task which was impossible. I couldn't even find my way home from the store to save my life, always ending up at our old house, puzzled about whose cars were in the driveway.

Another serious problem I had was several long-term memory issues. Sometimes someone would talk to me and the English language would not process. Individual words I understood but not what they were trying to say in a sentence. For example, one of my kids could be talking to me and all I would catch was "table, room, floor." I would be so confused and say, "What are you saying?" This time I would hear. "Someone threw a backpack on the table in the living room and knocked everything on the floor."

One afternoon, standing in our kitchen, Steve was talking to me and NOTHING was processing in my mind. I knew he was speaking English but I heard only random words. Inside my head I was saying to myself, "Come on, you know this!!" Steve must have noticed the complete lack of understanding and total confusion on my face and he offered his right hand towards me to shake and said, "Hello, I am Steve and I am your husband." That sentence went through the recognition process in my brain a couple of times and all of the sudden it made sense and I slowly said, "Yeah! I know that..." I was happy my brain figured that sentence out all by itself without him repeating it. He was just happy I remembered he was my husband.

In all seriousness, this accident caused me a lot of grief and pain. First, I lost my nursing job over it. I had worked for so many years to complete schooling as a single mom of four, marrying Steve only two months before graduation. Second, any newer friends I had made in the previous two years my brain could not remember. Apparently, I offended a few people. They probably thought I was being a snob by not speaking to them or saying hello at a kid's ballgame or the grocery store. I heard that I walked past supposed good friend as if I "didn't know them." Honestly, I didn't! It took several years for bits and pieces to come back to me and by then they did not want to talk. They never did hear my side of the story. Third, several things I had to re-learn such as doing the laundry, knowing my way around town, knowing what sports my kids took up in the previous two years. I remember picking up a picture and saying, "When did Chase play football?" Steve was used to this and said, "Last year, you went to several games." To this day I don't remember the games, just the pictures.

I had to learn to write everything on a calendar, but then the hard part was to remember to check it for schedules and appointments. When I made a sandwich, I needed to remember to eat it and not walk off for three hours leaving it untouched and the fridge wide open. It was a hard time. Still today I struggle with my head injury and forgetfulness. Thank goodness everyone knows that if there is something important, write it on mom's big calendar.

From my first marriage the lesson learned was not to count on anyone but myself. I thought that marriage would last forever and it was okay that I didn't have an education because it would be wasted if I were sitting at home raising kids anyway. The fact is that nobody has control over anything except their own lives and choices and I found myself an uneducated mom trying to figure out how to provide for my children. A completed education would have really come in handy! The opportunity to finally get my education was a gift courtesy of the divorce judge and I used it. However, with a head injury it didn't seem to matter now. All I have to show for it is a student loan I am still paying.

I did meet some amazing families during very traumatic times in their lives and had incredible and miraculous spiritual experiences as their loved ones teetered between life and death. I wish I could remember their names, but someday we will meet again.

Ella's Experience

When Ella was about three and a half, I had put her to bed and come into my room. Hardly any time had passed and she came running into my room, terrified.

"Jesus Christ is in my room. Jesus Christ! I no like him, Jesus Christ! He's scary." While she was saying this, she climbed me like I was a tree and her, a monkey. She wrapped her arms and legs around me tightly and was literally shaking. I had no idea she was so strong, squeezing me like a lifeline.

"Ella" I said, "How do you know it is Jesus?"

"He told me his name and he scary!" she kept saying, "I no like Jesus Christ! I no like him! I no like Jesus Christ in my room!"

"That's not Jesus in her room," I said to Steve, as we exchanged puzzled looks.

She had to be in our bed between us that night and it was difficult to sleep because she kept squeezing and wrapping around me, scared to death. If I would scoot away from her, she knew and would move closer. We never had referred to Jesus as Jesus Christ. If we talked about Jesus in our family home evenings, it was always just his first name. I didn't even know she knew that was his whole name. One thing I did know, Satan was appearing to my little girl and saying he was Jesus to scare her. We began saying night time prayers in Ella's bedroom and I would play music of primary songs from Sunday school on her cd player to fall asleep to. It seemed to keep whatever was evil away.

There was a twist to this story. Ella had a little LDS neighbor friend the same age. When I spoke to her mom, she told me a similar story. In her daughter's case it was some kind of scary frog man that kept coming into her room after she was put to bed. Her daughter would scream from her room, terrified, saying that the frogman told her he was her friend and she didn't want to be his friend. She said he was scary, too. This was the same timeframe as Ella's. Why were these appearances happening at the same time to these little girls?

Ella and Grandma B

Ella didn't have the same experiences with my mother that Savannah did as a little girl. Her experiences were at an older age. At seven years old, Ella came into my room after waking up and told me Grandma B was in her room.

At school in her 3rd grade classroom, she told me the class was sitting on their story rug, listening to the teacher read. She got up to use the restroom and when she returned to class, she was surprised to see Grandma B in the room, smiling at her. She told me she also saw her on the playground once at the school, watching her during recess. Grandparents truly watch over their grandkids. I know grandkids were the most important thing to my mom. She lived for my older siblings' kids. They were definitely loved more than her own.

One other experience Ella had was after the loss of a friend's older son. He was close to our family with a younger sister the same age as Ella. When the girls would play together, he would play, too. He was an amazing, incredible loving older brother. He died in an accident the year prior to her experience and with the grief the family had, we really hadn't seen them much since the accident. Ella came to me one morning and said, "Mom, I saw Evan in my room. He told me he was happy and not to worry about him and that he plays with Brianna all the time."

I asked Ella if she was worrying about Evan. She said, "Yeah, I didn't know if he was happy and I missed him so I have been praying to see him." I was really surprised. I had no idea she had been thinking about Evan or praying for him for that matter. I called Evan's mom and told her that Ella saw him and what she said. Evan's mom said, "That is funny you say that because Brianna told me that Evan comes and plays with her all of the time."

I had called Evan's mom about a month after the accident when I had an incredible dream about him. It was one of those visions, not really a dream. It was as if I were a fly on the wall, just invisible and watching. I was in a long hallway with white walls and white carpeting. It looked like the halls inside a LDS temple. Coming down and around the corner was Jesus Christ walking with Evan. Evan had his hands behind his back with one hand holding the other. Jesus was right next to him, walking and talking in clearly deep conversation. It was a teaching moment as I could see Evan was deep in thought as he walked, looking from the ground to Christ and back to the ground. Jesus was using one hand in his conversation, moving as he spoke and the other looked like a wing sort of as he had it behind Evan a little outstretched but not touching him. They looked like they had known each other forever and a big brother were teaching the younger one through the telling of a story. Evan nodded his head like he understood. They walked right past me and continued down the hall. Evan looked good and happy. He wasn't wearing the glasses he used to have either.

I hadn't told Ella this story, just Evan's mom who was relieved to hear that. It makes me wonder why I would have the experience. What I came up with was that the tragedy had shaken the family so hard that his mom was too devastated to receive the experience at that time, but God knew I would tell her so gave it to me. I hadn't even been thinking about his death when the experience occurred.

Reading Lips

One day I was driving down the freeway with the top down in my car when I realized I couldn't hear anything. I was deaf. I brushed it off as the wind in my face and ears and thought of giving myself a day or two to heal. Around the family and kids back home, their lips would move but I couldn't hear them. The only way to understand their needs was to read lips. I began to panic when it remained unchanged 2 days later.

Running to my doctor's office, she got on the phone with a colleague and then began a long series of tests behind my back to see if I could hear anything, but it was silent. She came to my face and mouthed to me that I had suffered from sudden sensorineural hearing loss, or sudden deafness. She said that the chances of getting any hearing back for normal people with the onset and time that had passed is about twenty-five percent, but mine would be slim to none since most sufferers have minimal hearing at onset and I was completely deaf. She said that 5000-7000 people a year acquire it and treatment has to be instant in hopes for some hearing recovery at all.

Out of the billions of people on this earth I have to be one of the 7000 to get this? Are you kidding me? Of course it's me! It is always me! I don't win the lottery, but I will get a rare kind of ear disease. Of course. I was devastated! My doctor put me on antibiotics and steroids in a last ditch effort to help but was sad with me as I left for home.

Returning home, I had my husband and kids talking to me but I had to tell them I couldn't hear anything they were saying and to write it down or look directly at me so I could attempt to read their lips. For the next couple of weeks I lived in a very silent world. It was such a weird thing to talk and not even hear myself. I was afraid and alone. Here I was, a prisoner in my own body. There was no one to talk to. My dreams were shattered of growing old and hearing my grandbabies saying "gramma" for the first time. The thought of not hearing those precious little voices killed me. That was my mom's whole happiness in this life, her grandkids, and I have looked forward to it forever. I cried a lot as my hearing did not return. It was very lonely watching my friends having conversations in front of me and I heard nothing. I smiled as I tried to read their lips but couldn't unless they were looking directly at me during the whole conversation.

Every night I was on my knees, begging God for my hearing back. I know it seemed selfish because so many are born that way and never have the opportunity to hear. How selfish was I to not be grateful for getting all of those years of hearing my own children's little voices. Again and again I told God thank you and I didn't mean to be ungrateful but "please let me hear again!" My heart ached and I held a new appreciation for the deaf. My heart goes out to them.

My thoughts changed to wondering what sign language classes were available for me to learn fast because at this moment I had nobody to talk to. It was so quiet and lonely in my body and I wanted out. Thankfully, Chandler had started sign language in high school and I thought how he would be the only one able to speak to me. My husband would have me silent for a while until he would learn sign language, too. The advantage? We won't argue about anything at all.

I read this old fable that got me thinking:

Two traveling Angels stopped to spend the night in the home of a wealthy family. The family was rude and refused to let the angels stay in the mansion's guest room. Instead the Angels were given a space in the cold basement. As they made their bed on the hard floor, the older Angel saw a hole in the wall and repaired it. When the younger Angel asked why, the older Angel replied..."Things aren't always what they seem."

The next night the pair came to rest at the house of a very poor, but very hospitable farmer and his wife. After sharing what little food they had, the couple let the Angels sleep in their bed where they could have a good night's rest. When the sun came up the next morning, the Angels found the farmer and his wife in tears. Their only cow, whose milk had been their sole income, lay dead in the field.

The younger Angel was infuriated and asked the older Angel, "How could you have let this happen? The first man had everything, yet you helped him," he accused. "The second family had little but was willing to share everything, and you let their cow die."

"Things aren't always what they seem," the older Angel replied. "When we stayed in the basement of the mansion, I noticed there was gold stored in that hole in the wall. Since the owner was so obsessed with greed and unwilling to share his good fortune, I sealed the wall so he wouldn't find it.

"Then last night, as we slept in the farmer's bed, the Angel of Death came for his wife. I gave him the cow instead. Things aren't always what they seem."

Sometimes this is exactly what happens when things don't turn out the way they should. If you have faith, you just need to trust that every outcome is always to your advantage. You might not know it until sometime later, though.

I took this story as maybe I could have lost my life, but the angels negotiated for me and took my hearing instead. It made me appreciate that I would still see my grandkids. I would have to teach them to sign. It would just be a new normal.

At Kate's house she was having a little party and one of her friends came up and started talking. I couldn't read her lips so said, "I'm sorry, I cannot hear." Just then, Kate said "This is Kayli, she is deaf." It made me gasp. The realization that I was now and forever truly deaf was frightening. They continued to talk and I couldn't get in on their conversation until I was able to read Kate's lips. She made me laugh by telling her friend, "She can't sign either. This just happened."

I said, "I am not only illiterate, I'm dumb! Awesome!" They both laughed.

Kate then told me her father was going to give me a blessing. It hadn't occurred to me to ask for one, but I was pleased she did. That evening, Kate's father laid his hands on my head and gave me a priesthood blessing. Of course I couldn't hear it, but Kate told me that he said I would eventually hear again. Really? Thank you, God! It took about a month and my hearing started slowly and partially coming back to the amazement of my doctor. I am definitely half deaf and regained all of the loud ringing in my ears, but how I appreciate what I have!

CHAPTER 10

The Spirit of Elijah

Turning of the Hearts to the Fathers

Deciding I wanted to be better about going to the temple more often, I spoke to my good friend Michelle. She had the same goals in mind that I did and we began going to the temple every Tuesday morning to help with other's family work.

As a few times turned into a few months we thought it would be best to start taking the new family history class going on at church. The class taught about how to start our family trees and then moving forward, how to do the work in the temple for those who had died. Our ancestors then would have a choice (agency) to decide whether or not they wanted to accept that work done for them. The teachers in the class asked why I wasn't doing my family tree. My answer was that my mother and sisters had already done Mother's side and that my dad was a bad person and wasn't going to heaven anyway so "Why do his work?"

"That is terrible!" was the answer to that. "You still need to do the work for him and your ancestors for them to have the same opportunity as everyone else."

Feeling a little guilty, I said, "Okay, I will do it."

To get this project started, I would have to call my father. It was after church on a Sunday night. Very nervous to call, I thought of all of the ways I would answer, relating to what different questions he may ask. I called him and said, "Hi Dad, its Kayli."

Surprised, he said, "Well, hello there."

"Dad, I started a genealogy class and barely started my family tree and realized I don't know anything about you or my grandparents, your parents. Can you tell me their names?"

He sat for a moment and then began to tell me. Next, I asked for their birthdays and death dates. He answered those, too. Then I asked for his grandparents. Starting with his father's side, he began to tell me a story of tragedy that broke my heart. His dad's mother first had a daughter named Viola. She was so close to her mom and so special. They were inseparable. Viola became very sick at five years old and died one night in her mother's arms of pneumonia. Viola's mother never recovered from losing her little girl. She went on to have three more boys but never another daughter. She was devastated by that loss and her sadness remained until the end of her life. My dad had tears in his voice when he finished this story. He said Viola was a true family tragedy of our past.

This was so sad for me. Here I was at the same time with my own five year old daughter who sounded exactly the same. Ella is so much of a mommy's girl as well. I would be devastated to lose her and vice-versa. She would be so sad without her mommy. This drove me to get their work prepared for the temple. I had to seal this family together. This little girl would not die in vain. Because of her, I was on a mission. The family was going to get their work done as far as I could go back into their line, my heritage.

As my dad continued with a few more names, he said, "Oh, wait a minute...Give me just a minute, I may have something. I think...Oh yes, I have these 3 notebooks from my uncle, Viola's brother. He came by once, your great uncle, to give me a record of our family history. He traveled around the world as some kind of minister, collecting information about our line. I believe in these notebooks there are about 75,000 names."

"What?" I gasped. I had hit the jackpot. "Dad, can I have those?" Ask and ye shall receive. He told me that he would send copies of them immediately. Frank gave me a few more names and information for the night, and we hung up. It was after midnight. I could not believe my luck.

The Most Amazing Family Reunion

Sunday night I finished entering the names my father had given me into an ancestry and Church website. This put the family ready to have their work done at the temple. Interestingly enough, a few names had been baptized through the Church already. The Church in 1905 and 1920 had taken pictures of their head stones with the information and did the baptismal work on them. These family members had been waiting to be found and connected to a family since then. Now, they were finally found and pulled into my tree. To complete the rest of their temple work, I prepped their names online for printing and went to bed.

Monday was a holiday from school and the kids were all home. Usually it is my cleaning day from the weekend, but instead the kids continued to make messes and enjoy another day home. Since mine and Michelle's pattern was to go to the temple on Tuesdays, Monday evening I called her to ask if we could postpone a day so I could clean the house Tuesday and go Wednesday. She replied, "I can't go on Wednesday but can you go on Thursday?"

"Yes" I said, "that works for me." I told Michelle about my good fortune with my father and we were excited to do work of ancestors that we knew a little something about instead of strangers.

My husband is a night owl and I am a light sleeper who likes to go to bed no later than 10:00 pm. I am a bear without enough sleep, so this makes a difficult combination when he stays up late with lights on working in bed and I toss and turn trying to sleep. This particular night I stayed up with him, trying to find some names through ancestry sites. At 1:00 am he finally turned off the lights. I was exhausted and quickly fell into a wonderful, deep sleep when I suddenly felt little hands pounding on my legs and heard a little girl's voice saying, "WAKE UP! GET UP! Things to do! Work to do! Get up!" With each word it was a pound, pound in symphony together.

"OWWWW!" I yelled out loud. I pulled my legs away from the pounding and felt one more pound on the bed that missed my legs. I quickly sat up and looked around. Angry at feeling bruises developing on my legs, I expected to see Ella next to the bed, but she wasn't there. Confused, I looked around and with Ella's room directly across the hall, figured she went back to her room since I had yelled. Our bedroom door was still closed. Ella may come into our room, but she never closes the door on the way back out. The hall I could see from under my door was still dark. Ella would have turned those lights on as well, but they were off.

"Steve! WHAT WAS THAT?"

"Huh?" he mumbled as he turned over and went back to sleep.

The clock read 3:15 am. I looked around for another minute, thinking maybe I had been dreaming, yet I could feel the bruises on my legs from the beating. Totally confused I lay back down, attempting to brush this all off as a weird dream and tried to go to sleep.

It should have been easy to fall back to sleep, given my two hours I had, but soon I heard all of this shuffling around in the room. It felt like a party had just walked in as quiet as they could to surprise me. Opening my eyes and expecting to see Ella back, dragging toys or a blanket, instead there was a group of adults just standing next to my bed, staring. As I looked at them, I wasn't afraid at all. They stood in the formation of bowling pins, both men and women, with one man wearing a red shirt and jeans standing the closest to me up front, then three people behind him and then maybe five behind them, all staring at me. A glance down toward the foot of my bed, I saw a woman and a little girl. My eyes went wide as I quickly sat up and all that came out of my mouth was, "I'm up!" My spirit knew what they wanted and who they were. I don't know how I knew that, but my soul remembered them. It was Viola with her mom and all of the grandparents and uncles I had put in for their work. I don't know the exact count of people present in my room, but I would say a dozen would be a fair number. Never had I seen any in pictures so nobody looked familiar to me, yet somehow I knew them. There would be no more sleeping for me. I had to get up and print their information off to prepare for the temple. I would definitely be going to the temple that day, not Thursday. I knew that for sure. As soon as I said "I'm up" they vanished.

I was tired and cranky. I had just seen angels or spirits or whatever they were and here I was murmuring as I climbed out of bed. Out loud, as if they were all standing there still, I said, "I know you don't have a body so don't need any sleep, but I do. I need sleep!" I opened my bedroom door and walked down the hall toward the office to print their cards for the temple and again said, "Seriously, you have all waited 100 years, what is two more days?"

Just then, the sweetest little soft temple lady voice said a little louder than a whisper, "You know when you're nine months pregnant and every day seems like another month?"

"Yes," I said out loud. Then there was like a long, slow sigh as if I was supposed to think about that. "OK" I said, "I get it!"

I started working on getting the names printed off to take to the temple. Now I knew why they woke me up so stinking early. It was my first time setting up the printer with this website and I couldn't do it. Over and over, I looked up ways to do it, but nothing worked. I could not print these names.

At 5:30 am my son, Corbin, got up to go to early morning seminary at the Church. He drove Michelle's daughter so I called him on the phone and told him to ask if Michelle was awake. Her daughter said she was, so I called her. Michelle answered the phone quickly and exclaimed, "Oh my Gosh, we HAVE TO go to the temple today!"

"I know. How do you know that?"

She began to tell me how she awoke around 3:15 am feeling like a crowd of people had come into her room. She didn't see anyone but felt like they were pushing her to go to the temple. She then looked over at her nightstand where her phone lit up as if I had called her and it even read 'Kayli Coffman.' "I KNOW you didn't call me at 3:15!"

"No, I didn't," I reiterated. "These people want us to go today."

Michelle came over at about 9:00am, which is when we usually leave. Finally at 10:00 am after calling around there was someone that knew how to get the printer working. We printed the information needed and took off towards the temple.

It was one of the worst weather days of the year with horrible rain and flooding. Cars had been swept off the road into ditches. My husband said, "Please don't go today. The news is telling everyone to stay off the roads."

"I have to go," I said. "Do you want these people coming back tonight? I don't!"

We left on very wet, slippery roads. My three younger kids all had orthodontic appointments that had been scheduled during their lunch time a month earlier so there wasn't much time to get this done. I felt like there were angels flying alongside the car as we traveled to make sure we would be kept safe.

The other side of our major six lane freeway had an accident that looked like a possible fatality. A huge truck had smashed a car which was on its nose with the tail in the air, smashed against the median by the large truck. It looked horrible and all six lanes were diverted to one as fire trucks and rescue crews were on the scene. I jokingly said to Michelle, "Okay, angels, I am doing this for you so clean up that mess so that we can get home on time!"

We got to the temple and I walked to the desk that processes ancestry information. They handed me five cards back and said, "These people need their baptisms done and we don't have anyone coming that can do it until a youth group on Friday. You can hold on to them or we can keep them and get the baptisms done Friday and keep them in an envelope for you."

I handed them back and said, "Well, if that is all we can do then I will leave them with you for Friday."

"These, here, need initiatories and the rest of these are ready for family sealings to be done," she said, handing me the rest of the cards.

"Great" I said, as we started heading toward the dressing room.

It had only been a minute when the lady from the front rushed to us, scratching her head and said, "The weirdest thing just happened. A group of people walked in to do baptisms just now that we weren't expecting. If you can wait five minutes, we can have these five cards ready for you, too."

We were really excited. This was definitely meant to be. Five minutes later she was back with the baptisms finished so we could take them to initiatory. We had no problem walking right in and getting those done. Then we headed to the sealing room.

Looking at my watch, we had about twenty minutes before time to leave, if that. Walking into the sealing room, our luck had gone out the window. The room was completely full of people. There was hardly a seat available. We had always come on Tuesdays and there were never this many people in there. This was like a Friday night. We handed my cards to the sealer and found a chair for the long wait. I whispered to Michelle that we probably were not going to get these done due to the crowd waiting for their own ancestors' sealings.

Just then the sealer said, "Sister Coffman, would you like to do your sealings?"

I thought I heard him wrong for a minute, but he was looking right at me. I said, "Umm, yes please."

I'm sure all of the people waiting in the room were wondering why in the world he called me since I had just walked in and they had all been waiting. He must have been very inspired and knew this work had to be done today for some reason.

I could feel the excitement from the spirits of my ancestors as we sealed all that were ready together. As I stood in proxy for Viola and Michelle for her mother, the sealer called up a random guy to stand in for the father. A young man who looked like a returned missionary walked up. Michelle and I were stunned. He looked identical to my Corbin, but a few years older. We both were staring at him as he took his place with us. If everyone has a twin in the world, that was Corbin's. Michelle kept whispering, "That is amazing, I can't believe how much he looks like Corbin!"

"I know, it's crazy" I said.

As soon as we finished the sealings Michelle said she heard Viola's mother's voice clearly in her ear whisper, "Thank you."

We left the temple in a hurry as it was getting close to lunch and the kids appointments. I could not help but think how fast we were in and out of that temple. Something was going on beyond what we can see on the earth. Everything had fallen into place completely until I remembered the freeway accident.

As we hit the freeway it had only been an hour and a half tops since we had come the opposite way of traffic. Expecting to get caught in the mess on the freeway we were surprised to find it clear, perfectly clear. In fact, something was amiss. There wasn't a car on it, anywhere. There were no cars going either way, just empty like a ghost town. As we looked around the city, seeing no movement, Michelle said, "I have lived here all of my life and have NEVER seen whatever this is."

I said, "Did a bomb go off while we were in the temple? Where is everyone? What did we miss?"

There was no explanation. We drove in an eerie silence trying to figure out what was happening. It wasn't until we got much closer to home that the cars started appearing on the roads. I have a feeling that the angels were keeping their part of the bargain and had us in some kind of twilight zone for about fifteen minutes to miss the gigantic pileup that was there. I've never experienced anything like that!

Let's think about this experience. That sweet little temple lady/Heavenly Mother voice said that EVERY one of our days was like another month to these spirits. So, does it seem right to reserve temple work that needs done instead of releasing it to either other family members or the temple so the work can be completed and these people can move on with their eternity? They are waiting and dependent on us for their future and eternity. Maybe we should all quit hoarding names and help them move on. They will certainly appreciate that.

Who Do You Think You Are?

With such a great experience under my belt, I was ready for more. Clearly these people wanted their work done. My goodness, they were stalking me for it. I was happy to do it for them, especially Viola. A few days passed and my dad, for once in his life, kept his word and two of three notebooks were copied and delivered to my house. They were awesome, showing graphs and pedigrees, names, birth dates, death dates and all. I began going up the tree further, filling in as many people as possible. The lines kept taking off different ways and it became a great puzzle I was putting together. I found us marrying into the Hershey chocolate family in Hershey, Pennsylvania. There was also Mark Twain and then I hit royalty, kings and queens. My father began to call every few weeks to see if I had found famous people. I felt if that was what made him give me more information, then that was fine with me. I was just looking to get their work done so they could be happy in Heaven and truly rest in peace. My father and I finally had something we could bond with and talk about. Strange as this may seem given our history, it was nice to finally get to know him as an adult.

More Ancestors

As I worked through my father's binders of ancestors and entered them into the ancestry sites and Church files for baptism, more and more spirits started showing up. This truly was God's work. Why else would all of these people start making appearances? It was like in the movie *Ghost,* when word gets around that Whoopi Goldberg could talk to spirits and they all start crowding her house. I was like the ghost whisperer or something and started feeling a little crowded, myself.

It's not like they were scary at all. I understood, they just wanted to move on in the afterlife and were at a stand-still in progression until someone helped them. It was a regular thing to walk out of a room and see someone just standing there, looking around the house as if he were a visitor.

Two of my boys have this "gift" of seeing them as well. One morning, as my son Chandler was waking up in his room, he looked over and saw a baby playing with some cars that he had on the floor. Near him was a young lady in an old-time nurse's outfit with the white dress and stockings and the little white hat. She wore a name tag that read "Mary." As soon as she saw Chandler watching them, she made kind of an "Uh-oh" with her face, quickly grabbed the baby, and vanished. We have many Mary's in our lineage as most people do, so it is hard to say who she was exactly and when she lived and died.

Chase had told me he wanted to start working on his own Coffman line, starting with his deceased great-grandparents. I helped him set up his account. He then called his grandma to get information about birthdays and death dates. He sat on one computer next to me as I worked on my line. Feeling satisfied that he had a few people put in, he finished his work. Barely a day or so passed when he came to me as I was cleaning the kitchen. There was a strange look on his face and he said, "Mom, do you believe in ghosts?"

"Spirits? Yes."

"I just came out of the game room upstairs and as I was walking across the hall toward my bedroom, looking toward the stairs, there was a man standing there in a white suit. He was an older man with his hair slicked back just standing there smiling at me."

I hadn't told the kids about my other experiences because I didn't want to frighten them, but now was a good teaching opportunity. These were his ancestors. After I had explained that the man was most likely one of his great-grandfathers that he had entered into the computer, he felt better. I told him that he had made it possible for them to get their work done so they could progress on the other side and clearly this man was very happy about Chase caring enough to do that. Chase felt a sense of pride and accomplishment. That changed his fear into relief.

Wet Mormons

For the non-believers out there reading my book, first of all I want to say that it is all true. Everything about our church, Christ's church, is in the King James version of the Bible. From the prophet, twelve apostles and saints to the building of temples, wearing of garments and baptisms for the dead, it's all there. Everyone seems to just skip over those parts even though it clearly states that God is the same yesterday, today, and forever. If you want to know if this is true instead of just assuming it isn't, pray. Pray consistently and deeply with faith that God will answer you. It may not be immediate—or maybe it will be—but He will answer you. Sometimes it is through a warm feeling inside and sometimes it is through someone else. Here are all of these spirits from different religions coming to me to get their work done. Why would they do that if it wasn't important or true?

What I can't figure out is why people have a problem with any Christian religion, especially the Mormons. We focus on the eternal family unit, honesty, being good people, loving one another, service, the community, the list goes on. When it comes to temple work for deceased ancestors, if we are wrong, what does it hurt? We got wet with good intentions in mind to help others. What if we are right? We just gave you, your family and posterity the greatest gift in this universe! You will be with your loved ones forever. What is bound on earth is bound in Heaven, but it has to be done by the proper authority with the true priesthood for that to be possible. This book would be twice as long if I wrote all of the spiritual experiences I have had in the temple getting this work done. It would make a believer out of anyone. My point is I have seen these people in their spirit form with my own eyes. It is real! This work is true! Make a call to the LDS missionaries and find out for yourself.

Little Levi

As the boys had become more sensitive to spiritual things, more miraculous events began to happen. There was a young boy I had come across named Levi in our line who died at ten years old in the 1800's. As he was entered in my "work to do at the temple" list, funny things began to transpire. Chase came to me one day and said, "Mom, I saw this kid peeking into my room as I was lying on my bed playing on my phone. He disappeared as soon as I saw him."

"I know exactly who that is. I just put him in to get his baptism done along with his father. He is probably just curious about you and modern technology since you are barely older than he. Don't worry, he isn't trying to scare you" I said.

Hopping into my big SUV one day in the garage to hurry out on errands, I looked into my rearview mirror to back out and in my 3rd row seat I saw a little boy duck down fast. I got out of my car. Knowing the kids were at school, I looked in the back anyway and of course nobody was there. It kind of freaked me out for a minute until I realized it had to be Levi. Chase came into my room one night and said he had been in his bed with the lights out except the hall and had his eyes closed to sleep. He just so happened to open them and saw a boy standing next to the bed staring right into his face. He jumped and the boy jumped and vanished. That time, Chase was really freaked out. I told him he obviously scared Levi as much as Levi scared him. Without me saying a word about seeing Levi in the car, Chase told me that when he and Chandler were in the car and I had run inside a building on a quick errand, he looked back and saw Levi duck down from the 3rd row seat. That was interesting since that is exactly what he did with me. He must really enjoy these cars from our time period. I passed it off about him being curious, but this kid needed to go! I felt that for sure after he startled me once again in my car. Chase began to complain about him after a couple more sightings. He was intrigued by that car and Chase for sure.

As a family, we went to the temple to do about a hundred baptisms, including Levi and his father. That was it. We never saw him again. That was a testament to me that the spirits really are waiting in limbo for progression which can only be made with our help by getting their work done at the temple.

The Trench Coat Man

After Levi had finally moved on, Chase and I were feeling relieved. After all, he was a little annoying and quite mischievous. An understanding came to me that all of these people, thousands in my line alone, wanted their work to be done for progression. There began to be an urgency welling within me. I have thought back many times of that visit with Lucifer and the voice, "Hurry, hurry! You've to hurry. There's not much time!" That voice of little Viola saying "Work to do" gets me motivated as well.

Plugging through and preparing names, I had just submitted those of a large group of men. Immediately after that, there was one in particular that I kept seeing in the house. He was a very tall, very thin man, probably about 6 feet, 5 inches tall and weighing 160 lbs. He wore a long, dark trench coat that went to his mid-calf.

Dropping off laundry upstairs one night, I was hurrying down our back stairs which are a tight 'U' shape to the laundry room. As I came around the last part of the 'U', he was right there in my face. He had one leg on the first floor travertine and the other stretched to about the 4th step, leaning forward on that leg with his head looking up as if to see if someone was coming down.

At that point I was right in his face and he mine. I totally jumped and almost fell down the last five stairs. Startled, too, he quickly vanished. My heart was pounding and I had to catch my breath. He scared the bajeebers out of me. Again and again, I saw him in the house for weeks. Knowing this would freak out my kids, I said nothing. One day, Chase came to me and said, "Mom, I keep seeing this man in the house."

"What does he look like?" I said.

"He looks like a stick-figure drawing of a man. He's really tall and super skinny and wears a coat," he said, just as I expected he would.

"Well," I reassuringly said, "You know it's a relative so don't be afraid of him. I've seen him, too. He kind of looks like your uncle, right?"

"Yes, exactly but even taller," Chase said.

Because Steve was working out of town, we couldn't get these men done at the temple. I was so pleased when one of the men in the ward asked if I had work to do for a big group of men going to the temple. So excited, I gave him eighty cards to work on. That exact day, Chase came to me saying he saw another heavier man waiting near our front door inside, as if he were a guest waiting for someone to come greet him. That following week, the men were gone. The work done at the temple cured the month-long sightings of the trench coat man. He moved on.

Miracles of Genealogy

There were so many people to enter into the computer for their work and they just kept showing up. It was getting a little claustrophobic and a bit crowded. Now, first of all I want to say, just because you do genealogy doesn't mean you will see people. This just happens to be a "gift" or a curse for myself and family. I know large amounts of people who religiously do genealogy and have never seen anyone. It just may not be the spiritual gift God gave to them, but theirs will be something I don't have.

Genealogy will bring ancestors very close to you whether you see them or not. There is a big possibility you will feel them and many friends have seen miracles associated with doing this. They are definitely instruments in helping you find them or other loved ones. When I get stuck with a family or on a particular person, I just start talking out loud. I know they are around, or their family members are, so I ask them to help me. Many times I have had some kind of inspiration to look for them a different way and have then, found them. They may have whispered in my ear or heavenly angels gave me the thought or idea, but I found them. "Ask and ye shall receive," the Bible says. If they aren't found, maybe they aren't ready so I keep track of their names to return to another time and move on. As long as I have done an exhausting search for them, really making my effort, that is enough for now.

After getting kids into bed at night several times I would decide to put in an hour of genealogy research. As soon as I entered a search site there would be my ancestors coming out of the woodwork. I know for a fact they were throwing themselves in my face to get their work done. There would be people I wouldn't even be looking for and their families appearing in these pop-ups. It was the craziest thing I had ever seen and it wouldn't stop. It was as if I had searched for them but the hunter becomes the hunted here. I repeatedly would say, "Whoa, whoa, slow down. I can't keep up." My right hand was exhausted because as one family would appear, their children's families would also and I would be writing down the order as to not forget about them. It was as if I were exploring a cave and leaving breadcrumbs to find my way back. Each new corridor led to fifteen more and I wanted to explore them all. It was miraculous and a bit crazy. I would find myself at 5:00 am still going strong because I couldn't stop due to all of the new information and people I had found. I had no idea how badly they wanted to be found! Truly, it is the Lord's work and everyone needs to find and help their ancestors. It is our duty.

President Wilford Woodruff had a vision regarding the desperate need to get our temple work done. He said, "In the night vision I saw him (the Prophet Joseph Smith) at the door of the temple in heaven. He came and spoke to me. He said he could not stop to talk to me because he was in a hurry. The next man I met was Father Smith; he couldn't talk to me because he was in a hurry. I met a half a dozen brethren who held high positions on earth, and none of them could stop to talk with me because they were in a hurry. I was much astonished.

By and by I saw the Prophet again, and I got the privilege to ask him a question. "Now," said I, "I want to know why you are in a hurry? I have been in a hurry all my life, but expected my hurry would be over when I got into the Kingdom of Heaven, if I ever did."

Joseph said, "I will tell you, Brother Woodruff, every dispensation that has had the priesthood on the earth and has gone into the celestial kingdom has had a certain amount of work to do to prepare to go to the earth with the Savior when he goes to reign on earth. Each dispensation has had ample time to do this work. We have not. We are the last dispensation, and so much work has to be done and we need to be in a hurry in order to accomplish it." (Discourse delivered at Weber Stake Conference, Ogden, 19 October 1896; as published in Deseret News Weekly, vol. 53, no.21.) Maybe that was the "Hurry, hurry" I heard with Lucifer.

Intruders

One genealogy all-nighter, I was in the office working on the ancestry site when I heard voices outside the office. First I thought they were right outside my window and was wondering if someone was going to try to break in or if it could possibly be teenagers toilet-papering our house. I stopped everything and listened. It was a male and female voice busily engaged in conversation, talking back and forth. All of the sudden I realized they weren't outside, they were already in the house. With Steve out of town, I panicked, "Oh my goodness, someone's in my house!" I think I had a heart attack as I looked around for something to use as a weapon, only finding a metal stapler.

Tip-toeing to my office door, I carefully looked out in the hall. They had sounded like they were walking closer toward the office from my kitchen, but now it all stopped. Either they had quit talking, had heard me and were hiding, or were gone; I didn't know which. There was nobody around and no sounds. I waited for probably ten minutes, holding my breath to not make a peep, and nothing. My heart had been pounding and calmed down. At that point I figured it was spirits I had maybe just been working on coming to hang around. They probably didn't realize I could hear their conversation and quit when they figured out I was going to hit them with a stapler or at least throw it through them.

Going back to my work and adding more people to the temple list, probably forty-five minutes had passed until I heard a sound. They were back, but now two female voices were talking in the hall right outside my office. "That's it!" I yelled, "I can hear you! I'm not doing any more work until you all learn to quit distracting me and freaking me out. I am done!" A few minutes later I felt bad, knowing they were just excited to be found so I said, "I really don't care so much and understand if you hang around, but I don't want to hear you talk and I prefer not to see you either, THANK YOU!" I closed up and went to bed for an hour or so until the kids woke for school.

The Pioneer Girl

In the morning before school I was waiting for the twins to finish getting ready and was cleaning up the guest room in preparation for company. As I came out of the bedroom toward the kids' rooms, focusing on the things in my arms, I raised my head slowly, looking in the direction I was walking. I saw boots in my peripheral vision on the carpet. Right at that moment, thinking it was Savannah, I glanced up toward her face. Her hair flung into her face as she took off into Savannah's room. I yelled, "Get your boots off of my carpet!" It is a big "no-no" to wear shoes in my house. That came from my Japanese experiences with exchange students and then my mission.

Savannah, I thought, was running into her room to pull her boots off quickly like she never had them on. I hurried in after her to do a shoe bust and catch her in the act of untying the many laces and the big surprise was she wasn't there. I went into her bathroom and then walk-in closet and no Savannah. "Savannah, where are you?" I yelled out.

"Downstairs, Mom," she calmly called back.

I went downstairs and she was standing in the hallway curling her hair in the mirror by the kitchen. Her lace-up boots were sitting by her backpack and gym bag, everything ready to go to school. Savannah has always been obedient and respectful so I was a little surprised and mad when I saw "her" dart off away from me into the room. Something was definitely unusual here. I asked, "How long have you been down here?"

"10 minutes" she answered while continuing to curl her hair.

I started thinking about what I had seen. The replay in my mind started with the boots I had first seen while raising my head. They were more old-fashioned than Savannah's and a bit taller and thinner. Similar to my daughter's, they laced-up like the 'combat' boots and take a bit of time to get on and off. The color was aged and not the same brown as the brand new ones Savannah had. Thinking about the girl now, I realized she was probably a year younger than Savannah and smaller in stature. Her hair was the same color brown but a bit shorter.

I feel bad that I must have scared this child to death (excuse the pun), chasing her down into Savannah's room, and yelling at her to get her boots off of my carpet. She had to have been from the 1800's as I think about the details from my memory of her and her boots. There were so many families at that moment I was, and still am, working on that unfortunately, I have no idea who she is.

Steve's Angel

In the wee hours of a morning something woke me. I am very sensitive to feeling like I'm being watched or there is someone present in the room. This is probably due to the threats I have made to the kids over the years about not waking me unless they have a true emergency which does not include needing a snack or watching cartoons. I have always had such a hard time sleeping that they are risking a very grouchy mom, if not corporal punishment, by needlessly waking me. The kids come into my room and just stand by my bed and stare at me in the face until I can feel their stare and wake up with a, "Can I help you?"

Anyway, I woke up and saw a man standing next to Steve's side of the bed this time. I actually thought it was Steve getting into bed. It took me a moment to adjust because he was just standing there, but then I saw that even though he had Steve's build, he was just a little bit shorter. Looking to my side, I saw Steve sound asleep. The spirit was very solid, unlike some that I had previously seen that were a bit transparent, like the trench coat man. With the large bay window behind, and the moon and backyard lights on, his shape had no transparency at all. It also made it difficult to see his face with those lights behind him. This is the first time I had seen angels or spirits on Steve's side of the bed. I had been working more on Steve's side at this time with Chase. Could this be the reason? Did he want his work done? This spirit had a very purposeful and serious stare straight on Steve. I sat up, intensely squinting, trying to get a good look at his face.

I said out loud, "What do you need?" He wouldn't even look at me. "What is your name?" I said, loudly.

Still the spirit said nothing, just a solid, unwavering stare at Steve. I was surprised he didn't quickly vanish like everyone else did. I sat up even more, about to get on my knees, leaning over Steve to get a better look at his face and said, "What do you want?" At that point, Steve woke and said, "Who are you talking to?"

"That guy standing right next to your side."

Steve turned to look and the man vanished. Again, I have no idea who he was, but someday we will know.

CHAPTER 11
Life After Life

Corbin and Suicide

This is a difficult section for me to write because it is still fresh and hurts a lot. To protect the family's privacy I will not go into some of the details surrounding his death.

After I dropped my son Chase at karate, my car randomly stalled. It was very strange as we had just purchased the car and it was perfect. The tow truck driver from the dealership was also surprised. I had Kate come pick me up to follow the truck and pick up a loaner car.

Just as we started to get on the freeway toward the dealership, my phone rang with agonizing news for the second time in my life. On the other end was my best (boy) friend forever Corbin's best guy friend from childhood. Happy to hear from him since it had been years, I joyfully asked how he was. He said, "Kayli, I wanted to let you know, Corbin died."

"Excuse me, what did you say?" I prayed I had heard that wrong, please God, let me hear that wrong. "Please tell me I didn't hear that correctly, what did you say?"

"Corbin killed himself," he explained.

"He wouldn't do that." I said in a confused tone. "He would NEVER do that! He would NEVER leave those kids." As the horror sunk in I could only repeat what I knew to be true, "He can't be gone, he wouldn't do that; he would never do that!"

"I know," he said, "I keep saying the same thing, but he's gone Kayli. He's gone. I can't believe it either."

"Oh my gosh, please tell me this is a bad joke! NO, GOD! He can't be gone! I just talked to him. He would never leave those babies; he wouldn't do that! He would never leave those kids no matter what, no matter what!" I just kept repeating.

"I want to talk to you about going to the funeral together. Let me give you some time to process this and I will call you back. I know its terrible news. I'm so sorry!"

We hung up and then I crumbled. Thank goodness Kate was driving or I know I would have crashed. I fell apart, screaming at God, "Don't take my Corbin, NOOOO!" I sobbed, "GOD, WHY? You've taken so much from me, don't take my Corbin! Please, God!"

I couldn't handle the intense pain. I felt like those cartoons where the person breaks into a million pieces and falls into a pile on the floor. My heart was going to stop any second. The pain inside was unbelievable. I couldn't even breathe. My mind switched over to his children, his parents, his sisters, then back to my own pain. I started hyperventilating, while I was sobbing, "No, no, no!"

My friend had pulled over and was rubbing my back saying, "I'm so sorry Kayli. I know how much you love Corbin."

I had forgotten that my six year old was with me and started asking questions. I again heard what I didn't want to as Kate answered Ella's question about what was wrong. "Your mommy's friend Corbin died and she is very, very sad."

I was in such disbelief and pain, for sure my heart would stop any minute but that would be a relief. Of course that would not happen, not to me. That would end my suffering.

In rush hour traffic it took us forty-five minutes to get to the dealership only to find that God really was watching out for us because nothing was wrong with my car. I truly believe I would have crashed with my daughter and been seriously injured if I had been driving when that call came in. Once we got to the dealership, it started immediately and has never had a problem since that exact day.

Corbin and I had just made plans for him to bring his family out to our place in Texas. We had it scheduled for a few weeks away, but Corbin was going to give me an exact date soon, since school had just ended. He wanted to fly a small plane into a private landing strip down the street from my house. I was seeking permission for him to do so from a family that lived in that neighborhood. He had looked it up on Google Earth and was super excited about it and the small, private runway. He thought it would be fun for our kids to hang out together as it had been six months since they had seen one another. We visited them last in Utah.

It didn't make sense to me. People who turn to suicide don't make plans! They are supposed to give things away, not make future plans! There were so many emotions in me. I was angry at myself thinking, how did I not know he was this unhappy? What kind of a friend am I to not know? Why didn't I feel I needed to call him that day, that time? Why didn't he call me? I was hurt and mad and sad, so many different emotions. Corbin and I had recently talked about some issues that were stressful for him, but he was so optimistic that things would get better and said he was going to hang in there and wait. He is patient and happy-go-lucky so I wasn't worried. I had been through so much intense stress with my life and had survived; he could do it, too.

Corbin has the best parents and such a great, loving support system with family and several very close friends. He could confide in any one of us and we would understand. He knew that! Why did he opt out? I was mad at him for leaving but then remembered I had been in those shoes so many times and knew the unbearable pain personally. Now I felt the other side of it. I missed him already and hoped he knew how much I loved him. My heart was just broken.

Facing a New Reality

I saw Corbin in a dream. It was right after he killed himself. He was standing next to his crumpled body, grabbing his head, pacing back and forth about a step from his body. He was a little freaked out and kept repeating "What did I do? Let me back in! Let me back! I made a mistake. What have I done?" I had never seen him like this as he was extremely distraught. This did not help with the grief I was feeling. It killed me to see him like that and not be able to help him or talk to him. I was worried and all I could do was pray. I told God that he knows Corbin has a heart of gold, has never done anything bad in his life, is one of the most perfect men on this planet and then said, "Please, God, let me take that pain from him, let me carry that burden so he doesn't suffer. I can't take it." The peace came into my mind, "Your brother Jesus already did that." I then asked God to please give him peace and happiness and take good care of him. He deserves so much more!

At The Funeral

I flew to Utah for the funeral. Everything seemed so surreal, like a dream. Unfortunately my dreams or visions are always real, never just dreams. It was so good to be with Corbin's family again. It made me feel close to him. His parents and sisters were still amazing.

When I arrived at the mortuary viewing, you would have thought a movie or rock star had died as the line was out the door, through the parking lot to the sidewalk and street. Who didn't love this guy? He really was the greatest! I felt so lucky he was my friend, my Corbin. He was so friendly and wanted everyone to feel special so wasn't comfortable being the popular guy. He ended up that way anyway because everyone was so drawn to his big smile and silly laugh. Corbin was wonderful and funny, but didn't need a lot of attention to be happy, just love.

When I saw him, like with Ryan, his body was an empty shell. It wasn't Corbin. I spent just a moment with that shell of him. I felt an indescribable emptiness again at the loss of him in my life.

The viewing area was packed but there was another area set up with all of his mission pictures of Scotland and the kilt he brought home and wore. Another area had a T.V. playing a video of his life. It started playing from when he was a baby to that cute little blond-haired boy, into the joy he had of marriage and fatherhood and the man he had become. A tissue box was on top of the television, but I didn't need one. I was all cried out and just hollow inside. There were several chairs in a semi-circle that you could sit and watch the movie play. His family wanted me to hang around until everyone left so we could go to his parent's home and talk. I sat in a chair, watching the video play over and over, kind of in a trance. I felt so numb and empty. People had come and gone several times, but I was alone, finally. Right at that moment of being by myself, I felt this bit of wind pass me to the chair next to me, as if Corbin just dropped himself in the chair next to mine. This broke my trance. I heard Corbin's voice perfectly loud and clear, "Can you believe all of this?" he laughed.

It was so unexpected to hear him and so shocking I flew out of my chair in disbelief. All of the people in line to see him must have thought I saw a mouse (or a ghost). Realizing what had just happened and in my embarrassment, I walked quickly and grabbed a tissue off of the T.V as if I needed one. I sat back down in the chair and said, quietly, "Corbin, I'm so sorry, come back, I want to talk to you. You just surprised me." I was sure he was sitting right next to me, but he didn't say anything else I could hear. I then did a more demanding stern voice, "Corbin, talk to me! Where are you?!" I heard nothing. That's when I began to cry again. I was mad at myself for flinching.

Corbin's Visit

My broken heart for Corbin wasn't healing at all. Between his sisters, mom, and I, we were a mess. I hit a severe depression. Barely able to eat or get out of bed after a month must have been enough for Corbin. He couldn't take it anymore.

One night, Corbin came to me in a dream. Not any ordinary dream, like all of my dreams, I know it was real. As soon as I saw him, I ran and threw my arms around him. Squeezing him as tight as I could, I quickly started kissing his right cheek, over and over. He began laughing, all embarrassed and a little uncomfortable.

"Stop it" as he laughed.

In all of the years I have known him, we have never kissed one another. He probably was surprised at the hundred kisses I planted on him. I could feel the sharp stubble on his cheek against my lips, but didn't care. He, still laughing, yet trying to wiggle away from my grip, said, "You are crushing me!"

I responded with, "I am never going to let you go." I stopped kissing him but had my forehead right up against his cheek, still squeezing him. That stubble was now against my face.

For some reason that surprised me that I could feel it. He even smelled like Corbin and it was wonderful. I felt him relax and he went silent. I pulled my head back to see him staring off. I knew he wanted me to look where he was looking so I did. It reminded me of the scriptures where it says, "Look. And I looked." That is exactly what I did. Looking off in the same direction, this window opened up. Within it I saw Corbin's mom. She was at the family business working in an office or some kind of room. She looked really cute in a stylish short skirt and sleeveless top. In her face I could see that her mind was somewhere else, not at work. She had a sadness that mirrored my own face.

Then Corbin looked again a bit to the left, and I looked. Another window opened up, it was his younger sister Ashley. She was getting kids dressed and ready for something. I recognized that her face was similar to her mother's. Her thoughts were elsewhere and a sense of sadness was present as she held things together to mask her grief. He looked a third time. I looked and saw his elder sister at a desk in an office, finishing a phone call. She then sat there for a minute, staring off and again the repeat of sadness across her face.

Corbin then said, "Why are you girls crying so much?"

"Because we miss you," I instantly answered.

"But I am right here. I am right here," he said, pointing down at the ground.

"But we can't see you!"

He said again, pointing exactly to the ground where we were standing, "I am RIGHT HERE!" He then began to disappear.

Panicked I said, "Corbin, don't leave! Come back!" That turned into a demanding voice, "Corbin, I am staying right here until you come back!"

It felt as if he were slipping through my fingers. No longer could I feel or see him. He was gone. Suddenly I found myself sitting up in bed with tears all over my face.

I believe God allowed Corbin to come to me so that I would know he was ok and tell his mom and sisters what had transpired. He didn't want us to suffer anymore. He couldn't take that, just as much as we couldn't take him being gone. He said that he would remain with us, never leaving. He was very clear that he was always next to us. Even if we didn't see him, hear him, or even feel him, his answer was, "But I am right here!"

From Angels to Devils—There is a Hell

My father had a stroke three months after Corbin had passed away. Because we had been bonding over genealogy together on the phone, this was upsetting. Finally I was getting to know my father and didn't want to lose him. On a plane to Oregon, I flew. My father was on life support. I stayed between Georgene's house and the hospital for several days. Dad wasn't getting better. The doctors said that even if he survived, half of his body would be paralyzed and he would need constant care, probably a nursing home. My father would not be happy with that. He was very independent.

For the last few years, father was lucky to have his step-son from his 3rd marriage and daughter-in-law living in his big house with him. His daughter-in-law, Stacy, was dad's favorite person in the world. He would still trade me or any and all of his real children for Stacy. She cooked for him, cleaned the house, and helped with anything needed. Stacy and my ex-step brother were both good at keeping him company. This was a tradeoff for rent while they attended school and Dad was retired. It was Stacy who noticed the stroke signs and took him to the hospital.

My father's only sister had traveled to come to the hospital that week, along with both 3rd marriage step-sons, their wives, my sister and her new fiancé and her kids who were all in their 20's now. We together made the decision to remove Dad from life-support. He had become completely unresponsive and the doctor said he would not be coming out of that. It's what he would have wanted.

The day came to remove life support. This very strong and powerful feeling came over me that I needed to leave. I couldn't shake it as it was repeated again and again. I had been a critical care nurse and had seen plenty of death so that didn't bother me. It was the very strong feeling, the Holy Spirit, which I needed to listen to this time. I told everyone that I needed to leave, fly home, and get my family. We would return for the funeral. At the risk of sounding crazy, I didn't say anything. Really, I didn't know these people anyway and wasn't quite sure why I was having the feeling. The accounts of what happened in that hospital room were a tiny bit varied by each person I interviewed who was present.

Father was removed from life support, struggled for a little bit which is a natural physical response, then died. The nurse stated she would get the doctor to call the time of death as she left the room. The room was full of people in tears, speaking amongst themselves. After the nurse left, the temperature in the room dropped several degrees. Stacy said she was freezing all of the sudden and had thought the air conditioning had just kicked on, blowing right on her. The room then became filled with a darkness that consumed it. As everyone was trying to figure out what was going on, Frank sat straight up in bed. You have to remember that he was old, weak, and supposedly paralyzed on one side. He sat straight up with his hands straight forward in front of him and his eyes opened wide, looking straight out with a look of horror as he made this horrible and loud, "Haaaaaaa!" exhale sound. He apparently sounded like all of the air was being sucked out of his body. You know in the movie *Ghost* when the demons come to get the bad guy?

"It was like he was being pulled out of his body by devils and he was so terrified that his spirit was trying to fight back and hold onto his body on the inside" was one account. Everyone jumped out of their skin, yelling and freaking out, as dad fell straight back on the bed and was gone. My sister claimed she jumped in the air with a scream and then thought this was all a horrible joke. She said she actually looked around for hidden cameras and began to laugh for a minute until she found out it was no joke at all. She then was terrified as to what had transpired. One other person I spoke to said, "I am never, ever going to speak about that experience. I'm going to tell myself it didn't happen and I won't speak about it."

Apparently, there isn't a warm light and friends waiting for everyone. The bad really do get what is coming for them. Maybe they all don't sit straight up when they are already dead, but demons do come for them.

What Is Private Will Be Made Public

Back at the house, we began to look through his things. Remember how I said that we were never allowed in his office when we were young. Apparently the rule still stood. My sister and I began going through his office a bit. One of us opened this small closet at the far end of the rectangular, skinny office. There, behind a bunch of books on a high shelf were some hidden scrapbooks. My sister pulled one out and began to look at it. She sounded concerned, "Kayli, look at this. What do you think this is?"

As I began to look, my eyes got wider with each page I turned. They were pictures of boys, lots and lots of little boys. That isn't the disturbing part. Every child was wearing the same exact shorts, no shirt, and posing as if to show their muscles with one leg stretching out forward; like a girl would pose, showing a leg. Beginning to get ill with each new page, I said, "What the hell is this?"

I grabbed another scrapbook and began looking. Some of the kids were goofing around and seemed fine, others had a look of horror on their faces and others looked like their soul was missing, empty, like a Holocaust picture. I almost threw up. Right then, I heard this chant coming from my sister, "The sin died with him. The sin died with him."

"What the freak are you saying? The sin did NOT die with him! What is this crap? What did he do? What the freak did he do to these boys?" Right then, Stacy walked in. I said, "Look at this!"

"What is it?" She opened the first page and said, "Ummm, kids camping?" She continued a few more pages. Her mouth dropped, "Oh my gosh! Oh my gosh! What the hell is this? What is this?" She then threw the scrapbook like it had caught on fire. She was screaming, "What is that?? What the hell??"

I heard the shredder and looked to see my sister pulling apart the books and shredding them. "Stop! Stop shredding them! We need to take these to the police!"

"The sin died with him. The sin died with him" she chanted, practically rocking back and forth. She was pushing me away, fighting for the books, destroying and shredding them as fast as she could as if to protect Father from prison somehow. We got in a huge fight and haven't spoken to this day.

Stacy's Encounter with Evil

A couple of days after my father died, Stacy came to me. She asked to speak to me about something privately. We stepped away from everyone and she said, "You are probably going to think I am crazy, but I wanted to ask you something."

"Try me. Nothing is crazy to me anymore."

"I went to bed last night and Shawn was already asleep. I went around the bed and climbed in when this darkness filled the room. I looked over toward the door and saw this creepy grim reaper looking black hooded figure come in. He had a chain attached to his bony wrist and the other side of the chain, Kayli, was attached to your dad. The second he came in, I was frozen. I couldn't reach Shawn for help. I wasn't able to scream. I was completely frozen. All I could do was watch this thing come from the door, past Shawn, circle the end of the bed, then come up the side towards me and I couldn't move. Your dad was screaming and crying saying, 'No, please! Please stop! Please don't!' This thing came right over the top of me and started strangling me. I couldn't breathe. I was gasping for breath and your dad was screaming hysterically for it to stop. It then let go and they both instantly vanished. I had been trying so hard to get away that when it let go, I flew into the air and landed right on top of Shawn. We both let out a yell. I then told him what had happened and he said it was a nightmare. Kayli, I'm telling you, I had not gone to sleep yet. I just got into bed. Shawn swears it was a bad dream, but I know it wasn't. What do you think?"

"I think you saw exactly what was going on. I don't think you are crazy! Stacy, my dad LOVED you. More than me, more than my siblings, he loved you. The worst hell for him would be to watch you get hurt. Maybe that is his hell so he can see how it was for others when he was hurting their loved ones. I don't know, maybe something like that."

Back home

There is a belief I have that when you are around evil, it can follow you home. There are bad spirits everywhere, but when you knowingly go into a place or situation that beckons those kinds of spirits, you have opened yourself up to it, invited "them" to be with you. I refuse to see horror movies, or paranormal television shows or go through haunted houses for that reason. Knowingly going to one, you are in some way wanting to be scared and know or hope you will see or feel evil. These spirits there are waiting for those who are inviting horror within, hoping to be able to remain with you. They are hoping you will invite them into your life or better yet, your soul. They do follow you home.

The fact I went back to my father's house was the only opportunity of invitation these spirits ever received from me. They jumped at the opportunity to follow me home, and did. I was home alone doing everyone's laundry from their suitcases. The family was off to school and work. I was still reeling from all of the horrible events at my dad's house when the hair on my neck stood up as music went on in the house. We have an intercom system throughout the house that you can play music through as well. It just went on, but not a pre-set channel we had, it was very loud classical music like my father would play. Nobody had played music on the system in months and certainly not that station.

Trying to remain calm, I went into the kitchen and turned it off. I looked to see if it was on a timer but it wasn't. If my dad was trying to send me a message, I didn't want it. It was so freaky, I left the house for the day. That kind of event never happened again.

Later I wondered if it really was my dad. It could have been since we had talked for a couple of years about him visiting us in Texas. A friend said to me that maybe he wanted me to know he was finally visiting but didn't mean to scare me. I wish that were the case, but he's got a sentence to carry out presently. Do I think there may have been evil spirits trying to get me to believe it was him so I would be deceived and allow them to stay in my home? That is probably more likely. Either way I cast them out. I have never seen, heard or felt Frank around me.

CHAPTER 12

The Not So Still Small Voice

Saving Chase

"And I was led by the Spirit, not knowing beforehand
the things which I should do."
(1 Nephi 4:6)

Chandler had such a fantastic, life-altering experience that I asked if I could share it here and he said I could. Chandler and Chase have rooms right next to each other with Savannah and Ella sharing one across the hall. The twins go to bed earlier than Chandler, since he is in high school and they are in middle school. The following is told from Chandler's writing:

My junior year of high school had been a very rough time for me. I was balancing church, seminary, a girlfriend, family, school, homework, practices and games, friends, time at the gym, and also sleep. I wasn't doing all that I should have been, when it comes to doing my duties at church. Up until this point in my life no profound promptings of the Holy Ghost or revelations have happened to me.

On a Tuesday night, my brother Chase and I went to a church activity. Chase being eleven years old at the time was in Boy Scouts, while I was with the priests. I noticed Chase sitting out of class in the church lobby on the couch so I went up to him and asked him what was wrong. He told me he wasn't feeling well and wanted to go home. We went home right after since it was almost over anyway.

When we got home, Chase decided to go straight to bed which was odd since he is usually the one to go to sleep the latest of anyone in our family. This didn't bug me too much so I just let him go and lay down.

I proceeded with my usual activities before bed such as getting something to eat and talking to my other siblings. It was only about thirty minutes after we got back that I went to my room. Roughly about five steps after entering into my room I heard a profound voice that seemed to be coming from the right side, next to me. It said, "Go check on Chase!"

It was very odd because I thought about how General Authorities in the church say promptings from the spirit are usually quiet whispers and feelings in your heart. This was definitely like someone was standing next to me, commanding me to go check on Chase.

Right then and there I turned around and, not questioning anything I had just heard, quickly walked out of my room and into Chase's. I proceeded to ask him how he was feeling because honestly I was still confused about what was going on.

Chase told me that he felt sick and thought he just needed some sleep. He then said, "I think my tongue is swelling up." I, being the paranoid big brother that I am, quickly went downstairs to tell my mom who is a nurse. I knew she would know what was wrong with him.

"Chase said he thought his tongue was swelling up." My mom, slightly panicking, forcefully told me to go get Chase and get to the car as fast as possible. I obeyed my mom, ran upstairs while she ran to get my stepdad and her keys. Mom, Chase and Steve rushed to the hospital while I stayed at home with the girls. The next day I found out that he had been going through some kind of anaphylactic allergic reaction and had to get immediate treatment to reduce the swelling to his throat and tongue. The doctor told my mom that his throat would have been completely swollen shut within thirty minutes after he had made it to the hospital. I can't even think about what would have happened if I had chosen not to listen to the Spirit. President Dieter F. Uchtdorf in April 2011 LDS General Conference said, "Let us strive to be among those who the Lord can rely on to hear his whisperings, and respond."

Chandler and Baseball

My son is an amazing baseball player. I am not biased; he is just a true natural and always has been. Little tiny baseballs instead of red blood cells run through his whole body, I am convinced. He LOVES the game!

When our family moved to Texas, Chandler stayed in Las Vegas with his dad for baseball and friends. After a year, he couldn't stand not seeing us and moved to Texas. It is a hard thing to move at fourteen, just starting high school. I thought this would be a 'stepping up' at least in baseball that he needed to push him to a higher personal level of greatness. The problem was his high school baseball coaches in Texas. They were the biggest disappointment ever!

The high school coaches, year after year, had Chandler benched, I believe, due to keeping the football players active in off season. This is Texas and football is everything. The team was horrible, constantly losing, as the real baseball players were bench-warmers. The worst part about it was the school didn't care, especially the coaches.

I have a very strong personal belief Chandler's coach was somehow jealous of his talent so didn't want him to make it big. The assistant principal's baseball kid got to play due to who he was. Politics also let some other school VIP members' kids play, but it was who you knew. Unfortunately, the assistant principal's kid wanted to play Chandler's position which was first base and pitching, so Chandler would forever be benched. Even though this other kid was terrible at baseball and would yell rudely at the coaches, even getting in trouble for marijuana, he played. In Texas, it is all politics and skewed in every way.

The one game Chandler got to play, batting only at the end as the last batter up, when we were losing, bases loaded and two outs, he knocked that ball into the outfield and brought two players in, winning the game for us. It was the only time I have ever recorded him playing in high school and was so excited with the result. In fact, I posted it on YouTube under, "Best high school baseball ending ever." (Yes, that is me screaming.)

That may have been the only game that crappy team won that year. Even so, he was benched the very next game and basically the rest of the season. This went on for all four years of baseball with those horrible coaches. His summer months he was so happy to play on select teams that appreciated his talent and played him plenty. The frustrating thing here is that after the summer season, he would have to wait a year to play select again, since the high school wouldn't let him play. Chandler became very depressed. He had played year round in Vegas and was very popular with coaches and teams. He didn't understand why they wouldn't play him or why they didn't like him. He is such a shy, yet extremely polite, kid and so amazingly talented. Just like his grandfather Thompson said about him being sensitive, he was. He came home a few times, so frustrated he was in tears, yelling, "I just want to play baseball!" The coaches at the beginning of every year tell the parents they "are not allowed to speak to them about their child playing or not playing during the season." You can guess why.

Long story short, after so much frustration, depression, and anger, I had a dream, a vision. I know how my visions work. They are truths that have happened, are happening now, or will happen in the near future. I know this experience was real! It was if I was a fly on the wall or just invisible. I was standing in the coaches' offices at the high school. There were four coaches together, discussing the players on the team. I recognized the head coach of the high school and Chandler's freshman coach but didn't know the other two. They were talking about who they would put on the junior varsity and the varsity teams. One coach that wasn't Chandler's usual and who I didn't know mentioned Chandler's name. Chandler's coach quickly spoke up with a very rude tone in his voice and said, "I'm not playing him! He's a Mormon kid!"

Was he totally discriminating against my kid due to him being a Latter-day Saint? Aren't we over that in America? Hadn't the Mormons been run out of towns and everything else in the 1800's? Are we really still there? That had never occurred to me. Texas is in the Bible Belt, a melting pot of Christian religions. Religious preference being a factor as to whether he played baseball or not, truly had never, ever crossed my mind. I immediately woke up and was like "Oh my goodness! This makes total sense now. Wow, how had I never thought of that? I have to tell Chandler. Now we know why."

Chandler took it very well. I think it was similar to when I asked my mother why my father hated me. I needed to know the truth and I could then move on and get over the pain. Chandler said very maturely, "Well, there's nothing I could have done about that then." He needed to know it wasn't anything he could change or that he did or didn't do right. He dropped out of baseball when senior year started after they gave his position to a freshman. Chandler said, "I'm not going through this anymore."

We knew now why this was happening. I have never allowed my kids to quit something, but this time, I not only didn't blame him, I supported him.

The Scouts

It was summertime again. It was time for select baseball teams to pick their players. Chan had his choice of teams as usual, but we had heard there were a large number of scouts for colleges and some professional teams coming to an invitation only try-out. The high school or select coaches can recommend a kid for the try-out. It was funny when we got there that Chandler's high school had no kids there. We laughed how "of course" that would be the case since the only ones that play are terrible football players. The coaches don't even like the baseball players. Chandler filled out the simple information questionnaire, pinned onto his shirt the number they gave him, and was ready to go.

Chandler's tryout was excellent, even though he was nervous. There were probably 30-40 scouts there. All eyes were on him. The head coach running the whole thing actually stopped the tryouts with fifty kids waiting in line for their turn when Chandler was pitching. This man walked onto the field and right up to Chandler and said, "What's your name son?"

"Chandler" he said.

"We will be calling you," the coach replied and then walked back to his chair on the field next to home plate to watch the remainder.

I loved seeing that big smile on my son's face again. The only time you see it that large is when he's on a baseball field, he truly glows! I'm actually pretty talented at not being biased about my kids. People think I am rude towards my children sometimes when I say how they weren't very good at something or messed up a play. I just tell the truth.

Very closely, I watched Chandler and every other player's moves that day, analyzing their talents or short-comings. I would say for this particular tryout, Chandler was in the top three out of probably one hundred kids there. One kid pitched better but was very slow at running. Two other boys could bat better but had a hard time with catching or running. For a 6'3" giant kid, you would think in relays he would be slow, but Chandler was actually very fast, in fact one of the fastest kids, running with these giant strides. Even I was surprised. Chan's batting was great! Pitching was obviously excellent since that was when the head guy approached him. There is no better first baseman than Chandler, at least at his age. All around, he's great.

The tryouts ended with the head telling the boys that they will get a call by the following Friday if they were wanted. I was 100% confident with Chandler getting the phone call. He was nervous but felt pretty good. There truly were several coaches following him around to evaluate his next activity. Finally, he was recognized for his talent.

This is where I think the mistake came in. I may have jinxed him. On the way home and seeing a strong possibility of Chandler getting signed on somewhere I said, "Maybe you aren't supposed to go on a mission. Maybe playing ball and being a leader that way will be better for you. Maybe that is Heavenly Father's plan for you. A Mormon baseball player in the public spotlight will be your mission." That was the first time in his life I had given him permission to *not* go on an LDS mission.

The longest week of Chandler's life was on, waiting for that phone call. When Friday came with no call, I was shocked and Chandler, devastated. Over and over in my mind it didn't make any sense. Everything from that day pointed to Chandler. They had to have lost or misplaced the one sheet of paper stating his information, number on his shirt, and phone number. There was no other explanation. That was it.

Now, I was upset because my son was hurting so bad. I couldn't understand why he couldn't catch a break in some way. God knew how he had suffered the last three years and that it wasn't fair. God knew how much Chandler loved baseball and wanted this. His pain was killing me. He had hit his all-time low. I wished so much I could take his pain away. I wanted to cry. I would give everything I had so my son could finally play baseball.

Going into my bedroom, locking the door, and dropping to my knees next to my bed, I began to pray. There was so much built up inside starting to boil over from years of seeing disappointment on his sweet face. The broken heart he had for three previous seasons on that high school team, only to grab the tiniest bit of hope again and having that smashed, I couldn't take his pain!

"Dear Heavenly Father" I started, "I come to you not for myself but as the mother of a son with a broken heart." Right when I got to that opening of my prayer, everything changed. Prayer is like a telephone, but you don't hear anything on the other side, usually. You are supposed to *feel* for the answer from God in your mind or heart, or, just have faith knowing and feeling nothing. Prayer sometimes feels like you are talking into the open abyss of space and nobody is receiving your telephone call.

Right at the spot on my prayer, though, someone started talking to me! The line was answered and they were doing all of the talking. I didn't even know that was possible. I had never even heard of prayer being that way before, ever!

I wasn't sure at the time but later realized it was Heavenly Father's voice I was hearing. He was talking right to me, as if in the room, loud and perfectly clear, as I was on my knees to talk to him. Knowing exactly why I was seeking him in prayer, knowing my every thought, He very matter-of-factly said, "Chandler has gotten off track from his real purpose in this life. He needs to re-focus on what is important. When he accomplishes his mission and all of the things he is supposed to do, he will receive ALL of the blessings he is supposed to receive."

It's as if I called to talk, But God did all of the talking and then hung up. I was sitting there on my knees, not sure what to do next. I had all of this pent up frustration and was ready to pour out my soul. What just happened? I didn't get to say anything! Just sitting there on my knees, I felt like the phone had been hung up. Do I say "Amen?" Do I try to say my prayer again?

Apparently Heavenly Father didn't want to hear my "squeaky wheel" so just shut down my whole complaint-fest with a few words and telling me the plan.

God doesn't force people into things, but our family always prays that he will direct our path and point us in the right direction. I think Father was answering that prayer right then. Just like the potter shaping the clay, molding it to become something beautiful, so was Father molding Chandler. God hadn't helped Chandler the way I wanted, or had he?

I have always wanted to do what God wanted me to. I have asked for help in the direction of my children's lives. Obviously I was wrong in what I had said to Chandler and baseball was not more important than going on his mission. Chandler had important work to do, like I had always believed. The thought came back about the blessing I received from Brother S. that Corbin and Chandler had to be born at that particular time for their own particular missions in this life. Maybe it literally meant their missions for the Church, not just their experience in life. Maybe God was helping in the way I had asked him to direct Chandler's life. He didn't want Chandler in baseball, at least right now. He wanted him to go on his mission. Then we will see what blessings he has in store for Chandler. After all, there is baseball in Heaven.

Chandler and the Dog

There is no explanation I can figure as to why Satan uses dogs as a means to get to people. Maybe he is just attempting to create something with four legs and a dog is the easiest to imitate, but he doesn't have the talent or power God has for creation. Satan comes up with the most grotesque creatures imaginable.

Corbin had left for college along with Michelle's oldest daughter and now Chandler was driving to seminary. Michelle's younger daughter was catching a ride with Chandler at 5:30am.

This particular ordinary morning, Chandler pulled into Michelle's driveway like he usually does and waited for her daughter to come out. However, after pulling in this time, there was a very large, black dog sitting on their porch, facing the door as if he had rung the doorbell and was waiting for someone to answer. As Chandler was looking at it, he said the dog turned around to look at him. It was dark and Chandler had the headlights on, but instead of the dog looking at the headlights, he looked above them, right at Chandler. It should have been very difficult to see him in the dark. Chandler said this was not a dog. It had a disgusting black gorilla face attached to a big dog body. He felt so frightened and said it was strange because he should have felt safe being in the car, but the dog looked like he could come right through the car at him. Chandler quickly sent a text to Madelyn that there was a dog on her porch waiting for her and to watch out. When he looked up, the dog took off into the dark. Michelle's husband later said that the dog should have triggered their security lights that Chandler said were not on.

My question is, was it waiting there to destroy Chandler? Was he to have the same experience as I did on my mission with the stripling warriors? Or was it waiting for Michelle's daughter? Whatever the case, Chandler was pretty shaken by it.

Again, what is Lucifer's deal with dogs? Every time he makes or attempts to create one it is so disfigured and ugly. A hint for you, Lucifer: leave the creativity to God. You are not an artist!

Here is another example of this. I attended Salt Lake City General Conference with my husband and two eldest sons last year. They drove down from BYU-I to meet us. We stayed at my favorite hotel right on Temple Square so we could walk everywhere. We had this amazing view of everything from the 12th floor. One morning I awakened to Chandler's hacking cough he brought with him from cold Idaho. As I opened my eyes to turn over, I saw a very large sheep in our room at the foot of our beds. I sat straight up so fast with eyes wide and loudly screamed, "Oh my gosh! Look at that thing!"

I scared the crud out of everyone as they flew out of bed. The sheep was more like a dog as it paused, looked at me, and began to run for the window. As it ran, my finger followed it as I yelled, "Look! Look at that thing!"

I could hear the pounding of its hooves on the carpet that sounded more like a horse than a dog. It ran right out the window, or more like through it, and was gone. Everyone was awake at that point and they said they could not see it after I kept saying, "Didn't you see it? Come-on, you had to have seen that. Did you hear it?" Nobody saw or heard it but me.

Everyone was unhappy I woke them, though. That dog looked like a large, dirty sheep that had some kind of gross dreadlocks covering its whole body and face. It appeared to be, I don't know, grazing on the carpet when I opened my eyes and spotted it. When it looked at me or towards me, since the eyes were hidden behind the dreadlocks, it had an abnormally long dog's snout. It was disgusting. I have no idea why it was in our room and why I saw it for about ten seconds while no one else could.

Attending another conference in Salt Lake City with my friend Wendy who has heard all of the stories, we decided to take a long walk or hike to the cemetery where many of the prophets were laid to rest. It was a true adventure because by the time we got there, it was dark. This made it even more fun. We were joking about how we hoped no "dogs" would get us in that dark place. We actually felt quite safe as we ran through the cemetery using the lights from our phones on a treasure hunt to find another prophet. It was truly a highlight of our trip. On our way to leave, we spotted several signs that stated, "No dogs allowed." We couldn't help but to burst out laughing at the irony.

Steve and Spirits

Everyone's talents are different. Some people have this great ability of playing instruments or making beautiful music. Others have a large voice and singing as their talent. Still others are artsy and creative, can paint, cook, sew or decorate. There are people who are excellent with special needs brothers or sisters, children or care-takers of animals, even those with incredible patience to be teachers of one kind or another or child-care givers. There is incredible bravery that make our world's heroes, and righteous leaders that never waiver. Everyone has something unique and special that many others don't have.

Gifts are a bit different. I am speaking about spiritual gifts here. In 1 Corinthians 12 it talks about the diversity of gifts but they are from the same spirit. In verse 7 it starts with:

But the manifestation of the Spirit is given to every man to profit withal. For to one is given by the Spirit the word of wisdom to another the word of knowledge by the same Spirit; To another faith by the same Spirit; to another the gifts of healing by the same Spirit; To another the working of miracles; to another prophecy; to another discerning of spirits(that is definitely one of mine); to another diverse kinds of tongues; to another the interpretation of tongues: But all these worketh that one and the selfsame Spirit, dividing to every man severally as he will.

Ephesians 3:7 *Wherefore I was made a minister, according to the gift of the grace of God given unto me by the effectual working of his power.*

Ephesians 3:8 *Unto me, who am less than the least of all saints, is this grace given, that I should preach among the Gentiles the unsearchable riches of Christ.*

1 Timothy 4:14 *Neglect not the gift that is in thee, which was given thee.*

1 Timothy 4:15 *Meditate upon these things; give thyself wholly to them; that thy profiting may appear to all.*

1 Peter 4:10 *As every man hath received the gift, even so minister the same one to another, as good stewards of the manifold grace of God.*

Moroni 10:7 *And ye may know that he is, by the power of the Holy Ghost; wherefore I would exhort you that ye deny not the power of God; for he worketh by power, according to the faith of the children of men, the same today and tomorrow, and forever.*

Moroni 10:8 *And again, I exhort you, my brethren, that ye deny not the gifts of God, for they are many; and they come from the same God. And there are different ways that these gifts are administered; but it is the same God who worketh all in all; and they are given by the manifestations of the Spirit of God unto men, to profit them.*

Moroni 10:9 *For behold, to one is given by the Spirit of God, that he may teach the word of wisdom;*

Moroni 10:10 *And to another, that he may teach the word of knowledge by the same Spirit;*

Moroni 10:11 *And to another, exceedingly great faith; and to another, the gifts of healing by the same Spirit;*

Moroni 10:12 *And again, to another, that he may work mighty miracles;*

Moroni 10:13 *And again, to another, that he may prophesy concerning all things;*

Moroni 10:14 *And again, to another, the beholding of angels and ministering spirits;*

Moroni 10:15 *And again, to another, all kinds of tongues;*

Moroni 10:16 *And again, to another, the interpretation of languages and of divers kinds of tongues.*

Moroni 10:17 *And all these gifts come by the Spirit of Christ; and they come unto every man severally, according as he will.*

Moroni 10:18 *And I would exhort you, my beloved brethren, that ye remember that every good gift cometh of Christ.*

Moroni 10:19 *And I would exhort you, my beloved brethren, that ye remember that he is the same yesterday, today, and forever, and that all these gifts of which I have spoken, which are spiritual, never will be done away, even as long as the world shall stand, only according to the unbelief of the children of men.*

Why do I quote all of these powerful scriptures? We all have a spiritual gift, or many, from God within us that need to be found and shared with others so that "all may profit" from it. Think about that again. God gave each of us a special gift. He didn't leave anyone out. It is our job to find that gift and share it so that we all may enjoy each other's gifts.

Steve had once told me he didn't believe in the Church, religion, spirits, etc. (Does he know who he is married to?) I told him to pray about it. He stated he would believe when he saw a spirit himself. Not everyone sees them. It is a spiritual gift and it most likely was not his, I told him. "Well. I will believe when I see." This was years ago.

One evening I had gone to bed along with Ella and Chase. Steve was up helping with Savannah's homework at the kitchen table. While I was working on my laptop in bed, Steve walked in with a puzzled look on his face. He looked back out to the hall and back at me again. Curious and intrigued as to why he had that weird look, I had to ask, "What are you doing?"

"Umm, how long have you been in here?"

"I don't know, for a while, why?"

"Did you just walk into the laundry room?"

"No," I said, becoming excited. "Did you see a spirit?"

"Well, I am just tired…" he began.

Right there I cut him off, "Do NOT discount what you saw! Do not discount it! You saw someone! Who did you see?" At this point I was super excited because he has to believe now.

"Well, I saw a woman with about your height and build walk past the kitchen, down the hall and into the laundry room. I thought it was you at first glance, but you didn't turn on the light and didn't come back out which seemed strange. I walked into the laundry room to see what you were doing in the dark and no one was there."

That is when I had to do the happy dance. Steve finally saw what Chase, Chandler, and I have been seeing.

Just Breathe

Many troubling things were going on in my life and I fell into a deep depression I couldn't pull out of. It had been years since this kind of hopelessness had shown its ugly face. If it wasn't for my children, I think I would have just disappeared. It got to a point I couldn't get out of bed, couldn't breathe. There was no energy to function. I felt like my chronic fatigue syndrome had supersized on me and I couldn't live another day like this. Several times I had been to my doctor, sometimes even vomiting as I went in but after pints of blood taken and multiple visits, nothing was found. My doctor said she knew something was indeed wrong with me and clearly I wasn't myself, but she couldn't find it.

The depression led my brain back to thoughts of suicide. Again, I didn't really want to be dead, just gone and non-existent. The heartache of those I had lost filled my head. I wanted my mom, missed Corbin and Ryan. What about my babies that had died? Were they boys or girls? The heartache consumed me. Crying was a daily occurrence as this grief became a chain on my soul.

This strong feeling came over me that I needed to get up and out of the house for a breather. I needed to get to Corbin's family. The feeling kept coming that I would find relief there. As I fell to my knees one day while the kids were at school, I sobbed about how I couldn't take this life and my pain and heartache any longer. Vividly I heard Corbin's voice as if he was sitting right next to me. He said, "Just breathe!"

I said out loud, "Corbin, I miss you so much. Can I see you one more time?" I heard nothing but I could still feel him there. Again the feeling came over me to go see his family. I contacted Corbin's sister Ashley and his mother who both told me I needed to come out immediately.

Even though I had purchased the ticket it was still a few days until departure. My room felt like a coffin for the living dead and I couldn't escape. Out loud I would say, "I can't do this. I can't be here anymore!" Again I heard the words, "Just breathe." Corbin was with me. Like he had told me before that he was "Right here" as he pointed to the ground where we stood, he wanted me to remember that.

The day before departure I was having a panic attack. So much was going on in my life personally and I was falling apart. Out loud I cried, "I can't do this Corbin! I am going crazy! I can't be here!" Clearly I heard his voice, "Go to my family. It's just a little longer. I'm right here." That got me through the night.

The next day, switching planes and walking through the Denver airport I started to have a panic attack. I began to hyperventilate and cry. I couldn't breathe. For a minute I didn't remember if I was going the right way in this huge airport and had to find the other terminal for my flight. I ran down different corridors until I was lost. My brain refused to work properly and terror set in. As I began looking around, I saw a red and white '57 Corvette model car on display directly in front of me at the bookstore. My entire brain focused on that car as I calmed down, walked into the bookstore and purchased it. I have never seen a small model of that exact car before. To me it was Corbin telling me that not only was he with me, but that I was going the right way in the correct terminal. He was walking with me on my journey to get to his family.

I found the flight and met his mom and sister at his grave where we spent hours talking about life. They loved the model car and also believed it was something Corbin knew would help me calm down and know he was there, helping me.

A Dangerous Situation

Apparently I am too feisty for my own good. I'm not afraid of anyone. I am a fighter. My upbringing taught met to hold my ground and never back down, especially in matters of justice. Total honesty is my personal motto. It is not in me to ever take from another and expect respect. If someone takes from me or my family, hellfire and damnation will come down. My wrath will be unleashed. I've never done well with people taking what isn't theirs, whether it was money, time, a parking space that I cleared, or especially my agency.

This has put me in a few dangerous situations and this was one of them. Sometimes I am so wrapped up in what is fair and not feeling like a "victim" by backing down that I don't see the danger or hear the spirit saying, "Get out of here!" I am not going into all of the details of this situation but will just say it was a very dangerous one in which I would not be bullied, nor back down. As I held my ground for what I believed was fair or right and the situation was escalated to its highest level, sirens screamed out yelling, "danger, danger" and I could not hear them. I am sure the still small voice was not so still or small as it quickly requested from God, "A little help here!"

The confrontation had turned to something similar to a "road rage" incident and this man had those "crazy" eyes—when someone is so angry that they almost look possessed? Their eyes just look psycho. That was this situation. I was in the right and will stand up for that. After all, that was learned in high school to not back down. I didn't want my children to see me as a victim. No one was going to bully me and get away with it because they were bigger or stronger. He clearly didn't know me and how feisty and mean I can be.

The man dared me to say one more thing and he was going to basically knock my head off. I saw those eyes and my spirit told me I should probably be afraid, but then I reminded myself that after my father, no one frightens me! I had just stepped into his face to say what he told me not to when all of the sudden a loud, commanding voice said to me, "Drop your eyes and walk away!" The voice was as thunder and it shook like an earthquake. I was actually surprised that no one else present in this small gathered crowd felt the incredible power or shaking of the quake.

Time stood still for just a few seconds. Everything was silent. There was no more yelling and hostility, just unusual silence. I felt like everything was frozen, like a movie, and I had opportunity to look around at everyone watching this situation including a few of my children who were with me. I looked toward the sky in the direction the voice came from and saw nothing, then at each face present. They were all frozen with eyes set on me, waiting for the next move. I just wanted to figure out what I had just heard and who said it. There was power behind that voice.

To me it felt for a second there wasn't a choice to obey; I had to, no, needed to for my best interest was at stake. Whose voice it was, I knew not. It was not recognizable to me at the time, at least with my earthly ears hearing it. Somehow my soul knew I needed to obey. There would be no standing up to that voice, just strict obedience. I still felt I had a choice to continue the fight, but my soul said, "I had better not." Those few seconds were very educational and changed my life forever.

The noise came back and I was standing in that same spot with eyes on me waiting for my next move at the challenge. What those present didn't know is the time I had right there to ponder the situation. Immediately, I dropped my eyes and walked away. Angry because of my stubbornness and confused and surprised as to why I was backing down, I left the situation.

The voice I couldn't get out of my head. Who was it? Why did I feel it had to be obeyed? Nobody makes me do anything I don't want to do, yet I walked. That wasn't what I wanted to do, but it was important and deep inside, I knew that but not why. There was a point to prove that I was right and the other person was wrong. Why did I obey? Still confused, I didn't want to eat that night or hang with the family so went straight to bed, knowing I would be up stewing for hours. Certainly I didn't expect what came next.

A Visit with God, Our Father

"Ye could not feel his words; Wherefore, he has spoken unto you like unto the voice of thunder, which did cause the earth to shake." (1 Nephi 17:45)

Not even tired, climbing into bed, my head must have just hit the pillow when suddenly I was sitting in what looked to be a bishop's office. Why did I not remember laying my head on the pillow in bed or thinking about things or even turning the lamp off or turning over to fall asleep? For some reason, suddenly I was sitting in this office.

There were no pictures on the white walls of Jesus or prophets or typical things found in a bishop's office. There was a large desk with someone sitting behind it. The chair I was in was not across from it like in a normal bishop's office, but right next to the side of the desk. Something was familiar about this office. "I've been here before," I slowly remembered.

A voice, strong, powerful and familiar said, "Let me show you what would have happened had you NOT listened to me!" Amazingly, it was God our Father. That is who the voice belonged to earlier in the evening, in that dangerous situation. It was my Heavenly Father getting involved and telling me to stand down!

This vision, like a movie screen, opened up and I watched the dangerous situation go very bad. In fact, seconds later, I was killed, right in front of my children. My body was lying on the ground. I could hear the screams of the children and that haunted me. I don't remember if my eyes were open, but it was clear I was dead.

There was a fast forward skip with the "movie" and I saw my funeral and then another skip to maybe a year later in which the children visited my grassed over plot and headstone at the cemetery. The perpetrator went to prison. The pain that my children had to bear losing their mother was heartbreaking. What my children, who had been witnesses, saw left forever scars. The sadness and sorrow that consumed my husband was unbearable and I begged Father to stop. There was nothing more I wanted to see. I understood.

There probably was a still small voice attempting to calm me down at that time of crisis, but certainly I hadn't heard it, and if I had, wouldn't have listened. Father *had* to get involved to stop the chain of events from unfolding. My question was why? People get killed every day so why would He get involved this time? Why did He care enough to stop this event compared to so many other bad situations that play out? Thinking about that question I realized that He probably does get involved with others. I still had a choice to listen or not.

The most amazing thing happened as I sat in that chair with God. I knew Him! I knew my Father and remembered Him. The lack of a relationship with my earthly father and not understanding the father-daughter relationship personally, I expected to be uncomfortable in the presence of men, especially God, but wasn't. This was my Father, all of ours. He was loving and gentle, protective and kind.

As one LDS authority at General Conference once said, when you get to Heaven, you will be surprised at how well you know Him. Yes, we know our Father and He knows us, very well. Another authority said, "He goes by many names; Elohim, God, the Almighty, but prefers to be called, just Father." That is what I called him so comfortably, "Father." As my memory of him and our relationship before this life slowly returned, I remembered talking to him before in that room, that very chair. Could it have been the time when I was stressed about my trials on the earth that Brother S. said I "was so disturbed I went and spoke to Heavenly Father about it?" There was one thing I knew for sure: every one of us on the earth has been in that chair and had a one-on-one talk with our Father. He lovingly talked to us about what we would endure on the earth, our family relationships, hardships and trials to come. We were able to go to him and talk to him about anything. Like a loving father he took time to spend with each of us individually, his special and beloved child. That was so normal and comfortable before this life, but as a human, it is mind boggling to think we could go into his office to speak to Father, or "God."

One interesting thing I failed to mention is what He looked like. I've seen Jesus, but Father—well, I wasn't allowed to look at his face. He didn't tell me not to, somehow I just knew.

Recently I came across a scripture about when Moses looked at God's face, what he said:

> Moses 1:11 *But now mine own eyes have beheld God; but not my natural, but my spiritual eyes, for my natural eyes could not have beheld; for I should have withered and died in his presence; but his glory was upon me; and I beheld his face, for I was transfigured before him.*

Could it have been since I was such an imperfect human and he was perfect, His goodness and glory would destroy me? That is what it sounds like, according to Moses. Not sure why, I just knew to keep my eyes down, almost in a respect for *and of* His power. He wasn't trying to make me feel less than Him; there was a physical reason that my soul understood but not my brain. His neck was exposed to his chest and I did look at that. He had a white gown-like shirt V-necked, similar to the kneeling spirit in my bedroom, but Father's sleeves were 3/4 length instead of short-sleeved. His forearms showed and his large and strong, masculine hands lay flat on top of the desk as if He was going to stand up or had just sat down. His nails were perfectly short and manicured. As we spoke I analyzed His hands and large fingers. They were so familiar as our Father in Heaven's hands. I knew I had seen them many times before. He had held and hugged me with those same strong hands.

Father, in silence, let me think and contemplate what had happened, where I was, who He was, and the million things running through my brain before He said anything more. He then spoke and said something that surprised me. "Ask me anything and I will give you the answer." I had been struggling so much with my husband being a convert to the Church but not really active and it had been a big part of my personal prayers for years. Father already knew my thoughts. I was just about to ask the question regarding that matter when the answer was already in my mind. Again I thought of my next question and as I opened my mouth, the answer was again in my mind. The more the questions came, the more the answers filled my head. If you were someone in the room you wouldn't have heard anything except me saying, "What about…Oh—Well. . . Oh! …Um, I see. Oh, okay." The whole conversation with questions and answers were going on telepathically. It was amazing.

I'm not going to disclose our whole question and answer session because it is personal and special to me, but I will say, with my husband's permission, that God knows the heartache of part member families of the Church. As much as I wanted Father to magically make my husband understand the importance of his role in the family and the Church, one thing Father will not do is take away our agency, our choices.

That is the most important rule in His kingdom, agency. This was what we all had voted for, Jesus Christ's plan to choose as we wish, and Father honors that plan with perfect respect. He did however show me what would happen if my husband chose against stepping up to his role in the family in the end.

Father said He would give me someone else to be my partner and lead my family after this life, if my husband's choice was not to do so. He would give me someone worthy of that calling. I started to tell him my concern with that. He needed to know how extremely and supremely picky I am and that I wouldn't be happy with any old person, but of course, He already knew that, too. The answer was immediately there.

Suddenly a man was standing in front of me, in front of Father and the desk. He had already lived on the earth and died without having the opportunity to marry. This man was absolutely beautiful and completely my type. He radiated with goodness and the priesthood like Christ did. My mouth fell open and I think I said, "Wow" out loud. I said something else to him that is personal and he blushed as he laughed a little bit at me and my boldness. He and Father exchanged a few words, he smiled at me, then left.

Father was reading my mind as I was thinking how amazing He was for knowing my type. As I sat there in awe for that moment, taking in this whole unbelievable experience, Father interrupted my thoughts and said out loud, "Don't you think I know you?" Father is full of surprises. In my head I had to think about that question for a moment with Father reading my every thought. I was thinking, "Well, I believe you knew OF me, of course, and you made me, but billions of others too, like an ant farm I guess. But, you are pretty busy and have billions of spirits, planets, and other things to do. Of course you are perfect and so you have to know everything, but you are untouchable and so far away. I mean really, pinch me, this seems unbelievable talking to you now."

I was thinking all of these wild things, trying to make sense of his question, wondering if He was chuckling at my craziness a little as He answered His own question in a strong deep voice with authority and boldness, "Of course I know you! You are my daughter, I created you. I LOVE you! You are mine!"

I was dumbfounded by that. His genuine and honest true love for me blew my mind. To comprehend His love for me was far past what my little imperfect earth brain could take in. His love could blow me into pieces it was so powerful and perfect. He had to hold back due to me presently in my weakened human form.

More questions were asked about current hardships I was going through that He already knew completely about. My thoughts then turned back to my husband and I asked Father what I should do about his anger toward the Church, for those bad men that wronged him within the Church, the reason that he left. Should we end things so I could move on since I didn't believe he would ever trust the Church again or return to it? Father opened a vision again.

My husband was standing there in a window as if frozen, like a picture. There were marks all over this "picture" all over and around my husband. It was as if I had taken a brown marker and did a little mark or check every time he did something that made me mad or that I felt was wrong. Now I was looking at him through a dirty window, but it didn't bother me; it was my husband on a normal day. Father didn't say it, but in my mind I knew that was how I was seeing my husband, completely flawed in every way. Father then ran his hand through the air like he was cleaning an imaginary chalkboard with one wipe and all of the marks were gone. The picture that had been so dingy was now perfectly bright and clear. The allergy commercials where the plastic film is pulled back on the screen and everything is extra clear came to my mind. There my husband stood in perfect clarity with no marks or imperfections. I gasped at his radiance.

Father didn't say anything verbally, but in my head I knew Father was saying this is how he saw my husband. Now, I saw him that way, too. He was glorious and beautiful as Christ was. I realized he was previously an amazing and valiant spirit in the pre-mortal life. He was perfect and would or could become this way again, if he chose. Father then said, "The only things that matter are his priesthood and testimony." Those were the only things I needed to worry about with my husband. A lot of thoughts came into my head about how I needed to stop picking my spouse apart for stupid little worldly things.

No wonder Father wants everyone to stay in their marriage relationships because all of the petty little things about each other are gone once we pass from this earth. Everything that we understand as important, simplifies. It doesn't matter at all. Father sees us so clearly and lets all of the little things just vanish. Jesus covers for the rest of our bigger imperfections. Things are going to be okay.

The answer that came to me through this experience was that all sons and daughters will have the opportunity to marry and Father knows our types exactly. No one on the earth needs to worry if they don't find that perfect person in this life because there are so many on the other side. If we do all that we can and are righteous, He will bless us with a companion that will blow our socks off. He is the perfect match-maker. No dating site can pick our spouse like God our Father can. He knows us better than we know ourselves.

A Few More Questions for Father

A few more questions about my trials on the earth came up. When they weren't going to go the way I wanted them to go on the earth, I was frustrated. Reading my frustration and impatience, Father said, "Don't you think I want you to be happy?" His questions amazed me with their simplicity, yet incredible depth and meaning.

"I don't know," I said, speaking honestly. It certainly didn't feel like it and especially with what my family had to recently endure in trials. Again he answered with the most tender care, "Of course I do! You are my daughter. I want you to have everything! I love you. You are mine!" I think tears came down my face that time. He meant every word of that and I felt it.

My heart longed to stay with Father, right there, with Him forever. Even writing this experience is hard for me because my heart remembers so vividly His love and I want to go back. I want to be with Father more than anything in this world. I miss Him! I love Him so much, we all do! If only we could all remember this, it would change everything and everyone.

There is a very important aspect to understand about the death of our loved ones. There are no "accidents." You have heard stories of people surviving incredible and impossible accidents. Their time was not up and they were protected. When our loved ones die in what we consider a true accident, it was their time to go. In fact, with children, many, if not most times, parents even knew about this great trial on earth and agreed to it. You are wondering why in the world would we do that? It is your trial to prove yourself to God, rock you to your core, humble and then strengthen you so that you will call upon God and come closer to him. It can destroy you if you let it and let Lucifer's whisperings in, but if you rely and trust our Father and brother, it will build your faith and make your family closer and stronger. In the preexistence you knew that families were forever and you would never really lose them, just be away for a short time. Their time was supposed to be short, but you still wanted them to be your child, so knew you were going to take the pain with the joy. It is the one trial and sacrifice that will give you exactly what you need to return back to Father and Mother.

The only problem is that we never had a body before and I told Father that I didn't know what I was getting myself into, probably you, too. I believed I could handle the pain and heartache and clearly failed that trial. It seemed to be too much for me. What I forgot, what we all forget, is that we are sons and daughters of GOD. We are sons and daughters of a King, of royal birth. We are so much stronger than we think.

I am talking about trials of all kinds here. It is Lucifer that whispers in our ears that we aren't good enough or that we have failed. As sons and daughters of God, we can never fail if we keep trying. Promise yourself that you will be perfect in one thing and that will be to never quit trying, always striving to do better. That is all I can promise Father and, funny enough, that is good enough. We are human and we are going to fall down. As the scriptures say, the natural man is an enemy to God and has been since the fall of Adam. Father gets it! That is the sole reason Jesus died for us. Father is not to be feared. Don't be a God-fearing Christian, be a God-loving one. There is nothing to fear with our wonderful and loving Father.

Again, it is Lucifer that desires us to be afraid of Father so that we give up and give in to him. Trials are there to bring out Christ-like attributes in us so that we may return to Father. We have been told to become like a little child. We need to have meekness, humility, long-suffering, charity, kindness, and love. Suffering trials gives us empathy and understanding of others. Once we overcome a trial we can reach out our hand to someone else that has just begun that journey. *Be patient in afflictions, for thou shalt have many; but endure them, for lo, I am with thee, even unto the end of thy days.* (Doctrine and Covenants 24:8)

Don't feel sad for your loved ones, they feel sad for you. They see everything and understand what we don't. They are in paradise while we suffer, but it breaks their hearts when we can't go on. They need us to so that they don't have to worry about us. Our time is short and we need to keep moving forward and striving for better, not falling apart and quitting.

When we pray the prayers don't disappear into the universe. Father hears each and every prayer as if He is sitting in the room with you as you pray. He is with you. What kind of father would not answer the cries of their child?

There were so many things running through my head. My mind opened up and an understanding of many questions flowed in. My earthly brain was attempting to comprehend His personal relationship with me when the answer came. What kind of Father would He be if He expected all of us on the earth to be these great, loving, involved parents but He, Himself, was a workaholic and absent father that didn't know us or spend time with His children? He is a far better parent than we could ever be. He is very involved in our lives and knows what we need and what we are going through every second. He is the Master. He knows us all perfectly to set us up in situations that would give us the most growth and education on this earth. We all carry His spirit genes within us and He created us to be strong enough to endure our trials on earth.

What I want everyone to understand is He truly is with us. He really knows us, completely. There isn't anything He doesn't know about His children. He could tell me my favorite ice cream, what I am afraid of, my favorite flower, color, what food I liked best, everything. Like we know the likes and dislikes of our children, what they are allergic to, their fears, anything, and we are imperfect, Father knows us perfectly. He is so awesome! Truly, He is the perfect Father. I miss Him every day. This has changed the way I pray to Him. Now, I just talk to Him during prayer. It isn't a practiced, boring typical prayer anymore, well at least privately. I can cry and tell Him what stresses me out because He already knows but wants to hear it from me, from all of us. It is the communication aspect He is looking for. Just like we know what may be bothering our children, we want them to open up and tell us. I am trying to put that experience of His love for us into words for every one of you, my brothers and sisters, hoping you can comprehend it in some way. It would change everything in this world if everyone could understand it.

Know who you are. You are His. You are precious, special, unique and individual. There was no mistake in the way you were made and He loves you for you! Oops, I forgot to ask Him about fixing the LDS singles program. My bad!

A Few Things About God and Agency

Even when Father commanded me to walk away, still I had my agency to stay and fight. I chose to listen, not knowing why. Had I not listened to Father due to my agency, He showed me the outcome. There was a choice for me here, to listen or not. Even Adam and Eve had the tree to eat from. In Moses 2:3 He commanded them not to eat of the tree of knowledge of good and evil but they could "choose for thyself, for it is given unto thee; but, remember that I forbid it," meaning agency.

The outcome would be that they had to leave the Garden of Eden. My outcome would have been I would have had to leave the earth as I know it (meaning physically, not necessarily spiritually). He may use his voice as a command, as in my situation, but will not take away our power, my agency to choose what decision to make.

Next thing, God doesn't let bad things happen to good people. People let bad things happen to good people. Again, agency is here. Our brothers and sisters in this world (people) take away agency of other brothers and sisters by using it to do bad things to good people. It breaks Father's heart. He will not take away their agency. He will, however, judge them on how they use their agency on earth and it will be very ugly for those who use it to hurt other people. The pain of our innocent brothers and sisters will be very short lived. Angels are always present with them during this awful experience to strengthen them and assist them through it and many times, to take them home to Heaven. They are not alone! Father will then make up to those who get hurt by someone else's poor use of agency. We may not and usually don't get satisfaction or a reward on this side, but the make-up on the other side is 1000x better than what we could receive or even imagine on the earth. Those who pass before their time will not lose the opportunity to do all of those things missed on the earth. They will still get to be married, have children, everything. God is fair and the universe balanced. That would not be fair if the innocent lost that opportunity because of other's agency to be evil. Have faith in his complete and perfect justice. He loves us all so much!

Lastly, because Father does not intervene in our agency, the scripture quote of "Ask and ye shall receive" has a whole new meaning for me. If we think we can do something by ourselves and don't ask for help, Father won't help. Isn't that what we asked for? When we finally get tired of falling on our face and humble ourselves enough to ask for help, then can Father help us. At that point, that is using our agency, to allow Him to help. Prior to asking, He won't intervene because of our desire to do it on our own. If you keep spoon-feeding your baby, how do they ever learn to eat? You give them a spoon to try and when they communicate to us they need our help and are hungry, we assist them with feeding themselves by holding the spoon together which teaches them to eat on their own. My point is, don't "expect" Father to jump into your problem and fix it because He "knows" what is going on or should fix it just because He is God. He can but usually won't intervene unless you ask. He doesn't want to and won't disrespect our gift of agency. Ask and ye shall receive, not always instantly but in the way that benefits you the most in the long run. Have faith in Him because Father truly does know best!

Does Father Weep?

There are no human or earthly words to describe God. The best I can come up with is glorious and beautiful, perfect and peaceful. Those words don't say what I want them to. Our Father in Heaven is indescribable and incredible, full of love in a complete and perfect form. He feels deeply for his children. He also hurts when we hurt, as a parent does. The book of Moses, chapter 7, is in my opinion the most perfect representation of God that we can comprehend as humans. Enoch sees God weeping and says in verse 28:

> *And it came to pass that the God of heaven looked upon the residue of the people, and he wept; and Enoch bore record of it, saying: How is it that the heavens weep, and shed forth their tears as a rain upon the mountains? And Enoch said unto the Lord: How is it that thou canst weep, seeing thou art holy, and from all eternity to all eternity? And where it possible that man could number the particles of the earth, yea, millions of earths like this, it would not be a beginning to the number of thy creations; and thy curtains are stretched out still; and yet thou art there, and they bosom is there; and also thou art just; thou art merciful and kind forever;*

Stop here for a second. It just came to me that Enoch is describing Him like I do. I love this. He is merciful and kind and there for us. Sorry for the interruption, read on.

> *And thou hast taken Zion and to thine own bosom, from all my creations, from all eternity to all eternity; and naught but peace, justice, and truth is the habitation of thy throne; and mercy shall go before thy face and have no end; how is it thou canst weep?*
>
> *The Lord said unto Enoch; Behold these thy brethren; they are the workmanship of mine own hands, and I gave unto them their knowledge, in the day I created them; and in the garden of Eden, gave I unto man his agency;*
>
> *And unto thy brethren have I said, and also given commandment, that they should love one another, and that they should choose me, their Father; but behold, they are without affection, and they hate their own blood;*
>
> *And the fire of mine indignation is kindled against them; and in my hot displeasure* (Stop. Notice his words, "hot displeasure." He doesn't

> want to do this but must in order to keep a perfect justice) *will I send in the floods upon them, for my fierce anger is kindled against them.*
>
> *Behold I am God; Man of Holiness is my name; Man of Counsel is my name; and Endless and Eternal is my name, also.*
>
> *Wherefore, I can stretch forth mine hands and hold all the creations which I have made; and mine eye can pierce them also, and among all the workmanship of mine hands there has not been so great wickedness as among thy brethren.*
>
> *But behold, their sins shall be upon the heads of their fathers; Satan shall be their father, and misery shall be their doom; and the whole heavens weep over them, even all the workmanship of mine hand; wherefore should not the heavens weep, seeing these shall suffer?*
>
> *But behold, these which thine eyes are upon shall perish in the flood; and behold, I will shut them up; a prison have I prepared for them.*
>
> *And that which I have chosen have pled before my face* (Jesus is who he is talking about). *Wherefore he suffereth for their sins; inasmuch as they will repent in the day that my Chosen shall return unto me, and until that day they shall be in torment;*
>
> *Wherefore, for this shall the heavens weep, yea, and all the workmanship of mine hands.*

All I can say to this whole section of scripture is "Wow." It is so profound. Here is our Father, God, the Creator of all, crying because of the poor choices made by our agency. As people, we hurt one another by lying, stealing, and killing when we are commanded to love one another. Is it fair to blame God for the bad things happening on the earth? No, it hurts Him too. He will make it right, but we must be patient and long-suffering like he has asked us to do.

Mother Earth and Natural Disasters

Does Father want to knock the evil right off of the earth? Yes, but He won't interrupt the plan we all agreed to that involved agency. Is He "itching" to clean it up? I would like to say yes but I will say no because He is perfectly patient, allowing our plan to go forward. The earth itself is 'itching' to clean itself up. That is why there are earthquakes and tsunamis, volcanoes and floods. In

Moses 2:5 God states that all things were created spiritually before they were naturally.

The earth was created in a spirit form first, what a concept. It is a spirit, made perfectly in glory and beauty. Like a dog trying to shake or scratch the flea infestation off of itself, so is the earth. The more filth on it, the more the disasters will happen. They will become a lot worse. In Moses 7:48 it reads,

> *And it came to pass that Enoch looked upon the earth; and he heard a voice from the bowels thereof, saying: Wo, wo is me, the mother of men; I am pained, I am weary, because of the wickedness of my children. When shall I rest, and be cleansed from the filthiness which is gone forth out of me? When will my Creator sanctify me that I may rest, and righteousness for a season abide upon my face? And when Enoch heard the earth mourn, he wept, and cried unto the Lord, saying: O Lord, wilt thou not have compassion upon the earth?*

The spirit of the earth begs to be cleansed from all of the sin thereon. As our bodies were made from the dust of the earth, so we will return as dust to the earth. We have not loved and respected our Mother Earth but have made it filthy with sin and all manner of wickedness. Of course earth wants to get rid of the filth upon it. Of course innocent people will perish as well as the wicked every time. Are there wars, famine, plague and disasters coming our way? All I can say is, we haven't seen anything yet!

Sin

In the movie *God's Not Dead* an exchange between an elderly mother, suffering from dementia, and her selfish, arrogant son provides enlightenment. Her son observes that after all of her years of praying and believing, she has benefitted very little.

"You are the nicest person I know. I am the meanest person and I have everything and am happy."

"Sometimes the devil allows people to live a life free of trouble because he doesn't want people turning to God. Their sin is like a jail cell, except it is all nice and comfy and there doesn't seem to be any reason to leave. The door is wide open. Till one day time runs out and the door slams shut and suddenly it's too late to get out," his mother replies, not even recognizing it is her son she is talking to.

What a profound and true thought about the great deceiver, our brother Lucifer. He makes evil in the world look very comfortable until time runs out and he has those souls encaged. Don't let this happen to you.

CHAPTER 13

For the Followers of Christ

Food Storage, Do It!

The prophets have told us to get our food and water storage. They aren't kidding! If you think they are going to come out the Sunday before a disaster and tell you details such as "This Friday at 9:00 pm there will be an earthquake across all of North and South America and there won't be any available food so get your food this week," think again. It's called obedience. They have been more than patient and generous telling us time and time again. If you haven't listened by now, you have not been obedient and are going to be hungry.

The amount of disobedient members of Christ's church is mind-boggling. That is why they have told us so many times, hoping maybe this time you will listen. You will only have yourself to blame when your children cry for food, not the prophets or God, yourself! Take responsibility and get it together, now!

Bad Mormon Behavior: Quit It!

One thing about members of the Church of Jesus Christ of Latter-day Saints, they know stuff! They know that they are supposed to represent Jesus Christ in word and deed. They are supposed to go the extra mile and act even better than what is expected. So let's just talk about my Mormon neighbor Megan (name changed). Here is your typical transplanted Utah Mormon, living in my neighborhood in Las Vegas. My little Corbin liked to play with her son. Corbin came home crying one day and said, "I can't play with Brenten anymore. His Mom said it's because you and Daddy are divorcing."

What?? Are you kidding me? Shame on you, Megan! What kind of person would turn a five-year-old little boy away, whose parents are divorcing? I would have gone out of my way, if the tables were turned, to give your child extra love and attention through a difficult time. I would have let my home be a place of refuge for your little boy! Again, what kind of person would do that? Let me answer that…a very, very bad person. If there is one thing I can't stand more than thieves and liars, it is wolves in sheep's clothing, the hypocrites!

Megan held a compassionate service calling when I was in the car wreck that almost took my life and gave me traumatic head injury. She sent no meals in to my family, probably telling the Relief Society president that she had. She was sure to be the one that put a noose around my neck and kicked the chair out, pinned the scarlet A's to all of my clothing when I was pregnant with the twins, and the one that insisted everyone bring their bag of stones to the town square for my stoning. She is one of the very worst examples I have seen, EVER, of a member of Christ's church. This is the same Megan that when I took myself, unmarried, and children to church and put the twins in nursery, she came up to me and said, "Nobody wants your little bastard children here."

Unbelievable, right? Yet, Megan would smile and pat them on the head when anyone walked down the hall past us. She also made sure my children were ostracized from the neighborhood carpools so they would be the only ones not invited. She then pulled up to my middle school son, Corbin, one day with a car full of our neighborhood kids and challenged him to a race. My kid who wasn't wearing a bike helmet because it wasn't mandatory, she challenged to a race with an auto full of children she was responsible for to take home! Megan told him she would give him $20 if he beat them to the corner stop sign. What twelve-year-old boy wouldn't try to win that? Not only did she make sure he didn't win with all the kids in the car watching, she hit him! Yes, she hit him with her car. He crashed and she took off. He walked his broken bike and bloody body home. His new shirt I had just bought for him, torn and bloody. That was it! I called the police and the school. I was done with whatever her problem was with me and my children. Finally I was done turning the other cheek and when the police came to her house and the school (she was on the PTA of course) called her in, she was livid, calling me, screaming and yelling, to which I yelled back and hung up on her. This time, I fought back and she wasn't used to it.

When I got to a Relief Society dinner activity shortly after the bike accident event, she was sitting at the table I usually sit at with the women I talk to, trying to keep me from telling what had happened. Knowing what she was up to, I sat at another table with the wives of the bishopric and about five others. She couldn't keep her eyes off us, wondering what we were talking about. I told the table what had happened and everyone was gasping. She knew it was the story she didn't want out and came over and in such a disgustingly sweet way and said, "Kayli, I think there has been a horrible misunderstanding..."

I cut her off and said, "There is no misunderstanding, Megan! You challenged my child with no helmet on a race against your car full of neighborhood children! You then hit him and drove away! There is no misunderstanding and don't you EVER, EVER come near my children again or you will answer to me!"

Funny enough, and thank goodness for everyone, she moved back to Utah right after that where the majority of those Mormons stem from. God will take care of people like that.

Megan is the perfect example of a LDS member that drives people out of the Church. The worth of souls is great in the sight of God, every soul! I wouldn't want to answer to Father for that. For those of you injured by a Megan, come back. There are so many truly good members that are here to help you and bring you back to the safety of the fold with open arms. Don't let a Megan keep you from all of the blessings you and your family deserve. There are so many promises God has in store for you. Jesus will leave the ninety-nine sheep (members of his church) to search for the one (that has been lost from/never been part of his fold). I love the symbolism he teaches by. It shows your incredible worth.

I have a very close friend that lives in a typical nice neighborhood in Salt Lake City with her husband and four children. She is the great granddaughter of a prophet who passed on many years ago. Because her parents left the church, she wasn't raised in it and has almost no knowledge of its teachings.

Can you believe that? A prophet's great granddaughter knows nothing about the Church except when I asked her she responded, "He was a prophet. I guess that it's a big deal in your church."

"YEAH" I said. "Huge!"

When asking about their neighborhood she responded, "Nobody talks to us because we aren't Mormon."

My heart is very sad about that. I am sure our beloved prophet would love to have a family befriend his great granddaughter and teach them about the Church. The funny thing is, if I revealed who she was and where she lived, everyone would want to be her best friend. Why? She shouldn't be treated any differently than any other person or family living on your block. Why can't we treat everyone like that? They are all God's children. Wouldn't we want to fellowship God's son or daughter who knows nothing about the Church and teach them the gospel, too?

One thing I know about Jesus is he did not hang around with "members" or join the "members-only" club but instead preferred the company of widows, lepers and prostitutes. He went to help and serve those who were abandoned, alone, and truly humble. If we want Jesus in our own lives, we need to follow his example.

Glass Houses

A word to the rest of the LDS people: Do not sit in your glass houses, looking down and throwing stones at others. Quit buying your cases of Windex to polish your glass to see better. Shame on you!! Repent!

For those of you that do not let your children play with other neighbor kids who aren't LDS, stop it!! That is so cruel! This church was built on converts. Your ancestors were converts. All of the pioneers or their parents were converts, so quit thinking your "good-ol-boy" Mormon blood somehow makes you better or more superior than anyone else. That "born into Mormon blood" WILL NOT SAVE YOU! Remember that the "First shall be last." Do you all really want to be last? Yes, I am talking to you, quit thinking about your neighbor right now and look at yourself! Quit pointing your finger because three fingers are pointing right back at you!

Would Jesus run that little child of divorce off? No, he would have taken him into his arms and said, "I am so sorry for your pain, so sorry!" Jesus would have wept with my child, not ostracized him. What would Jesus do to those Catholic or Protestant children and parents that just moved in to an all-Mormon neighborhood? He would welcome them with love and bread. He would invite them into his home. He would comfort them, befriend them, and most of all, love them! Again, repent! I am so tired of apologizing while sitting on airplanes with regular people, hearing stories of terrible behavior by judgmental Latter-day Saints, especially in Utah. These families feeling unwelcome and shut out of neighborhoods because they were not LDS has got to stop. You all have the biggest responsibility to rally around, love and nurture these families. There is a reason God put them right there in your neighborhood, for you to love and to teach. That is your personal assignment. Make an effort. When that doesn't work, make a greater effort! If that still doesn't work? Try harder! You will be judged on how you handle that opportunity. Never quit. You may be the only chance they have on the earth to hear about Christ and his restored church.

Are you really going to pull out your Windex right now? They, not knowing anything about the gospel, are better off than you. You know the gospel and don't share it or even worse, don't act it? Is that what you are teaching your children? That they are to judge and turn people away? Do you love your children at all? Do you want them to make it back to our Father? Stop it now! Stop teaching them Satan's way. Who are you serving? When the hurricanes come, your pretty little glass house will crash and fall and so will your family! That is a promise!

Defended

I recently met a wonderful transvestite from New York that lives in Amsterdam, Netherlands. She is now named Ashlie. On a blog with hundreds of people making jokes about Mormons and "magic underwear," I had said that they were not secretive, but sacred. That fueled rage and hate in which Ashlie stood up to the lynch mob, demanding respect for our religion, covenants and sacredness of our holy garments. It was such an amazing act of courage and love on behalf of someone not familiar with our religion.

Ashlie went on to say how she is treated by the LDS people with hate, judgement and disdain but hopes her example of respect will teach us to offer the same for others. She still stood firm, demanding respect for what was holy to us as LDS members.

Amazed at her love and Christ-like attributes, I contacted her and told her that if members of the Church treat her unkindly and have "disdain" for her, they are not true members of Christ's church. Christ didn't judge others and throw people out. Christ didn't have disdain for anyone, except maybe the hypocrites. I thanked her for standing up for our beliefs and her respect of that which is special to us. Then, I assured Ashlie that she was special and truly loved by our Father and our brother, Jesus. She "is welcome at my dinner table any time." She responded by an, "Awwww...thank you." Our job is to love all of our brothers and sisters—that is it!

One more chastisement for all: Inside the church, people have problems. Marriages end in divorce. Teens get pregnant. Members have substance abuse problems. People make mistakes. QUIT JUDGING! If that was your sister going through the divorce, would you ostracize her? No, you would feel terrible, not gloat. You would love her, try to comfort her, be there for her. Do you turn her children away? They would need you at that time the most to listen and to love them. Take them out for ice cream. Let them know you are there for them, that it's not their fault. Love them! When your niece gets pregnant do you shut her out? Do you pull out your bag of stones and start the death sentence? I should hope not. Your sins may be different than her sins but we all have sins. You help her through the process. If she gives up the child, you support her. If she keeps that baby, throw her a shower. Love her! When you find out your own teenager has been using cocaine or meth, do you disown them or throw them on the streets? NO! Get them the help they need. Support them. Love them! Stop being so hard on "imperfect" families in difficult situations! Maybe your life and your marriage are going smooth right now. It can change in one day. I felt as if my marriage was almost perfect. It changed in one day. You are not immune. It may seem so now, but you are not. Quit it! We are all truly brothers and sisters. When you get that through your head, you will stop this bad behavior.

I tell you hard things because I care. Don't think I am not talking to myself, too. I am farther from perfect than most. I love my brothers and sisters of this earth (well, most of them. I need to work on that) and want all of us to make it back to Mother and Father's table for dinner. My motto is "no empty chairs." Please understand that in no situation in this book am I boasting or think in any way I am better than you. In fact, I have probably more sins and more things to learn than most anyone. I believe that is why I have to have a bit more hand-holding than most through this life by Father and Mother. Please accept my apology if it comes across that way. In the New Testament John 20:29 it reads:

> *Jesus saith unto him, Thomas, because thou hast seen me, thou hast believed: blessed are they that have not seen, and yet have believed.*

I rest my case.

This book with many of my spiritual experiences is to share that there is a daily, even minute by minute war going on for your soul. Every choice you make puts you on either the good or bad side. It is hard when the world has numbed most people on the earth to feeling for that light of Christ. Remember that Satan is the ruler of this world for now and is allowed to tempt and try us. That was OUR choice to allow. Don't blame our Father. This is for our good. Once you touch a hot stove and are burned as a child, you won't touch it again. You learned from that experience. This life is a series of learning adventures, but don't let Satan take hold of your heart or numb you to Father or our brother, Jesus. I know what is going on all around us on earth and the other side. I've seen much more than I have written. This is my soul to keep and I will not allow Lucifer to encage it after our brief life. Never cease calling on God for deliverance from evil. He will not forsake you. I have seen ancient armed warriors from Heaven with my own eyes, standing guard to protect me from Satan and his followers on more than one occasion. I felt the evil coming for me and asked, then received. I pray that I have included each of the experiences Father wanted me to as I dedicate this book to Him.

We are all equal in the eyes of our Heavenly Father and Mother. I just want to help you if I can by sharing my experiences. Know you are loved, important, always watched over and thought about.

This is my work and my glory, to assist our Father, to bring to pass the immortality and eternal life of man, or you and your ancestors, my brothers and sisters.

Homesick

The other day was a rough one for me. In fact the prior three days were also bad. I became so down and discouraged. After crying most of the day, and then cleaning and organizing the house I retreated to bed at 2:00 am. In bed, tears ran down my face as I silently prayed to God. I said, "Father, I feel so down and sad. I don't want you to think I am ungrateful for the time you already spent with me because it was the highlight of my life on earth. I just miss you and home. Do you hug your children? As you know, I have never had a Father's hug. I sat with you and you never touched or hugged me. I didn't ask why because I didn't think about it. I feel so down and could really use a hug from you right now."

I had just said that as my husband completely asleep scooted over and hugged me like I have never been hugged before. He is not a touchy, feely guy by any standard and this was not like he was making a pass at me. He wrapped his arms around me and pulled me in tight, really tight. In fact I have never felt strength and power from him like that. He held me tight for about ten minutes as my quiet tears soaked the pillow. He then let go and rolled away. I whispered, "Thank you, Father."

The next morning I asked my husband if he remembered that he hugged me the night before. He answered, "Really? I did that?"

I knew it wasn't him. It was definitely our Father.

Final Message

My dear brothers and sisters, there will be days and nights when you feel overwhelmed, when your hearts are heavy and your heads hang down. Then, please remember, Jesus Christ, the Redeemer, is the Head of this Church. It is His gospel. He wants you to succeed. He gave His life for just this purpose. He is the Son of the living God. And He will help you.

—President Dieter F. Uchtdorf
Church of Jesus Christ of Latter-day Saints

Now What?

The day after I finished this book my doctor called. Now it seems I have cancer. I called Chaney and the first thing she said, "Of course you do! Everything happens to you. Why leave out cancer?" This starts a whole new chapter in my life's adventures. Will there be another book? Not a chance!

Author can be reached by email at Mysoultokeepbook@gmail.com

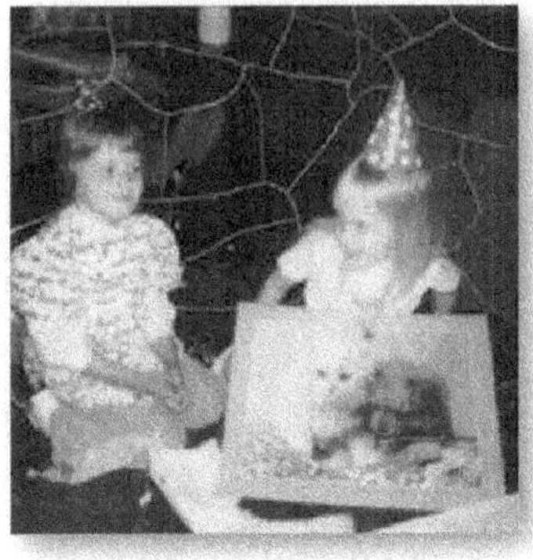
Kim and I at Kim's 3rd birthday party.

Donald and Tootie, Kim's wonderful parents

My best friend, Chaney

Grandpa on the farm with Shep #10

Georgene and I prior to a concert in Portland, OR.

Corbin's dad's awesome car. Great memories!

On my mission in beautiful Japan

Christian on his mission in Chicago

Mom and Glenda

Kitty Idol

A little ocean time with Beverly

Pammy and I going for a ride on her horses

Visiting with Kim and her parents after high school

My last picture with mother

The sunshine in my life and proof that God really does love me. My kids.

www.ingramcontent.com/pod-product-compliance
Lightning Source LLC
Chambersburg PA
CBHW030823090426
42737CB00009B/844